COLUMBIA CRITICAL GUIDES

William Shakespeare

Othello

EDITED BY NICHOLAS POTTER

Consultant editor: Nicolas Tredell

COLUMBIA UNIVERSITY PRESS NEW YORK

6/2002

Columbia University Press
Publishers Since 1893
New York
Editor's text copyright © 2000 Nicholas Potter

First published in the Icon Critical Guides series in 2000 by Icon Books
Ltd.

Library of Congress Cataloging-in-Publication Data

William Shakespeare : Othello / edited by Nicholas Potter.
   p. cm.—(Columbia critical guides)
   Includes bibliographical references.
   ISBN 0–231–12428–7 (cloth)—ISBN 0–231–12429–5 (paper)
    1. Shakespeare, William, 1564–1616. Othello. I. Potter,
Nicholas. II. Series.

PR2829.W46 2001
822.3'3—dc21   2001042379

⊗

Casebound editions of Columbia University Press books are printed on
permanent and durable acid-free paper.

Printed in the United States of America

c 10 9 8 7 6 5 4 3 2 1
p 10 9 8 7 6 5 4 3 2 1

Contents

INTRODUCTION

THIS GUIDE is intended to assist the student to make his or her way through the mass of opinion that has accumulated about Shakespeare's great tragedy *Othello*. The play has elicited contrasting responses, from Thomas Rymer's famously dismissive response to much more favourable accounts. It has almost never provoked unqualified praise, except from playgoers perhaps. Critical reflection has almost always found itself perplexed at some point, and this Guide will seek to show how and why and try to discern a shape to the critical history of the play.

What is criticism?

Criticism is no more than the articulated responses of the critic to the work. The critic is no more than a person who takes his or her response to a work seriously enough to want to articulate it and to explore its implications. In recent times, criticism been subject to scrutiny from practitioners of English who feel that the practice has been insufficiently examined. Catherine Belsey's *Critical Practice* and Bernard Bergonzi's *Exploding English* may be consulted for differing views on the discussion.[1] New critical approaches have developed, especially in respect of Renaissance Studies and of Shakespeare Studies in particular. Brian Vickers's *Appropriating Shakespeare*[2] gives a hostile but illuminating account of some of these. The work of the practitioners of these new approaches is their defence. The lesson one learns from the study of critical history itself is well put by Brian Vickers writing of the criticism of the eighteenth century in *Shakespeare: The Critical Heritage*.

■ In studying the reception of Shakespeare, or of any other major writer, over a long historical period the modern reader is involved in a constant series of adjustments and comparisons. We work with a triangle, consisting of Shakespeare in his age, the eighteenth-century writers in theirs, and ourselves in our own: which, no less than the others, has a critical and aesthetic system that is inherited, consciously or not, and shaped by many influences. We can juxtapose our understanding of Shakespeare with the eighteenth century's understanding of him, and with our understanding of them. This triple process of comparative interpretation ought to make us see that our position is also time-bound, and culture-bound, ought to prevent us from feeling any easy sense of superiority. Another age will arise that may look at our Shakespeare criticism with reactions ranging from indulgent apology to disbelief and contempt. One aim of studying the critical judgments of the past is to make us aware of the relationship, in their work as in our own, between judgment and interpretation, and the critical assumptions or methodology that – often unconsciously – produce those judgments. We will not be led into a complacent sense of progress.[3] □

It is equally important to avoid being led into an easy relativism. The critic has a responsibility to what he or she believes and should be certain that indulgent apology is not a cover for the failure to accept that responsibility. The effort is to understand and the difficulty of doing so grows at least in the same degree as distance from the past increases. John Dennis was aware of this at the end of the seventeenth century.

■ [T]o set up the *Grecian* Method amongst us with success it is absolutely necessary to restore not only their Religion and their Polity but to transport us to the same Climate in which *Sophocles* and *Euripides* writ; or else, by reason of those different Circumstances, several things which were graceful and decent with them must seem ridiculous and absurd to us, as several things which would have appear'd highly extravagant to them must look proper and becoming with us.[4] □

The proportions of this Guide give preponderance to the views of the twentieth century. This is because criticism is a developing process (which is not the same as progress), the beginnings of which in the English cultural tradition can be discerned in the seventeenth century. The eighteenth century sees the tradition first put itself forth in its new-found strengths; the nineteenth century builds upon those strengths; the twentieth century examines and questions. This Guide will not attempt to guess at what may come after.

Whenever quotations from the play itself have been used in extracted material (and regardless of the version of the play from which the original quotation came, or even if the critic himself or herself has quoted sometimes from memory and not always accurately) the act, scene and line number that follow them in square brackets have been standardised to the Arden Shakespeare, third edition, edited by E. A. J. Honigmann.

CHAPTER ONE

Restoring Order: *'The Tragedy of the Handkerchief'*

IN A sense that this Guide will shortly explore, criticism is a growth of the period following the Restoration in 1660 of Charles II to the throne of England after twenty years of civil war and various forms of parliamentary rule.

Shakespeare's own period was far from exempt from political excitement; Martin Coyle's Guide to *Richard II* in this series explores the close relationship between Shakespeare's company and the events of the rebellion of the Earl of Essex in 1601.[1] Nevertheless it has been widely observed that the period sometimes known as the Interregnum enjoys a special significance. When T. S. Eliot remarked in his essay entitled 'The Metaphysical Poets' that 'in the seventeenth century a dissociation of sensibility set in, from which we have never recovered', he was signalling a re-examination of the previous three centuries of English history that would radically adjust the way the past was thought about for much of the twentieth century.[2] Eliot's phrase 'in the seventeenth century' is disingenuous; the most obvious feature of that century to the casual observer is the period of civil war.

It would be difficult to trace the development of which Eliot speaks to the civil wars in any direct way; to try would also be to overlook the significance of other factors such as the developments in what would become science and the formation of intellectual habits that will flourish as Rationalism. None the less it is necessary to bear in mind the stresses and strains in English culture that are associated with the period; it is enough, perhaps, to remember that John Milton lost his property and much of his liberty, and could have forfeited his life because he served the revolutionary government during the Interregnum.[3]

Criticism of *Othello* may much less controversially be said to have begun with the Restoration because Thomas Rymer chose *Othello* to bear the brunt of his attack on English drama in his *A Short View of Tragedy*

(1693). Before Rymer there is nothing really in the way of criticism of *Othello* – and not only of *Othello*. Brian Vickers, to whose *Shakespeare: The Critical Heritage* every student of the critical history of Shakespeare's plays is indebted, comments:

■ I print no contemporary allusions in the text proper, since it seems to me that none of these amount to sustained criticism of any great value.[4] □

The selection of material in this Guide accords with Vickers's category of 'sustained criticism', but it is necessary to consider his categories more fully before proceeding. He says that 'in addition to regular critical essays and poems to or about Shakespeare' he has included:

■ The adaptations of Shakespeare's plays, of which over a hundred appeared in the period 1660–1820; theatre criticism, dealing with performances of both the original plays and the adaptations; notes and comments from the editions of Shakespeare.[5] □

In doing this he is making a very important critical point: 'Shakespeare' now exists as an agglomeration of views and versions; performances, critical theories, historical commentary, editorial controversy. It is even possible to suspect, as Gary Taylor does in *Reinventing Shakespeare*, that Shakespeare is a sort of cultural mirage, or a chimera more exactly; both a mythical creature and a composite.[6] *Othello* was not adapted and that fact makes the task easier. The adaptations are enormously significant for the study of Shakespeare but do not concern the student of *Othello*. The editorial debate has not been as heated and controversial as has that over *King Lear* or *Hamlet*. This is not to say that there are no editorial controversies; this Guide will consider them but it does not have to grapple with the problem of whether or not there is more than one play answerable to the title.[7] The problem with *Othello* is more concentrated, but that does not make it any less complex.

The problem is in two parts, as it is with any play. First, is it a reading play or a performance play? Second, whichever it is, what does one make of it? The first part of the problem can be addressed by saying that it is not a problem at all but an artificial distinction: who, after all, would confuse a film script with a film? The theatrical script can then be examined as the basis of possible performance, as the score of a musical work might similarly be considered. This is simple but ignores two facts, one inconvenient, the other more important: there has been a tradition of reading Shakespeare since at least 1623 when John Heminges and Henry Condell of the King's Men published the first Folio edition of Shakespeare's plays; Heminges and Condell published their edition seven years after Ben Jonson had published in 1616 a Folio edition of his plays.

Jonson was determined to have his plays taken seriously and to him that meant as literature. The stage may come and go, but literature remained. In defiance of public opinion Jonson published his Folio edition to establish his work as literature, to be read. Heminges and Condell merely took up his lead. In doing so they confirmed Jonson's view and Shakespeare took his place in the nation's literature. Of course he did not thereby renounce his place in the nation's dramatic repertory, which he has kept. The question that arises is that of the relationship between the dramatic tradition and the literary tradition and, after the Restoration, the critical tradition.

Terry Eagleton identifies the emergence of the critical tradition in England with the social-political conditions of the early eighteenth century.[8] Criticism, literature, jurisprudence, divinity, were, he argues, the common concern of a group in English society, the homogeneity of which was unprecedented. In English society previously, though there had been always a polite culture, aloof from the rest, it can be argued that there was more continuity, or greater opportunity for continuity, between the various elements of English society.

Such a view underlies E. M. W. Tillyard's *The Elizabethan World Picture* and it may seem a conservative assumption but Robert Weimann has argued a similar view from a Marxist perspective.[9] The Restoration saw the development of two cultures – a popular culture and a polite culture. These were divided by literacy and an expanding publishing industry catering to the literate, but also in that arena in which the classes had mingled in Shakespeare's time, the theatre. Brian Vickers comments:

■ Whereas in Shakespeare's London there were from five to eight theatres open at any one time, and a weekly audience of some 18,000 to 24,000, in November, 1660 only two companies were licensed by the crown: the Duke's Men, managed by Sir William D'Avenant, and the King's Men, run by Thomas Killigrew. Indeed in 1682, due largely, it seems, to a decline in the status and quality of actors available, and hence of audiences attracted, the two companies amalgamated into one (though they returned to two in 1695). The theatres were much smaller than the open-air public theatres of Shakespeare's day; they accommodated about four hundred people, at much higher prices, in late afternoon and evening performances. Although there are enough references to rowdyism and violence within the Restoration theatres for us not to make the mistake of equating them with a decorous court-theatre or the kind of intimate circle which Gibbon records around Voltaire, it is nonetheless true that by comparison with Shakespeare's this was a more socially select audience, of fashionable or would-be fashionable people, their hangers-on and their servants.[10] □

The distinctions here are crucial; 'socially select' must not be confused with 'decorous', and the meaning here of 'decorous' must certainly not be confused with the more modern meaning of the word.

Vickers's mention of Voltaire offers an opportunity to make the distinction more clear. Voltaire was stung by a comparison he had heard that Lord Kames had made between a passage in Racine's *Iphigénie* and the passage in *Hamlet* that features the phrase 'Not a mouse stirring'. Voltaire explodes:

■ Oui, monsieur, un soldat peut répondre ainsi dans un corps de garde; mais non pas sur le théâtre, devant les premières personnes d'une nation, qui s'expriment noblement, et devant qui il faut s'exprimer de même. [Yes sir, a soldier may reply in this manner in a guardroom; but not at all in the theatre, before the foremost personages of a nation, who express themselves nobly, and before whom one must express oneself in the same manner.][11] □

'Il faut' carries the force of the fullest notion of *decorum*; of what it is fitting to do. For Voltaire the necessity is imposed by the presence of 'les premières personnes d'une nation' and there should be a much fuller discussion before the notion of the 'first' persons of a nation should prove acceptable. None the less, Voltaire provides an example, if extreme, of an insistence upon due decorum. This has nothing to do with being 'genteel' as that word, in its turn, became debased, with overtones of the finicky, or precious. It has to do with a sense of congruity, of appropriateness that the 'genteel' attempted to mimic. Court theatre was inextricably involved with the ritual processes of the court as a whole and the 'intimate circle which Gibbon records around Voltaire' was inextricably involved with the counterparts of those processes in the French Academy.

'Socially select' makes a different point and this is another area in which great care must be taken. 'Decorous' refers to behaviour; 'socially select' to class. The 'socially select' may or may not behave 'decorously' and, according of course to the standards by which social selection is accomplished, may or may not jeopardise their status as 'socially select'. Brian Vickers offers the reminder that even the socially select are not immune from 'rowdyism and violence'. The late seventeenth and early eighteenth centuries had different standards of behaviour to those to which we may appeal in this present time.

It is an obvious point but one to stress; behaviour that should be found unacceptable in the present age would in another age, one which prided itself on its decorousness, be found quite acceptable. This is true of racism, for example, and Voltaire provides an illustration.

■ Dans une tragédie de Shakespeare nommée *Othello*, cet Othello, qui est un nègre, donne deux baisers à sa femme avant de l'étrangler. Cela paraît abominable aux honnêtes gens; mais des partisans de Shakespeare disent que c'est la belle nature, surtout dans un nègre. [In a tragedy by Shakespeare, called *Othello*, this Othello, who is a Negro, kisses his wife twice before strangling her. This seems abhorrent to honest persons; but devotees of Shakespeare say that this is true to nature, especially in a Negro.][12] □

It is ironic that Voltaire should choose to describe his tribunal by the epithet 'honnêtes' as the word 'honest' is so abused by Iago in the play, but it is only too familiar that the 'honnêtes' should happily identify someone as 'un *nègre*' (Larousse defines '*nègre*' as '*de la race noire*') and talk about the 'nature' of such a person. Racism consists in the identification of groups of people by their characteristics; this identification may become antagonistically discriminatory or it may not but as Patricia Williams detailed in her Reith lectures for 1997 racism begins in the unthinking recognition of racial characteristics as the identifying character of a person.[13] Othello himself has to deal with this in the play and no critic of *Othello* can avoid dealing with it in turn.

Criticism is no more than the fully articulated judgements a society makes upon its productions. Specialised judgement has developed in many areas leaving the word criticism to apply to literature, music, theatre, art and so on. The fuller meaning should not be forgotten in the narrower use prevalent today. Criticism still entails the full armoury of judgement. The critical tradition is answerable, ultimately, to the cultural tradition as a whole – that is, to a concern with questions of life and not merely questions of 'literature' or 'theatre' as though there could be a satisfactory account of either that took no account of the rest of existence.

The relationship between the theatrical and the literary tradition is part of the rest of existence: the critical tradition, ultimately, should always have that in mind. The emergence of the critical tradition in the wake of the Restoration is certainly enabled by the homogeneity to which Terry Eagleton points, but it is also a reflection of the divergent opinions within that group and of its own sense of the fragility of its authority that the formal emergence of such a tradition was accounted a necessity.

The sense in which the Restoration period may be said to have invented criticism derives from its enthusiastic adoption of Neo-classicist views that it had borrowed from sixteenth-century France and that sixteenth-century France had acquired from fifteenth-century Italy. Curt A. Zimansky, editing Thomas Rymer's *Works*, claims that Rymer's position can be traced to a few key works in the French school, the *Poëtique* (1640) of Jules de la Mesnardière; *La Pratique du théâtre* (1657) by the

Abbé d'Aubignac; René Rapin's *Réflexions sur la poëtique* (1674), Rymer's translation of which was published in the same year; André Dacier's edition of Aristotle's *Poetics* (1692).[14] To say this is not to undermine Rymer; far from it, it shows his orthodoxy. This is what is so interesting about him because his background and surroundings do not always point in this direction. His schoolmaster was an ardent royalist but his father was a parliamentary supporter who prospered during the Interregnum, became implicated in the Farnley Wood uprising and was hanged, drawn and quartered at York Castle for treason on 7 January 1664. His political connections were mainly with prominent Whigs and William I made him Historiographer-Royal. *A General Draught and Prospect of Government in Europe* (1681) supports the rights of parliaments against royal prerogative. Such a set of contradictions suggests either a timeserver or a paradox: Zimansky wisely comments that 'it is surely safer to look for the source of his ideas of royal decorum in critical theory and the practice of heroic tragedy rather than in a personal fanaticism for which there is no other evidence'.[15]

The heart of Rymer's work is the concept he borrowed from the French school but can claim the credit for naming in English, 'poetic justice', by which he means that ideal justice that cannot be expected on earth but must be demanded in poetry. His whole insistence is that literature, and theatre, must reflect the ideal; what better way of explaining the paradox than by the hypothesis that this was a man committed to an ideal of justice he knew he could not expect to find in the earthly world?

Rymer's reputation is itself interesting:[16] Macaulay famously dismissed him as 'the worst critic that ever lived'; Pope thought him 'on the whole, one of the best critics we ever had'. Pope's word may be thought more reliable than Macaulay's on matters of criticism, but it is best not to take any one's word. Dr Johnson thought him an ungenerous critic in comparison with Dryden; Scott opined:

■ Nothing can be more disgusting than the remarks of Rymer, who creeps over the most beautiful passages of the drama with eyes open only to their defects, or their departure from scholastic precept.[17] □

This would be useful if he had said anything about 'beautiful' and something about 'defects'. It may be suspected that he had in mind some dewy-eyed notion of beauty enhanced by defects and that rather spoils the effect. 'Scholastic' is an interesting epithet: it recalls Duns Scotus (*Doctor Subtilis*) and the murky world of ill-understood mediaeval pre-occupations with the number of angels that might be gathered upon the head of a pin. It is an especially interesting epithet because Rymer had, in a way, anticipated this criticism. Speaking of 'the Fable or Plot' he is concerned to show in *Tragedies of the Last Age* (August 1677) that 'common sense' is the only guide one needs to find out 'the Rules':

■ And certainly there is not requir'd much learning, or that a man must be some Aristotle, and *Doctor* of *Subtilties*, to form a right judgment in this particular; common sense suffices.[18] □

Common sense guided Corneille, says the later essay:

■ Corneille tells us, in the *Examen* of his *Melite*, that when first he began to write, he thought there had been no Rules: So he had no guide but a little *Common sence*, with the Example of Mr. *Hardy*, and some others, not more regular than he. This *Common sence* (says he) *which was all my rule, brought me to find out the unity of Action to imbroyl four Lovers by one and the same intreague.*[19] □

This is not mere propaganda: *The Cambridge History of English Literature* put it thus:

■ French drama of the seventeenth century, and especially French tragedy as written by Corneille and Racine, had developed in obedience to supposed classical laws and strictly respected the unities of time, place, action and kind – all very good things, for their other names are continuity, stability, simplicity and congruity.[20] □

French tragedy . . .

■ . . . was accepted everywhere but in England as the model . . . Shakespearean tragedy developed, not from examples of classical restraint, but from the realism of the 'miracles' and the horrors of Seneca.[21] □

In fact, the precepts were anything but scholastic. Renaissance scholarship in Italy had developed the enthusiasm; Dacier and his colleagues were following Castelvetro and his.[22] Most importantly, their argument was that 'the Rules' were not precepts but observations from Nature and accessible to Common Sense, and that they were precisely not 'scholastic'. Curt Zimansky cites A. O. Lovejoy:

■ The presumption of the universal accessibility and verifiability of all that it is really needful for men to know implied that all subtle, elaborate, intricate reasonings about abstruse questions beyond the grasp of the majority are certainly unimportant, and probably untrue.[23] □

Doctrines appealing to common sense have always made this appeal and always will, by definition because common sense is what we all believe. It is ironic, then, for Scott to suggest that Rymer is 'scholastic' because it was as important for Rymer (following Dacier, who was following

Castelvetro) to identify *Doctor Subtilis* as a bogeyman as it was for Scott to suggest that Rymer was just that bogeyman himself and for the same reasons – both were appealing to common sense.

Rymer begins his essay with an observation:

■ From all the Tragedies acted on our English Stage, *Othello* is said to bear the Bell away.[24] □

This is borne out by other commentators of the period; Gerard Langbaine, whose *An Account of the English Dramatick Poets* was published in 1691, says:

■ Othello, *the Moor of* Venice *his Tragedy*. This is reckoned an Admirable Tragedy; and was reprinted 4°. *Lond.* 1680. and is still an entertainment at the Theatre-Royal.[25] □

This is, no doubt, why Rymer singles *Othello* out for such a scathing attack; his opinion of *Julius Caesar* is no higher but his vituperation is reserved for *Othello*. His theoretical basis is laid out straight away:

■ The *Fable* is always accounted the *Soul* of Tragedy. And it is the *Fable* which is properly the *Poets* part. Because the other three parts of Tragedy, to wit the *Characters* are taken from the Moral Philosopher; the *thoughts* or sence, from them that teach *Rhetorick*: And the last part, which is the *expression*, we learn from the Grammarians.[26] □

This is controversial already and shows clearly Rymer's principles and his indebtedness to the classical tradition. Gascoigne and Puttenham[27] from the earlier age would have been pleased to think that they had this influence over their contemporaries in the theatre but would have been the first to acknowledge that, in their view, lamentably, they did not. Ben Jonson would have been pleased to think that his friend had worked in this way but he knew that he did not:

■ Thou hadst little Latin and less Greek.[28] □

Rymer immediately criticises Shakespeare for altering Cinthio's 'Fable', especially for raising the status of Cinthio's Moor (who is unnamed) and for giving him the title 'The Moor of Venice':

■ We say the Piper of *Strasburgh*; the Jew of *Florence*; And, if you please, the Pindar of *Wakefield*: all upon Record, and memorable in their Places. But we see no such cause for the *Moors* preferment to that dignity. And it is an affront to all Chroniclers, and Antiquaries, to top upon 'um a *Moor*, with that mark of renown, who yet had never faln within the Sphere of their Cognisance.[29] □

He objects too to the elevation of Desdemona, who in Cinthio is a simple citizen, to the status of a Senator's daughter. These may seem trivial objections but they will form part of Rymer's grand design. He summarises the Fable efficiently and impartially:

■ Othello, *a Blackmoor Captain, by talking of his Prowess and Feats of War, makes* Desdemona *a Senator's Daughter to be in love with him; and to be married to him, without her Parents' knowledge; And having preferred* Cassio, *to be his Lieutenant (a place which his Ensign* Jago *sued for)* Jago *in revenge, works the Moor into a Jealousy that* Cassio *Cuckolds him: which he effects by stealing and conveying a certain Handkerchief, which had, at the Wedding, been by the Moor presented to his Bride. Hereupon,* Othello *and* Jago *plot the Deaths of* Desdemona *and* Cassio, Othello *Murders her, and soon after is convinced of her Innocence. And as he is about to be carried to Prison, in order to be punish'd for the Murder, He kills himself.*[30] □

And he comments:

■ What ever rubs or difficulty may stick on the Bark, the Moral, sure, of this Fable is very instructive.
　First, This may be a caution to all Maidens of Quality how, without their Parents' consent, they run away with Blackamoors . . .
　Secondly, This may be a warning to all good Wives, that they look well to their Linnen.
　Thirdly, This may be a lesson to Husbands, that before their Jealousie be Tragical, the proofs may be Mathematical.[31] □

This gives us the manner. Rymer's choice of *Sarcasm* ('a biting irony') is a deliberate rhetorical choice; he needs to destroy by ridicule. It is this manner that brought most of the critical reaction down on his head, from Dryden's objection to his 'Ill-Nature and his Arrogance'[32] to Scott's finding Rymer's comments 'disgusting'. It is instructive to compare Dr Johnson's views on the moral of the play as these are recounted by Boswell from Friday 12 April 1776:

■ I observed the great defect of the tragedy of *Othello* was, that it had not a moral; for that no man could resist the circumstances of suspicion which were artfully suggested to Othello's mind.

JOHNSON. 'In the first place, Sir, we learn from *Othello* this very useful moral, not to make an unequal match; in the second place, we learn not to yield too readily to suspicion. The handkerchief is merely a trick, though a very pretty trick; but there are no other circumstances of reasonable suspicion, except what is related by Iago of Cassio's warm expressions concerning Desdemona in his sleep; and that depended entirely upon the assertion of one man. No, Sir, I think *Othello* has more moral than almost any play.'[33] □

Even taking into account Johnson's delight in talking controversially, and in contradicting Boswell (who often describes himself deliberately proposing views he knows Johnson will contradict!) these views are not contradicted by Johnson elsewhere. Eighty years later than Rymer, Johnson is describing more or less the circumstances Rymer describes but puts a very different construction upon them and draws a very different, indeed an entirely opposite, conclusion.

Rymer regards the explanation of Desdemona's love for Othello with incredulity. He quotes Act I, Scene iii, lines 135–46 and comments:

■ This was the Charm, this was the philtre, the love-powder that took the Daughter of this Noble Venetian. This was sufficient to make the Black-amoor White, and reconcile all, tho' there had been a Cloven-foot into the bargain.

A meaner woman might be as soon taken by *Aqua Tetrachymagogon* [a 'medicine' widely advertised in London a few years earlier].[34] □

The Duke's 'I think this tale would win my daughter too' does not impress Rymer: '[I]t seems, the noble Venetians have an other sence of things.'[35] He takes this further:

■ The Character of that State [Venice] is to employ strangers in their Wars; But shall a Poet thence fancy that they will set a Negro to be their General; or trust a *Moor* to defend them against the *Turk*? With us a Black-amoor might rise to be a Trumpeter; but *Shakespear* would not have him less than a Lieutenant-General. With us a *Moor* might marry some little drab, or Small-coal Wench; *Shake-spear*, would provide him the Daughter and Heir of some great Lord, or Privy-Councellor: And all the Town should reckon it a very suitable match: Yet the English are not bred up with that hatred and aversion to the *Moors*, as are the Venetians, who suffer by a perpetual Hostility from them . . .[36] □

He concludes that . . .

■ . . . never was any Play fraught, like this of *Othello*, with improbabilities.[37] □

He objects to the characters, most of all to Iago:

■ But what is most intolerable is *Jago*. He is no Black-amoor Souldier, so we may be sure he should be like other Souldiers of our acquaintance; yet never in Tragedy, nor in Comedy, nor in Nature was a Souldier with his Character . . . *Shakespear* knew his Character of *Jago* was inconsistent. In this very Play he pronounces,

If thou dost deliver more or less than Truth,
Thou are no Souldier [II, iii, 215–16].

This he knew, but to entertain the Audience with something new and surprising, against common sense, and Nature, he would pass upon us a close, dissembling, false, insinuating rascal, instead of an open-hearted, frank, plain-dealing Souldier, a character constantly worn by them for some thousands of years in the World.

Tiberius Caesar had a Poet Arraign'd for his Life: because *Agamemnon* was brought on the Stage by him, with a character unbecoming a Souldier [the story is told in Suetonius, *The Twelve Caesars*, in *Tiberius*].[38] □

Desdemona is no more convincing:

■ This Senators Daughter runs away to (a Carriers Inn) the *Sagittary*, with a Black-amoor: is no sooner wedded to him, but the very night she Beds him, is importuning and teizing him for a young smock-fac'd Lieutenant, *Cassio*. And tho' she perceives the *Moor* Jealous of *Cassio*, yet will she not forbear, but still rings *Cassio*, *Cassio* in both his Ears.[39] □

He passes over the *Thoughts*:

■ [F]rom such *Characters*, we need not expect many that are either true, or fine, or noble.[40] □

Nor does he like the *Expression* much either:

■ In the *Neighing* of an Horse, or in the *growling* of a Mastiff, there is a meaning, there is as lively expression, and, I may say, more humanity, than many times in the Tragical flights of *Shakespear*.[41] □

He instances Roderigo and Iago outside Brabantio's window in I, i. He does not object to the language itself but to its placing: it is inappropriate that the news of his daughter's elopement should be broken to him in such a manner. He is one of, to use Voltaire's phrase, 'les premières personnes d'une nation'.

■ In former days there wont to be kept at the Courts of Princes some body in a Fools Coat, that in pure simplicity might let slip something, which made way for the ill news, and blunted the shock, which might otherwise have come too violent upon the party.

Aristophanes puts *Nicias* and *Demosthenes* into the disguise of Servants, that they might, without indecency, be Drunk; And Drunk he must make them that they might without reserve lay open the *Arcana* of State; And the Knavery of their *Ministers*.

After King *Francis* had been taken Prisoner at *Pavia*. *Rabelais* tells of a Drunken bout between *Gargantua* and Fryer *John*; where the valiant Fryer, bragging over his Cups, amongst his other flights, says he, *Had I liv'd in the days of Jesus Christ, I would ha' guarded* Mount Olivet *that the Jews should never ha' tane him. The Devil fetch me, if I would not have ham string'd those Mr. Apostles, that after their good Supper, ran away so scurvily and left their Master to shift for himself. I hate a Man should run away, when he should play at sharps. Pox on't, that I shou'd not be King of* France *for an hundred years or two. I wou'd curtail all our French Dogs that ran away at* Pavia.

This is address, this is truly Satyr, where the preparation is such, that the thing principally design'd, falls in, as it only were of course.[42] □

Rymer's notion of 'course' needs some clarification. The whole essay is governed by carefully thought out standards of decorum that are grounded in a conception of class that is much more radical than any that might be met with today. Rymer's first illustration in the preceding passage gives some idea of this.

It is paradoxically true that some news might be better broken in the manner he describes – that is, let slip by 'some body in a Fools Coat' in 'pure simplicity', than that it be broken by a peer. This is because one's relationship with a peer involves a mutual respect whereas one's relationship with 'some body in a Fools Coat' involves nothing at all; in fact one does not have a relationship with 'some body in a Fools Coat'. One is not looking into the eyes of one's peer. There is no loss of face. Mutual respect, mutual regard, mutual *watchfulness* is the central characteristic of a culture based upon conceptions of Honour. It is degrading to Brabantio, and, perhaps more importantly, to his position, to be apprised of his daughter's elopement in this manner. The events can not be regarded as intended to be satire, because satire must observe appropriateness as well, and Rymer illustrates this from Rabelais where the satire is directed against the braggart Friar John. There is no satire directed against Iago and Roderigo in *Othello* Act I, Scene i because the whole effect of the scene is vitiated by the outrage to decorum. It may well be Shakespeare's point to show Brabantio degraded and his position set at nothing but it is Rymer's argument, implicitly, that such a point should not be made on stage.

Rymer is much less offended by the breach of the Unity of Place than might have been presumed:

■ For the *Second Act*, our Poet having dispatcht his affairs at *Venice*, shews the Action next (I know not how many leagues off) in the Island of *Cyprus*. The Audience must be there too: And yet our *Bays* had it never in his head, to make any provision of Transport Ships for them.

In the days that the *Old Testament* was Acted in *Clerkenwell*, by the *Parish Clerks* of *London*, the Israelites might pass through the *Red sea*: but, alass, at this time, we have no *Moses* to bid the Waters *make way*, and to Usher us along. Well, the absurdities of this kind break no Bones. They may make Fools of us; but do not hurt our Morals.[43] □

The thinking behind this kind of objection seems to be that the initial imaginative acceptance of place should not be stretched by asking the audience to accept a change of place; though it may appear to be naïve realism it is in fact more subtle than that. Dr. Johnson, too, wished that the first scene had not been set in Venice. Rymer's deeper point is that: '[T]he absurdities of this kind break no Bones. They may make Fools of us; but do not hurt our Morals.'[44]

His essay presses on towards the points at which, he believes, our morals are hurt. The 'improbabilities' he exposes and ridicules not for themselves but as a cover for far more serious breaches of decorum. He pours scorn on the opening of Act II as absurdly concerned with an exchange between Cassio and Montano about Othello's marriage and the character of Desdemona:

■ I thought it enough that *Cassio* should be acquainted with a Virgin of that rank and consideration in *Venice*, as *Desdemona*. I wondred that in the Senate-house every one should know her so familiarly: yet; here also at *Cyprus*, every body is in a rapture at the name of *Desdemona*: except only *Montanio* who must be ignorant; that *Cassio*, who has an excellent cut in shaping an Answer, may give him the satisfaction.[45] □

Desdemona's entrance does not improve matters: Cassio's courtesy strikes Rymer as absurdly inflated and her backchat with Iago offensive:

■ Now follows a long rabble of Jack-pudden farce betwixt *Jago* and *Desdemona*, that runs on with all the little plays, jingle, and trash below the patience of any Countrey Kitchin-maid with her Sweet-heart. The Venetian *Donna* is hard put to't for pastime! And this is all, when they are newly got on shoar, from a dismal Tempest, and when every moment she might expect to hear her Lord (as she calls him) that she runs so mad after, is arriv'd or lost. And moreover.

> *. . . in a Town of War,*
> *. . . the peoples Hearts brimful of fear . . .* [II, iii, 209–10]

Never in the World had any Pagan Poet his Brains turn'd at this Monstrous rate. But the ground of all this Bedlam-Buffoonry we saw [earlier in the essay], in the case of the French *Strolers*, the Company for Acting *Christs Passion*, or the *Old Testament*, were Carpenters, Coblers, and illiterate fellows; who found that the Drolls, and Fooleries inter-larded by them, brought in the rabble, and lengthened their time, so they got Money by the bargain.

Our *Shakespear*, doubtless, was a great Master in this craft. These Carpenters and Coblers were the guides he followed. And it is then no wonder that we find so much farce and *Apochryphal Matter* in his Tragedies. Thereby un-hallowing the Theatre, profaning the name of Tragedy; And instead of representing Men and Manners, turning all Morality, good sence, and humanity into mockery and derision.[46] □

This is a serious charge and some answer must be given to it. First, though, it is worth asking whether or not the account Rymer gives of 'the Drolls, and Fooleries' to be found in English drama before the Restoration is a true one. *The Cambridge History of English Literature* has already been cited:

■ Shakespearean tragedy developed, not from examples of classical restraint, but from the realism of the 'miracles' and the horrors of Seneca.[47] □

Part of the 'realism' of the Miracle Plays had been their intermingling of the elevated and the lowly, which can be a Christian symbolism of a pro-found kind where, for example, the Nativity of Christ is concerned. Rymer's account is a *post-hoc* rationalisation, designed to appeal (if he did not believe it) to a gentlemanly audience that would be pleased with a picture of the low, grasping cunning of ordinary workmen. Shakespeare's own presentation of the Mechanicals in *A Midsummer Night's Dream* gives us a better picture, satirical as it is, and droll, as it is meant to be, of the impulses that went into the making of popular theatre and of his sympathy with it.

Rymer then takes the reader through Acts II and III at quite a clip; Scott's description of Rymer 'creeping' is as insulting as it was surely intended to be but it is inaccurate. Take Rymer's dismissal of III, iii, 350–60 for example:

■ The Indians do as they ought in painting the Devil White: but says *Othello*:

OTHELLO. . . *Her name, that was as fresh*
As Dian*'s Visage, is now begrim'd and black,*
As mine own face . . . [III, iii, 389–91]

There is not a Monky but understands Nature better; not a Pug in *Barbary* that has not a truer taste of things.

OTHELLO . . . *O now for ever*
Farewel the tranquil mind, farewel content;
Farewel the plumed troop, and the big Wars,
That make Ambition Vertue: O farewel,
Farewel the neighing Steed, and the shrill Trump,
The spirit stirring Drum, th'ear-piercing Fief,
The royal Banner, and all quality,
Pride, Pomp, and Circumstance of glorious War,
And, O ye Mortal Engines, whose wide throats
Th'immortal Joves great clamours counterfeit,
Farewel, Othello's *occupation's gone* [III, iii, 350–60].

These lines are recited here, not for any thing Poetical in them, besides the sound, that pleases. Yet this sort of imagery and amplification is extreamly taking, where it is just and natural. As in *Gorboduck*, when a young Princess on whose fancy the personal gallantry of the King's Son then slain, had made a strong impression, thus, out of the abundance of her imagination, pours forth her grief:

MARCELLA . . . *Ah noble Prince! how oft have I beheld*
Thee mounted on thy fierce, and trampling Steed,
Shining in Armour bright before the Tilt,
Wearing thy Mistress sleeve ty'd on thy helm.
Then charge they staff, to please thy Ladies Eye,
That bow'd the head piece of thy friendly Foe?
How oft in arms, on Horse to bend the Mace,
How oft in arms, on foot, to break the Spear;
Which never now these Eyes may see agen?[48] ☐

It may seem absurd – and even to be an act of effrontery, insolence or deliberate perversity – to a modern reader to make a comparison between Shakespeare's verse and that of *Gorboduc*. Thomas Sackville and Thomas Norton had made a giant leap forward from their predecessors but once Marlowe, Kyd and Shakespeare had caught the idea, the earlier work seems now at least to be only historical in its importance. Yet the end of the preceding chapter of *A Short View of Tragedy* praises it highly:

■ But early under Queen *Elizabeth,* our dramatick Poetry grew to something of a just symmetry and proportion. In 1566. *Geo. Gascoigne* of *Grays-Inn* translated the *Supposes,* from *Ariosto,* which was there acted: as also his *Jocasta* Englished from *Euripides,* the Epilogue written by *Chr. Yelverton.*

And after that were reckon'd for Comedy, *Edward* Earl of *Oxford;* for Tragedy amongst others, *Thomas* Lord of *Buchurst,* whose *Gorboduck* is a fable, doubtless, better turn'd for Tragedy, than any on this side the *Alps* in his time; and might have been a better direction to *Shakespear* and *Ben. Johnson* than any guide they have had the luck to follow.[49] □

True to his lights, Rymer praises 'the regularity and roundness of the design' to which all else is subordinate. If the Fable is got right the rest only has to fit in; if the Fable is not got right then nothing else will fit. Othello and Desdemona are out of proportion and all Rymer has to do is to show how, again and again, this lack of proportion leads to absurdity. It has to be said that a lack of proportion does lead to absurdity. If audiences and readers do not think Othello a grand character then what he says will seem absurd. The question is, can one simply ignore Rymer's claim that it is not in proportion?

Rymer is the first to publish a critical account of the play that notices the apparent discrepancies in the time-scheme:

■ DESDEMONA *How now, my dear* Othello,
Your Dinner, and the generous Islanders
By you invited, do attend your presence.
OTHELLO *I am to blame.*
DESDEMONA *Why is your speech so faint? Are you not well.*
OTHELLO *I have a pain upon my Fore-head, dear* [III, iii, 283–8].

Michael Cassio came not from *Venice* in the Ship with *Desdemona,* nor till this Morning could be suspected of an opportunity with her. And 'tis now but Dinner time; yet the *Moor* complains of his Fore-head. He might have set a Guard on *Cassio,* or have lockt up *Desdemona,* or have observ'd their carriage a day or two longer. He is on other occasions phlegmatick enough: this is very hasty. But after Dinner we have a wonderful flight:

OTHELLO *What sense had I of her stoln hours of lust?*
I saw't not, thought it not, it harm'd not me:
I slept the next night well, was free and merry,
I found not Cassio*'s kisses on her lips . . .* [III, iii, 341–4].

A little after this, says he,

OTHELLO *Give me a living reason that she's disloyal.*
JAGO *. . . I lay with* Cassio *lately,*
And being troubled with a raging Tooth, I could not sleep;
There are a kind of men so loose of Soul,
That in their sleeps will mutter their affairs,
One of this kind is Cassio*:*
In sleep I heard him say: sweet Desdemona,
Let us be wary, let us hide our loves:
And then, Sir, wou'd he gripe, and wring my hand,
Cry out, sweet Creature; and then kiss me hard,
As if he pluckt up kisses by the roots,
That grew upon my Lips, then laid his Leg
Over my Thigh, and sigh'd, and kiss'd, and then
Cry'd, curs'd fate, that gave thee to the Moor [III, iii, 412–27].

By the Rapture of *Othello*, one might think that he raves, is not of sound Memory, forgets that he has not yet been two nights in the Matrimonial Bed with his *Desdemona*. But we find *Jago*, who should have a better memory, forging his lies after the very same Model. The very night of their Marriage at *Venice*, the Moor, and also *Cassio*, were sent away to *Cyprus*. In the *Second Act*, *Othello* and his Bride go the first time to Bed; the *Third Act* opens the next morning. The parties have been in view to this moment. We saw the opportunity which was given for *Cassio* to *speak his bosom* to her; *once*, indeed, might go a great way with a Venetian. But *once*, will not do the Poets business; The *Audience* must suppose a great many bouts, to make the plot operate. They must deny their senses, to reconcile it to common sense; or make it any way consistent, and hang together.[50] □

He has noticed earlier that the discussion between Iago and Cassio at II, iii, 328–37 . . .

■ . . . implies an experience and long conversation, the Honey-Moon over, and a Marriage of some standing. Would any man, in his wits, talk thus of a Bridegroom and a Bride the first night of their coming together?[51] □

He has also noticed that Roderigo has had an unusually hard time of it:

■ The last thing said by him in the former *Act* was,

RODERIGO *. . . I'll go sell all my Land* [I, iii, 380].

A fair Estate is sold to *put money in his Purse*, for this adventure. And lo here, the next day.

RODERIGO *I do follow here in the Chace, not like a Hound that hunts, but one that fills up the cry: My Money is almost spent. I have been tonight exceedingly well cudgell'd, I think the issue will be, I shall have so much experience for my pains, and so no Money at all, and with a little more wit return to* Venice [II, iii, 359–63].

The Venetian squire had a good riddance for his Acres. The Poet allows him just time to be once drunk, a very conscionable reckoning![52] □

Later he comments on Desdemona's anxious conversation with Emilia in III, iv.

■ The *third Act* begins in the morning, at noon she drops the Handkerchief, after dinner she misses it, and then follows all this outrage and horrible clutter about it. If we believe a small Damosel in the last *Scene* of this *Act*, this day is effectually seven days.

BIANCA . . . *What keep a week away! seven days, seven nights,*
Eightscore eight hours, and lovers absent hours,
More tedious than the Dial eightscore times.
O weary reckoning! [III, iv, 173–6]

Our Poet is at this plunge, that whether this *Act* contains the compass of one day, of seven days, or of seven years, or of all together, the repugnance and absurdity would be the same. For *Othello*, all the while, has nothing to say or to do, but what loudly proclaim him jealous: her friend and confident *Emilia* again and again rounds her in the Ear that *the Man* is jealous: yet this Venetian dame is neither to see, nor to hear; nor to have any sense or understanding, nor to strike any other note but *Cassio, Cassio*.[53] □

III, iii does not impress him:

■ [T]hen comes the wonderful Scene, where *Jago* by shrugs, half words, and ambiguous reflections, works *Othello* up to be Jealous. One might think, after what we have seen, that there needs no great cunning, no great poetry and address to make the *Moor* Jealous. Such impatience, such a rout for a handsome young fellow, the very morning after her Marriage must make him either to be jealous, or to take her for a *Changeling*, below his Jealousie. After this *Scene*, it might strain the Poets skill to reconcile the couple, and allay the Jealousie. *Jago* now can only *actum agere*, and vex the audience with a nauseous repetition.

Whence comes it then, that this is the top scene, the Scene that raises *Othello* above all other Tragedies on our Theatres? It is purely from the *Action*: from the Mops and the Mows, the Grimace, the Grins and Gesticulation. Such scenes as this have made all the World run after *Harlequin and Scaramuccio* . . . Had this scene been represented at old *Rome*, *Othello* and *Jago* must have quitted their Buskins; They must have played *bare-foot*: the spectators would not have been content without seeing their Podometry; And the Jealousie work at the very Toes of 'em. Words, be they Spanish, or Polish, or any inarticulate sound, have the same effect, they can only serve to distinguish, and, as it were, beat time to the *Action*. But here we see a known Language does wofully encumber, and clog the operation: as either forc'd, or heavy, or trifling, or incoherent, or improper, or most what improbable. When no words interpose to spoil the conceipt, every one interprets as he likes best. So in that memorable dispute betwixt *Panurge* and our English Philosopher in *Rabelais*, perform'd without a word speaking; The Theologians, Physicians, and Surgeons, made one inference; the Lawyers, Civilians, and Canonists, drew another conclusion more to their mind.[54] □

Gerard Langbaine, cited earlier, records the popularity of the play; Rymer confirms that it was popular, and that Act III, Scene iii was widely noted. Abraham Wright (1611–90), Vicar of Okeham, was a keen playgoer, and he left a list of plays for his son James's use; he comments:

■ A very good play both for lines and plot, but especially the plot. Iago for a rogue, and Othello for a jealous husband 2 parts well pend. Act: 3 the scene beetwixt Iago and Othello, and the I sce: of the 4 Act between the same shew admirably the villanous humour of Iago when hee persuades Othello to his jalousy.[55] □

Robert Gould wrote in *The Play-House. A Satyr* (1685):

■ When e'er I *Hamlet* or *Othello* read,
My Hair starts up, and my Nerves shrink with dread!
Pity and *Terrour* raise my Wonder high'r,
'Till betwixt both I'm ready to expire!
When curs'd *Iago* cruelly I see
Work up the Noble *Moor* to *Jealousy*,
How cunningly the Villain weaves his Sin,
And how the other takes the Poison in.[56] □

Such examples tend to confirm the view that this aspect of *Othello* was noted. It is worth considering two entries in the diary of Samuel Pepys, himself an enthusiastic playgoer. In October 1660, Pepys notes two outings – the first on 11 October and the second the day after next, on 13 October:

■ 11th. [T]o walk in St. James's Park – where we observed the several engines at work to draw up water, with which sight I was very much pleased.

Above all the rest, I liked best that which Mr Greatorex brought, which is one round thing going within all with a pair of stairs round; which being laid at an angle of 45 doth carry up the water with a great deal of ease. Here in the park we met with Mr Salsbury, who took Mr Creed and me to the Cockpitt to see *The Moore of Venice*, which was well done. Burt acted the Moore; by the same token, a very pretty lady that sot by me, cried to see Desdimona smothered.

13th. I went out to Charing Cross, to see Major-Generall Harrison hanged, drawn, and quartered – which was done there – he looking as cheerfully as any man could do in that condition. He was presently cut down, and his head and heart shown to the people, at which there was great shouts of joy. It is said that he said that he was sure to come shortly at the right hand of Christ to judge them that now had judged him. And that his wife do expect his coming again.

Thus it was my chance to see the King beheaded at White-hall, and to see the first blood shed in revenge for the blood of the King at Charing-cross.[57] □

What links these three events is 'seeing'. Pepys remarks of the engines in St. James's Park, 'with which sight I was very much pleased'; he goes with Mr Salsbury and Mr Creed 'to the Cockpitt to see *The Moore of Venice*' and to Charing Cross 'to see Major-Generall Harrison hanged, drawn, and quartered'. These events are all Spectacles, and it may be that Gerard Langbaine and Abraham Wright are applauding *Othello* as spectacle as well. Rymer, then, does not disagree with them on a matter of evaluation but on a matter of identity. They identify spectacle and he identifies something else. They are not evaluating the same thing differently but seeing different things.

The matter may be even more subtle than this, for there are grounds for thinking that Rymer knew what his contemporaries thought of *Othello* and was not mistaken about what they thought it was either; he wanted to show them the consequences of thinking along those lines. The last part of his essay is the most important.

Rymer moves on to Act IV. Pausing to glance at the moment in Act IV, Scene i, when Iago arranges to have Othello hide away while he questions Cassio about Bianca, he ironically calls the device 'a Stratagem never presented in Tragedy' and comments:

■ So to work they go: and *Othello* is as wise a commentator, and makes his applications pat, as heart cou'd wish – but I wou'd not expect to find this Scene acted nearer than in *Southwark* Fair.[58] □

He comments on Iago's part in the murder plans:

■ *Jago* had some pretence to be discontent with *Othello* and *Cassio*: And what passed hitherto, was the operation of revenge. *Desdemona* had never done him harm, always kind to him, and to his Wife; was his Country-woman, a Dame of quality: for him to abet her Murder, shews nothing of a Souldier, nothing of a Man, nothing of Nature in it. The *Ordinary* of *New gate* never had the like Monster to pass under his examination. Can it be any diversion to see a Rogue beyond what the Devil ever finish'd? Or wou'd it be any instruction to an Audience?[59] □

He complains that Lodovico's behaviour is unnatural, arguing that the Venetians, the danger passed, could easily arrest and certainly would have arrested Othello for his treatment of Desdemona. He thinks Roderigo absurdly credulous and Desdemona unconvincingly docile.

■ With us a Tinkers trull wou'd be Nettled, wou'd repartee with more spirit, and not appear so void of spleen.[60] □

Above all, though, it is the accusation that she has given Cassio the handkerchief Othello gave her to which Rymer directs his fiercest disapproval:

■ But hark, a most tragical thing laid to her charge.

> OTHELLO *That Handkerchief, that I so lov'd, and gave thee,*
> *Thou gav'st to* Cassio.
> DESDEMONA *No by my Life and Soul;*
> *Send for the man and ask him.*
> OTHELLO . . . *By Heaven, I saw my Handkerchief in his hand* . . .
> . . . *I saw the Handkerchief* [V, ii, 48–9, 62, 66].

So much ado, so much stress, so much passion and repetition about an Handkerchief! Why was not this call'd the *Tragedy of the Handkerchief*? . . . We have heard of *Fortunatus his Purse*, and of the *Invisible Cloak*, long ago worn thread bare, and stow'd up in the Wardrobe of obsolete Romances: one might think, that were a fitter place for this Hand-kerchief, than that it, at this time of day, be worn on the Stage, to raise every where all this clutter and turmoil. Had it been *Desdemona*'s Garter, the Sagacious Moor might have smelt a Rat: but the Handkerchief is so remote a trifle, no Booby, on this side *Mauritania*, cou'd make any consequence from it.[61] □

Worse is to follow:

■ OTHELLO . . . *O heavy hour!*
Methinks it shou'd be now a huge Eclipse
Of Sun and Moon, and that the affrighted globe
Shou'd yawn at Alteration [V, ii, 97–9].

This is wonderful. Here is Poetry to *elevate* and *amuse*. Here is sound All-sufficient. It wou'd be uncivil to ask *Flamstead*, if the Sun and Moon can both together be so hugely eclipsed, in any *heavy hour* whatsoever. Nor must the spectators consult *Gresham* Colledge, whether a body is naturally *frighted* till he *Yawn* agen. The Fortune of *Greece* is not concern'd with these Matters. These are Physical circumstances a Poet may be ignorant in, without any harm to the publick. These slips have no influence on our Manners and good Life; which are the Poets province.

Rather may we ask here what unnatural crime *Desdemona*, or her Parents had committed, to bring this Judgment down upon her; to Wed a Black-amoor, and innocent to be thus cruelly murder'd by him. What instruction can we make out of this Catastrophe? Or whither must our reflection lead us? Is not this to envenome and sour our spirits, to make us repine and grumble at Providence; and the government of the World? If this be our end, what boots it to be Vertuous?[62] □

He suggests an alternative:

■ Desdemona dropt the Handkerchief, and missed it that very day after her Marriage; it might have been rumpl'd up with her Wedding sheets: And this Night that she lay in her wedding sheets, the *Fairey* Napkin (whilst *Othello* was stifling her) might have started up to disarm his fury, and stop his ungracious mouth. Then might she (in a Traunce for fear) have lain as dead. Then might he, believing her dead, touch'd with remorse, have honestly cut his own Throat, by the good leave, and with the applause of all the Spectators. Who might thereupon have gone home with a quiet mind, admiring the beauty of Providence; fairly and truly represented on the Theatre . . .

But from this Scene to the end of the Play we meet with nothing but blood and butchery, described much-what to the style of *the last Speeches and Confessions of the persons executed at Tyburn*: with this difference, that there we have the *fact*, and the due course of Justice, whereas our Poet against all Justice and Reason, against all Law, Humanity and

Nature, in a barbarous arbitrary way, executes and makes havock of his subjects, *Hab-nab*, as they come to hand. *Desdemona* dropt her Handkerchief; therefore she must be stifl'd. *Othello*, by law to be broken on the Wheel, by the Poets cunning escapes with cutting his own Throat. *Cassio*, for I know not what, comes off with a broken shin. *Jago* murders his Benefactor *Roderigo*, as this were poetical gratitude. *Jago* is not yet kill'd, because there never yet was such a villain alive. The Devil, if once he brings a man to be dipt in a deadly sin, lets him alone, to take his course: and now when the *Foul Fiend* has done with him, our wise Authors take the sinner into their poetical service; there to accomplish him, and do the Devils drudgery.

Philosophy tells us it is a principle in the Nature of Man *to be grateful*.

History may tell us that *John an Oaks, John a Stiles*, or *Jago* were ungrateful; *Poetry* is to follow Nature: Philosophy must be his guide: history and *fact* in particular cases of *John an Oaks*, or *John of Styles*, are no warrant or direction for a Poet. Therefore *Aristotle* is always telling us that Poetry is . . . more general and abstracted, is led more by the Philosophy, the reason and nature of things, than History: which only records things higlety, piglety, right or wrong as they happen. History might without any preamble or difficulty, say that *Jago* was ungrateful. Philosophy then calls him unnatural; But the Poet is not, without huge labour and preparation to expose the Monster; and after shew the Divine Vengeance executed upon him. The Poet is not to add wilful Murder to his ingratitude: he has not antidote enough for the Poison: his Hell and Furies are not punishment sufficient for one single crime, of that bulk and aggravation.

> EMILIA *O thou dull Moor, that Handkerchief thou speakest on,*
> *I found by Fortune, and did give my Husband:*
> *For often with a solemn earnestness,*
> *(More than indeed belong'd to such a trifle)*
> *He beg'd of me to steal it* [V, ii, 224–6].

Here we see the meanest woman in the Play takes this *Handkerchief* for a *trifle* below her Husband to trouble his head about it. Yet we find, it entered our Poets head, to make a Tragedy of this *Trifle*.[63] □

This long passage has been left to speak for itself at first because it is the heart of Rymer's argument. The entire rhetorical strategy of the chapter leads up to it. It is only possible to give a fair hearing to the argument that there is at all a rhetorical strategy if it is accepted that the heart of the argument is serious and worth attending to. There are two points to be made. First, Rymer's argument picks up speed, direction and concentration once he has reached Act IV. Having rather loosely and casually laid about him as he wanders through the play up to this point he starts to pick up some of his key points and make them more frequently. He especially redoubles his efforts to identify *Othello* with the extraordinary. He does this in two ways. He identifies *Othello* with a traditional culture, as he has done before, mentioning the London Parish Clerks performance of the *Old Testament*, only he stresses the popular cultural aspect of traditional culture more here, mentioning *Southwark Fair* and some of the stock devices of Romance, such as *Fortunatus his Purse* and the *Invisible Cloak*; he also introduces *New-gate* and *Tyburn*, places of imprisonment and execution, associated with a popular tradition of tales of crime and last confessions. Introducing Tyburn allows him to introduce a key argument: with this difference, 'that there we have the *fact*, and the due course of Justice'.

What unites Southwark Fair, Newgate and Tyburn is that they are places where the extraordinary is gathered; the marvels and spectacles of the Fair and the villainies of the imprisoned and executed are alike marginal to, and affirmative of, the ordinary business of society. They affirm the ordinary business of society simply by being, and by being identified as, extraordinary and hence unlike the ordinary business of society. They are identified by being exhibited at special places where their exhibition is expected. Thus one expects to find at Southwark Fair or at Tyburn the extraordinary; it follows then that what one finds at Southwark Fair or Tyburn will be extraordinary. If one found something about which one was uncertain one could set one's mind at rest by reflecting that one had found it at this place and so it was extraordinary.

This matters where there may be some doubt about what is extraordinary. Rymer concludes his account of *Othello* with an interesting reflection:

■ What can remain with the Audience to carry home with them from this sort of Poetry, for their use and edification? how can it work, unless (instead of settling the mind, and purging our passions) to delude our senses, disorder our thoughts, addle our brain, pervert our affections, hair our imaginations, corrupt our appetite, and fill our head with vanity, confusion, *Tintamarre*, and Jingle-jangle, beyond what all the Parish Clarks of *London*, with their *old Testament* farces, and interludes, in *Richard* the seconds time cou'd ever pretend to? Our only hopes, for the good of their Souls, can be, that these people go to the Playhouse, as they do to Church, to sit still, look on one another, make no reflection, nor mind the Play, more than they would a Sermon.

There is in this Play, some burlesk, some humour, and ramble of Comical Wit, some shew, and some *Mimickry* to divert the spectators: but the tragical part is, plainly none other, than a Bloody farce, without salt or savour.[64] □

The exhibitions of Southwark Fair or Tyburn do not have this effect because one goes to Southwark Fair or Tyburn for the extraordinary and to the Theatre, as to the Church, for the ordinary. 'Ordinary' here does not mean 'uninteresting'; it means 'orderly'.

The whole of Rymer's argument may be summarised by his phrase:

■ *Poetry* is to follow Nature; Philosophy must be his guide.[65] □

It may be said that he takes this from Aristotle but he is not copying Aristotle; he is using Aristotle's authority. The task of the Theatre for Rymer is to establish what is Nature; Philosophy teaches the Theatre and the Theatre teaches the Audience. Nature is not History; History is *fact* and you may get all the *facts* you want at Tyburn. It is tempting to explain this emphasis with a reference to the civil wars, and Rymer mentions Richard II in his conclusion; Richard was deposed and executed. The temptation should be resisted unless a clear explanation presents itself, such as Rymer's proven loyalties, but these are not proven. His anguish had another cause: 'If this be our end, what boots it to be vertuous?' is a revealing question. He knew that one needed the reassurance that there was some purpose to be served by being virtuous if not necessarily a purpose to one's own immediate and practical advantage, and he saw that *Othello* suggested that the world was disorderly and pointless.

Isaac d'Israeli saw him as a sort of Don Quixote:

■ Rymer grasped the new and formidable weapon of modern criticism. Armed at all points with a Grecian helmet and a Gallic lance, this literary Quixote sallied forth to attack all the giants or the windmills of the English theatre.[66] □

In the spirit of Rymer, one is moved to ask how one can be armed 'at all points' with 'a Grecian helmet and a Gallic lance', but that can pass; d'Israeli has seen something important. Rymer really does do criticism. He looks closely; he quotes; he gives exact references; he analyses what he quotes (sometimes). It is remarkable that the answers to him in his own time do nothing of the kind and not one attempts to rebut his points about *Othello*. Dr Johnson compared him to Dryden in his *Life of Dryden* and must have known his judgment of the moral of *Othello* and yet Boswell does not record that Johnson reflected upon the closeness of his judgment of that moral to Rymer's, with the obvious difference that the values are reversed.

With the flowering of the Augustan age, Rymer passes into literary history, but his ghost appears in T.S. Eliot's essay on *Hamlet*, in his remark in passing that he had never read 'a cogent refutation' of Rymer.[67] This attitude lies behind his essay on *Othello*, as shall be seen later.

CHAPTER TWO

The Age of Johnson: The Triumph of Reason

THE 'COGENT refutation' of which Eliot noted the lack certainly was not attempted by Rymer's contemporaries; Charles Gildon took on the general argument in a spirited and not ineffective essay, but did not really answer the case against *Othello*. However, he does make some good specific points. He answers Rymer's objection that Othello could not have risen to command the Venetian forces.

■ [T]he Character of the *Venetian State* being to employ Strangers in their Wars, it gives sufficient ground to our Poet to suppose a *Moor* employ'd by 'em as well as a German; that is, a *Christian Moor*, as *Othello* is represented by our Poet, for from such a *Moor* there cou'd be no just fear of treachery in favour of the *Mahometans*. He tells us –

I fetch my Life and Being
From Men of Royal Siege [I, ii, 21–2.].

Supposing him therefore the Son or Nephew of the Emperor of *Monomotopa*, *Æthiopia* or *Congo*, forc'd to leave his Country for Religion (or any other occasion), coming to *Europe* by the convenience of the *Portugueze* Ships, might after several Fortunes serve first as a Voluntier till he had signaliz'd himself and prov'd himself worthy of Command; part of this may very reasonably be drawn from what the Poet makes him say. Now upon this Supposition it appears more rational and probable the *Venetians* shou'd employ a Stranger who wholly depended on themselves, and whose Country was too remote to influence him to their prejudice, than other Strangers whose Princes may in some measure direct their Actions for their own Advantage. But that *Othello* is suppos'd to be a Christian is evident from the Second Act, and from these words of *Iago*:

> *– And then for her*
> *To Win the* **Moor**, *were't to renounce his* **Baptism**, *&c* [etc.] [II, iii, 337–8].

Why therefore an *African* Christian may not by the *Venetians* be suppos'd to be as zealous against the *Turks* as an *European* Christian, I cannot imagine. So that this bustle of *Littora littoribus Contraria*, &c. is only an inconsiderate Amusement to shew how little the gentleman was troubled with thought when he wrote it.[1] □

This sturdy argument is an excellent instance of two separate but related themes that converge compellingly on *Othello*: one is the increasing tendency among critics to look for more detail in the story and to supply it from supposition when it is not given ('part of this may very reasonably be drawn from what the Poet makes him say'); the other is the way in which *Othello* and what 'the Poet' makes Othello say lends itself to this tendency. These two themes are brought to fruition in the work of A. C. Bradley (see Chapter Three), and the reaction against it by modernist critics is a marked feature in early twentieth-century criticism.

It also shows a most interesting dilemma. The more reasonable Othello's position is made to appear, the less purpose there seems to be in making him a Moor at all, and the less the critical account comes to square with the play's insistence on Othello's difference. Gildon goes on to give a very good answer to Rymer's pugnacious assertion that a *'Negro'* could never have risen as high as Shakespeare makes out that Othello has risen. In doing so he demonstrates a very neat argumentative tactic, turning Rymer's own argument on himself:

■ 'Tis granted, a *Negro* here does seldom rise above a Trumpeter, nor often perhaps higher at *Venice*. But then that proceeds from the Vice of Mankind, which is the Poet's Duty, as he informs us, to correct, and to represent things as they should be, not as they are. Now 'tis certain, there is no reason in the nature of things why a *Negro* of equal Birth and Merit should not be on a equal bottom with a *German, Hollander, French-man*, &c. The Poet, therefore, ought to show Justice to Nations as well as Persons, and set them to rights, which the common course of things confounds. The same reason stands in force for this as for punishing the Wicked and making the Virtuous fortunate, which as *Rapin* and all the Critics agree, the Poet ought to do though it generally happens otherways. The Poet has therefore well chosen a polite People to cast off this customary Barbarity of confining Nations, without regard to their Virtue and Merits, to slavery and contempt for the meer Accident of their Complexion.[2] □

Emboldened, Gildon proceeds to deal with Rymer's objections to

Shakespeare's displaying Desdemona's love for Othello:

■ Unless he can prove that the Colour of a Man alters his Species and turns him into a *Beast* or *Devil* 'tis such a vulgar Error, so criminal a fondness of our Selves, to allow nothing of Humanity to any but our own Acquaintance of the fairer hew that I wonder a Man that pretends to be at all remov'd from the very Dreggs of the thoughtless Mob should espouse it in so public a manner! A Critic, too, who puts the Poet in mind of correcting the common corruptions of Custom. Any Man that has convers'd with the best Travels, or read any thing of the History of those parts on the continent of *Africa* discover'd by the *Portugueze*, must be so far from robbing the *Negroes* of some Countrys there of *Humanity* that they must grant them not only greater Heroes, nicer observers of Honour and all the Moral Virtues that distinguish'd the old *Romans*, but also much better Christians (where Christianity is profess'd) than we of *Europe* generally are. They move by a nobler Principle, more open, free and generous, and not such slaves to sordid Interest.

After all this, *Othello* being of *Royal Blood*, and a Christian, where is the disparity of the Match?[3] □

Where indeed? And where, then, is the mainspring of the action of *Othello*? According to Gildon, experience shows us that Iago had nothing to go on and Othello no grounds for anxiety:

■ Experience tells us that there's nothing more common than Matches of this kind where the Whites and Blacks cohabit, as in both the *Indies*. And Even here at home Ladys that have not wanted white Adorers have indulg'd their Amorous Dalliances with their Sable Lovers, without any of *Othello*'s Qualifications, which is proof enough that Nature and Custom have not put any such unpassable bar betwixt Creatures of the same kind because of different colors; which I hope will remove the improbability of the Person, especially when the powerful Auxilarys of extraordinary Merit and Vertues come to plead with a generous Mind.[4] □

Unfortunately, Gildon has forgotten that he is arguing from Nature to confound Rymer with his own first principle, and here argues from History. As a consequence, he shows how easy it is to get into a tangle when arguing about this matter. His argument from Nature should have sufficed (and does suffice); that he goes on to argue from History might be taken to suggest that he is not really sure of his position.

Gildon later abandoned this position on the play and in his 1710 Preface to Rowe's edition took to supporting and propagating Rymer's views:

■ I have drawn the Fable with as much favour to the Author as I possibly cou'd, yet I must own that the Faults found in it by Mr *Rymer* are but too visible for the most Part. That of making a *Negro* of the Hero or chief Character of the Play wou'd shock any one, for it is not the Rationale of the thing, and the Deductions that may thence be brought to diminish the Opposition betwixt the different Colours of Mankind – that wou'd not be sufficient to take away that which is shocking in this Story, since this entirely depends on Custom which makes it so. And on common Women's admitting a *Negro* to a Commerce with her every one almost starts at the Choice. Much more in a Woman of Vertue; and indeed *Iago*, *Brabantio*, &c. have shewn such Reasons as make it monstrous. I wonder Shakespeare saw this in the Persons of his Play and not in his own Judgment. If *Othello* had been made deformed, and not over young, but no Black, it had removed most of the Absurdities; but now it pleases only by Prescription. 'Tis possible that an innocent tender young Woman who knew little of the World might be won by the brave Actions of a gallant Man not to regard his Age or Deformities, but Nature – or what is all one in this Case, Custom – having put such a Bar as so opposite a Colour it takes away our Pity from her, and only raises our Indignation against him.[5] □

It is depressing to see how much Gildon's thinking about race has changed in sixteen years. Equally depressing is the complacency of 'Nature – or what is all one in this Case, Custom'. When they were expressed, Rymer's views were a challenge to established opinion, and they have that virtue that belongs to an attempt to shake people out of complacency; here they have become the staple of the worst kind of complacency – that which takes the way things are as the way things ought to be. There can be no doubt that the *Remarks on the Plays of Shakespeare* are more sophisticated writing than the enthusiastic but imperfectly organised and sometimes inarticulate earlier piece. There can also be no doubt that what Gildon gained in confidence as a critic he lost in humanity; the assertion of orthodoxy is smug.

It was not always this way; the age was certainly taken up with 'the Rules', though this did not deter practitioners who felt constrained by them from complaining against their attempted imposition; indeed, Congreve, Vanbrugh, Farquhar all wrote against them.[6] It is also possibly a mistake to see Neo-classicism as short-sightedly concerned with regimentation for its own sake. John Dennis opines that:

■ [W]riting Regularly is writing Morally, Decently, Justly, Naturally, Reasonably.[7] □

And that is a powerful claim. Dennis's refutation of Rymer makes some very useful points, though it does not deal with *Othello*. His opening paragraph is an important acknowledgement that the critic must be sensitive to history:

■ Upon reading Mr. *Rymer's* late Book I soon found that its Design was to make several Alterations in the Art of the Stage, which instead of reforming would ruin the *English Drama*. For to set up the *Grecian* Method amongst us with success it is absolutely necessary to restore not only their Religion and their Polity but to transport us to the same Climate in which *Sophocles* and *Euripides* writ; or else, by reason of those different Circumstances, several things which were graceful and decent with them must seem ridiculous and absurd to us, as several things which would have appear'd highly extravagant to them must look proper and becoming with us.[8] □

The cardinal difficulty with the Rules seems to have been Shakespeare and Fletcher. Curt Zimansky observes that:

■ Corneille could reject Hardy and other predecessors and work, albeit uncomfortably, in conformity to the critical standards then developing. Dryden could not reject Shakespeare and Fletcher, whose plays were still acted regularly and whose dramatic techniques could still furnish guidance. In France the greatest drama arose with or after the criticism; in England it preceded.[9] □

This is really important, though it is saying two quite different things. The plays were still acted regularly, which means that audiences were used to them and liked them; but Dryden could have struck out on his own if he wanted to. More importantly the plays could still furnish guidance, which is to say that Dryden liked them. He wrote to Dennis:

■ I cannot but conclude with Mr. *Rymer* that our *English* Comedy is far beyond any thing of the Antients. And notwithstanding our Irregularities, so is our Tragedy. *Shakespeare* had a Genius for it; and we know, in spite of Mr. *Rymer*, that Genius alone is a greater Virtue (if I may so call it) than all other Qualifications put together. You see what success this Learned Critick has found in the World, after his Blaspheming *Shakespeare*? Almost all the Faults which he has discover'd are truly there; yet who will read Mr. *Rymer*, or not read *Shakespeare*? For my own part, I reverence Mr. *Rymer's* Learning, but I detest his Ill-Nature and his Arrogance. I, indeed, and such as I, have reason to be afraid of him, but Shakespeare has not.[10] □

'Genius' is to argument about Shakespeare in this age what *deus ex machina*[11] can be to the Theatre: when you need to get out of an awkward situation you invoke it. Appeals to 'Genius' usually mean that critical discussion, if it has begun, falls silent; it effectively stops it before it starts. Yet Dryden is appealing to a fact:

■ Almost all the Faults which he has discover'd are truly there; yet who will read Mr. *Rymer*, or not read *Shakespeare*?[12] □

There is almost a note of exhaustion in this; what is Theory in the face of Facts? Charles Gildon highlights the apparent absurdity of Dryden's view:

■ This unaccountable Biggotry of the Town to the very Errors of *Shakespear*, was the Occasion of Mr. *Rymer*'s Criticisms, and drove him as far into the contrary Extream. I am far from approving his Manner of treating our Poet; tho' Mr. *Dryden* owns that all or most of the Faults he has found are Just, but adds this odd Reflection: And yet, says he, who minds the Critick and who admires *Shakespeare* less? That was as much as to say, Mr. *Rymer* has indeed made good his Charge, and yet the Town admir'd his Errors still: which I take to be a greater Proof of the Folly and abandon'd Taste of the Town, than of any Imperfections in the *Critic*. Which in my Opinion expos'd the Ignorance of the Age he liv'd in.[13] □

Gildon is right on two counts: he has got the reasoning behind Rymer's tone and manner; he has also got Rymer's intention right, though it may well be that it was not only the Ignorance of his Age but the moral danger in which that ignorance placed it that Rymer hoped to expose.

He is also right about Dryden's comment. It is an odd reflection. It may mean that there are more beauties than faults or at least as many (this was a common view – Dennis expressed it); this may be what 'Genius' means. Or 'Genius' may mean something else, like 'power' perhaps; something other than 'beauty'. In either case it would help if someone had done what Rymer did – that is, take us through it critically. No one does, at least where *Othello* is concerned, refute Rymer. Dryden may mean something else altogether; he may mean that theatregoers are not interested in criticism, as suggested earlier. It may be that criticism and theatre are at the moment governed by different criteria. Certainly criticism is in its infancy; this is the importance of Rymer. It may be that the critical techniques have yet to develop to deal with something like *Othello* and that Dryden, who has a foot in both the critical and the theatrical camps, is caught in this dilemma. Further exploration will show whether or not this is true.

Not everything merits or demands the attention of criticism; it would not be right to think theatregoers uncritical, as Gildon seems to. It may be argued that some things do not have to meet critical standards set for other kinds of work. After all, *Much Ado About Nothing* will not repay the kind of attention that should be given to *King Lear* or even to *Twelfth Night*. This will not do for Rymer's attack on *Othello* however; if something more is to be claimed for that play it must meet critical attention. This is what is most important about Rymer.

Refutation on specific points is provided, either directly as refutation or indirectly as addressing the point but not mentioning Rymer. Thus, for example, John Hughes, writing in *The Guardian* (23 April 1713) discusses Act III, Scene iii:

■ The deep and subtle Villany of *Iago*, in working this Change from Love to Jealousie in so tumultuous a Mind as that of *Othello*, prepossessed with a Confidence in the disinterested Affection of the Man who is leading him on insensibly to his Ruin, is likewise drawn with a Masterly Hand. *Iago*'s broken Hints, Questions, and seeming Care to hide the Reason of them; his obscure Suggestions to raise the Curiosity of the Moor; his personated Confusion and refusing to explain himself while *Othello* is drawn on and held in suspence till he grows impatient and angry, then his throwing in the Poyson, and naming to him in a Caution the Passion he would raise

– *O beware of Jealousie!* – [III, iii, 167]

Are inimitable strokes of Art in that Scene which has always been justly esteemed one of the best which was ever represented on the Theatre.[14] □

Hughes also discusses the handkerchief:

■ But there is nothing in which the Poet has more shewn his Judgment in this Play, than in the Circumstances of the Handkerchief, which is employ'd as a Confirmation to the Jealousie of *Othello* already raised. What I would here observe is that the very slightness of this Circumstance is the Beauty of it. How finely has *Shakespeare* expressed the Nature of Jealousie in those Lines which on this occasion he puts into the mouth of *Iago*:

Trifles light as Air
Are to the Jealous Confirmations strong
As Proofs of Holy Writ [III, iii, 325ff.].

It would be easie for a tasteless Critick to turn any of the Beauties I have here mentioned into Ridicule; but such an one would only betray a Mechanical Judgment formed out of borrow'd Rules and Common-place Reading, and not arising from any true Discernment in Human Nature and its Passions.[15] □

Unfortunately, Hughes reveals in this last remark that he has Rymer in his sights but the only form of attack he has is the assertion that any one who disagrees with him is insensitive; this is not an argument. Lewis Theobald takes on Rymer directly:

■ The Groundwork of this Play is built on a Novel of *Cinthio Giraldi* . . . who seems to have design'd his Tale a Document to young Ladies against disproportion'd Marriages: . . . That they should not link themselves to such against whom Nature, Providence, and a different way of Living have interpos'd a Bar. Our Poet inculcates no such Moral, but rather that a Woman may fall in Love with the Virtues and shining Qualities of a Man and therein overlook the Differences of Complexion and Colour. Mr. *Rymer* has run riot against the Conduct, Manners, Sentiments, and Diction of this Play: but in such a strain that one is mov'd rather to laugh at the Freedom and Coarseness of his Raillery than provok'd to be downright angry at his Censures . . . Thus this *Critick* goes on, but such Reflexions require no serious Answer. This *Tragedy* will continue to have lasting Charms enough to make us blind to such Absurdities as the Poet thought were not worth his Care.[16] □

He exerts himself more over the handkerchief:

■ Because this Episode of the *Handkerchief* has been attack'd by Snarlers and Buffoon-Criticks I am tempted to subjoin an observation or two in Justification of our Author's Conduct. The Poet seems to have been aware of the Levity of such Judges as should account the giving away an Handkerchief too slight a Ground for Jealousy. He therefore obviates this, upon the very Moment of the Handkerchief being lost, by making *Iago* say:

> *Trifles light as Air*
> *Are to the Jealous Confirmations strong*
> *As Proofs of Holy Writ* [III, iii, 325ff.].

Besides this, let us see how finely the Poet has made his Handkerchief of Significancy and Importance. *Cinthio Giraldi*, from whom he has borrowed the Incident, only says that it was the *Moor's* Gift, upon his

Wedding to *Desdemona*; that it was most curiously wrought after the *Moorish* Fashion, and very dear both to him and his Wife . . . But our Author, who wrote in a superstitious Age (when *Philtres* were in Vogue for procuring Love, and *Amulets* for preserving it), makes his Handkerchief deriv'd from an *Inchantress*; *Magick* and *Mystery* are in its *Materials* and *Workmanship*; its *Qualities* and *Attributes* are solemnly laid down; and the Gift recommended to be cherish'd by its Owners on the most inducing Terms imaginable, *viz.* the making the Party amiable to her Husband, and the keeping his Affections steady. Such Circumstances, if I know anything of the Matter, are the very Soul and Essence of *Poetry*. *Fancy* here exerts its great *creating* Power, and adds a Dignity that surprizes to its Subject. After this, let us hear the coarse Pleasantries of Mr. *Rymer* . . . Whether this be from the Spirit of a *true Critic* or from the Licence of a *Railer* I may be too much prejudiced to determine, so leave it to every indifferent Judgment.[17] □

This, though, does not argue against Rymer's point; it merely asserts the contrary. Rymer's strength is not the Rules; it is his possessing a coherent theory of which the Rules are a part, a theory of the practice of Art and the practice of criticism governed by a philosophical outlook and a morality grounded in an ultimate vision: 'If this be our end, what boots it to be vertuous?' Hughes is humane and Theobald is scathing, but neither is clear about the authority from which their pronouncements derive. It may be liberal to understand that Shakespeare wrote in 'a superstitious Age' but Rymer's angry contempt is directed at the folly and wickedness of superstition; Theobald's understanding seems scholarly and remote and even patronising in comparison. At least Rymer cares. Theobald is not superstitious; his careful formulation does not allow us to conclude that he believed Shakespeare superstitious; does he believe Othello to be superstitious, or Desdemona? Iago cannot be superstitious; he sees the handkerchief as a trifle. There are questions here to be answered and neither Theobald nor Hughes can answer them, except to say that the play is obviously good and anyone who cannot see this is insensitive. But that is not reasoned criticism.

Dr Johnson's comments on *Othello* are frequently rich. He corrects Pope, for example, who had, with characteristic freedom, changed 'antres vast and deserts idle [I, iii, 141]' to 'antres vast and deserts wild':

■ Every mind is liable to absence and inadvertency, else Pope could never have rejected a word so poetically beautiful.[18] □

Even Homer nods. Gildon (in his earlier essay) had enthused over this image:

■ What an Image does *Desarts* IDLE give? That very Epithet is a perfect *Hypotyposis*,[19] and seems to place me in the midst of one where all the active hurry of the World is lost.[20] □

Garrick dropped the image from his presentation and added instead:

■   Of my redemption thence;
Of battles bravely, hardly fought: of victories,
For which the conqueror mourn'd, so many fell;
Sometimes I told the story of a siege,
Wherein I had to combat plagues and famine;
Soldiers unpaid; fearful to fight,
Yet bold in dangerous mutiny.
All these to hear
Would *Desdemona* seriously incline . . . [21] □

Johnson's unexplained 'poetically beautiful' has here a kind of explanation by contrast: Garrick's verse is pedestrian.

The age was in some ways very literal and prided itself on its rationality; this sometimes leads to a short-sighted approach, especially to imagery. Shakespeare balances the epithets 'vast' and 'idle' much as Marvell balances the well-known lines from 'To His Coy Mistress':

■ But at my back I alwaies hear
Time's winged Chariot hurrying near:
And yonder all before us lye
Desarts of vast Eternity.[22] □

The contrast in Marvell is between, on the one hand, the complex idea of Time's Chariot 'hurrying' – a contrast in itself between grandeur and everyday bustle – and the emptiness of eternity (to the present mind of the poet); the contrast in Shakespeare is between the grandeur of size and the futility of uselessness. This is a moral idea in *Othello*: images of sterility abound.

William Dodd, whose anthology of excerpts from Shakespeare was the form in which Goethe first encountered Shakespeare's work and who was executed for forgery, comments on this speech, 'The simplest expressions, where nature and propriety dictate, may be truly sublime; such is all this fine speech of Othello'.[23]

Johnson noted the apparent discrepancies in the time-scheme of the play. Commenting upon Emilia's ''Tis not a year or two shows us a man' [III, iv, 104], he says:

■ From this line it may be conjectured that the author intended the action of this play to be considered as longer than is marked by any note of time. Since their arrival at Cyprus, to which they were hurried on their wedding night, the fable seems to have been in one continual progress, nor can I see any vacuity into which a *year or two*, or even a month or two, could be put. On the night of Othello's arrival, a feast was proclaimed; at that feast Cassio was degraded, and immediately applies to Desdemona to get him restored. Iago indeed advises Othello to hold him off a while, but there is no reason to think that he has been held off long. A little longer interval would increase the probability of the story, though it might violate the rules of the drama.[24] □

The time-scheme does not provoke the degree of scepticism it provoked in Rymer; Johnson speaks merely of a longer interval increasing the probability of the story. It is not improbable as it stands. Johnson's being of his time emerges most strongly in his comment on the lines 'I must weep,/But they are cruel tears. This sorrow's heavenly;/It strikes where it doth love' [V, ii, 20–22]. He glosses these lines as follows.

■ This tenderness, with which I lament the punishment which justice compels me to inflict, is a holy passion.

I wish these two lines could be honestly ejected. It is the fate of Shakespeare to counteract his own pathos.[25] □

The exact probity of Johnson's position is a measure of his greatness as a critic; he expresses his desire, his hope, and the knowledge that he cannot have it because of the conflicting demands of his critical sensibility and his scholarly obligation. He expresses, too, a profound judgement of Shakespeare's work as a poet in the medium of drama that is a profound comment on his own beliefs; Othello's depiction of his condition as one in which an honest man has to inflict just punishment against his softer feelings and his depiction of this contrast as a 'holy passion' (in Johnson's phrase) is an outrage against the idea of holiness. It is, moreover, an outrage Shakespeare could not help; it is his fate.

Johnson's general observations are a model of sound critical observation:

■ The beauties of this play impress themselves so strongly upon the attention of the reader that they can draw no aid from critical illustration. The fiery openness of Othello, magnanimous, artless, and credulous, boundless in his confidence, ardent in his affection, inflexible in his resolution, and obdurate in his revenge; the cool malignity of Iago, silent in his resentment, subtle in his designs, and studious at once of his interest and his vengeance; the soft simplicity of Desdemona, confident of merit and conscious of innocence, her artless perseverance in her suit, and her slowness to suspect that she can be suspected, are such proofs of Shakespeare's skill in human nature as, I suppose, it is vain to seek in any modern writer. The gradual progress which Iago makes in the Moor's conviction and the circumstances which he employs to inflame him are so artfully natural that, though it will perhaps not be said of him, as he says of himself, that he is *a man not easily jealous*, yet we cannot but pity him when at last we find him *perplexed in the extreme*.

There is always danger lest wickedness, conjoined with abilities, should steal upon esteem, though it misses of approbation; but the character of Iago is so conducted that he is from the first scene to the last hated and despised.

Even the inferior characters of this play would be very conspicuous in any other piece, not only for their justness but their strength. Cassio is brave, benevolent, and honest, ruined only by his want of stubbornness to resist an insidious invitation. Roderigo's suspicious credulity and impatient submission to the cheats which he sees practised upon him, and which by persuasion he suffers to be repeated, exhibit a strong picture of a weak mind betrayed by unlawful desires to a false friend; and the virtue of Emilia is such as we often find, worn loosely but not cast off, easy to commit small crimes but quickened and alarmed at atrocious villainies.

The scenes from the beginning to the end are busy, varied by happy interchanges, and regularly presenting the progression of the story; and the narrative in the end, though it tells but what is known already, yet is necessary to produce the death of Othello.

Had the scene opened in Cyprus, and the preceding incidents been occasionally related, there had been little wanting to a drama of the most exact and scrupulous regularity.[26] □

Johnson's comments are not made in an essay on *Othello* but as part of his edition of Shakespeare, and it is worth making some comments on this undertaking to put the comments in context. Edmond Malone commented on Johnson's indebtedness to the Neo-classicist heritage for his overall critical outlook:

■ Dr Johnson sat down to write this admirable preface with a mind fraught with all that had been written by Dennis, Gildon, Rymer, Guthrie &c on the same subject; whose pamphlets he had recently read.[27] □

Additionally, Brian Vickers points out that Johnson largely ignored the work of contemporary writers such as Theobald, Upton, Hurd, Roderick, and Webb and Kames.[28] The consonance with Rymer may be suggested by glancing at Johnson's comments of *Twelfth Night*:

■ The marriage of Olivia and the succeeding perplexity, though well enough contrived to divert on the stage, wants credibility and fails to produce the proper instruction required in the drama, as it exhibits no just picture of life.[29] □

The first of two important themes in this comment is the lower status of the stage. 'Well enough contrived to divert on the stage' suggests that it is not well enough contrived to divert the mind engaged in reading the play rather than seeing it on stage. Johnson held that 'a play read affects the mind like a play acted', though he allowed that a little heightening or diminution of affect might be experienced as the play was well or badly performed. The second important theme is the comfortable assumption that it is the 'requirement' of drama to produce 'the proper instruction', which it does by exhibiting a 'just picture of life'. Johnson takes Rymer's objections to the stage a little further in this comment but the rest is entirely in keeping with Rymer's views – that is, with Neo-classical criteria as Rymer imported and expressed them in his own work. Johnson does not make these comments about *Othello*, however, and it may be assumed that he did not find that play wanting in this important respect. Indeed, his comments to Boswell already noted suggest as much. Brian Vickers points out that Johnson objected to the deaths of Ophelia and Cordelia and comments:

■ Johnson is just as upset by the death of Desdemona, but since he does not in this case wish for poetic justice that must mean that he thinks it just.[30] □

There is no reason to think that it 'must' mean that; Vickers shows admirably clearly how inconsistent Johnson's work in this edition is, if only because it took shape over so long a period with so many interruptions.[31] It is, however, an interesting and profound departure from Rymer at least (and Dennis and Gildon had not challenged Rymer on his views of *Othello*). That Johnson did think the picture just is clear from his comments recorded by Boswell. How can this be explained?

It is worth here recalling Theobald and Hughes and asking again why their comments do not amount to an effective refutation of Rymer. Both critics seize upon Iago's 'Trifles light as air' as a counter-quotation to Rymer's use of Emilia:

■ EMILIA *O thou dull Moor, that Handkerchief thou speakest on,*
I found by Fortune, and did give my Husband:
For often with a solemn earnestness,
(More than indeed belong'd to such a trifle)
He beg'd of me to steal it [V, ii, 224–7].

Here we see the meanest woman in the Play takes this *Handkerchief* for a *trifle* below her Husband to trouble his head about it. Yet we find, it entered our Poets head, to make a Tragedy of this *Trifle*.[32] □

It may well be true that jealous persons exaggerate the significance of trifles; Rymer can only be answered by showing that the exhibition of the historical fact that they do produces 'the proper instruction required in the drama', a 'just picture of life'. Martin Coyle points out that:

■ The underlying thrust of most Neo-Classical criticism is towards didacticism; the purpose of art is not only to entertain, but also, through entertainment, to instruct.[33] □

Sir Philip Sidney's definition of poetry as a form of imitation whose purpose is 'to teach and to delight' may be recalled here.[34] Rymer's most important point is that:

■ *Aristotle* is always telling us that Poetry is . . . more general and abstracted, is led more by the Philosophy, the reason and nature of things, than History: which only records things higlety, piglety, right or wrong as they happen. History might without any preamble or difficulty, say that *Jago* was ungrateful. Philosophy then calls him unnatural.[35] □

If he is to be refuted it will have to be shown that the play is led 'by the Philosophy, the reason and nature of things', or it will have to be shown that the purpose of art is not 'not only to entertain, but also, through entertainment, to instruct'.

Two essays on Jealousy in *Othello* (one in 1747 possibly by Mark Akenside, the other unattributed so far) make the cardinal mistake of referring to documented cases showing striking similarities to the circumstances laid out in *Othello*. The error can be easily revealed:

■ The Question is, whether our Poets are justified in this; that is to say, whether they follow Nature or outrun her; whether in cases of this kind they draw the true Picture of a jealous Man or a hideous *Caracatura* of *Jealousy*, and consequently, whether they deserve to be commended or condemned. I must for my own part confess that it seems to me they are much better acquainted with the human Mind than those who have taken upon them to censure them; and that it may be very justly affirmed that the boldest Poets have not ventured to feign Actions more out of the Road of Reason than are related as Matters of Fact upon the same Topick by the most authentick Historians. Now if this can be made out, that is to say, if it can be shown from the Records of History, which are no other than *written Experience*, that when Men are stung with Jealousy they really act as wildly, as absurdly, and as inconsistently as the Poets represent them acting, then all Ground and Foundation of Criticism in this Respect will be taken away, and the Poets must be allowed to be better acquainted with the true Force of the Passions than those who have taken upon them to find Fault with their Productions, and even to chastise the Publick for the Applause they have vouchsafed to those Productions as supposing them just Representations of Nature.[36] □

No. The reviewer triumphantly produces a piece of *'written Experience'*, but to no effect, on Rymer's position, at least:

■ *History* may tell us that *John an Oaks, John a Stiles*, or *Jago* were ungrateful; *Poetry* is to follow Nature: Philosophy must be his guide: history and *fact* in particular cases of *John an Oaks*, or *John of Styles*, are no warrant or direction for a Poet. Therefore *Aristotle* is always telling us that Poetry is . . . more general and abstracted, is led more by the Philosophy, the reason and nature of things, than History: which only records things higlety, piglety, right or wrong as they happen. History might without any preamble or difficulty, say that *Jago* was ungrateful. Philosophy then calls him unnatural.[37] □

Nature cannot be discovered from History; that is precisely Rymer's point. Until that point is dealt with, Rymer is not refuted. Again and again writers are driven back on the position that everyone knows it is a good play and anyone who says that it is not does not know what they are talking about. But, again, that is not reasoned criticism. Until there is another theory, the problem will remain. Until then it is not clear what, if anything, distinguishes a good play from an entertaining spectacle.

Dr Johnson's remarks deserve careful presentation, not least because there are some signs of the almost unconscious development of a body of critical theory capable of refuting Rymer that can be discerned in his comments. This body of theory will not take full shape until articulated by A. C. Bradley and by that time its weaknesses will be showing but it is an important viewpoint and must be carefully traced. For the sake of convenience it can be linked with the term 'Realism' and it may be considered together with the taste that encouraged the development of the Novel in English culture. Vickers points out that Johnson evaluates behaviour as he would in real life.[38] This is not a trait peculiar to Johnson. Consider Charlotte Lennox's discussion of Emilia:

■ *Cinthio* shews this Woman privy, much against her Will, to the Design on *Desdemona*; and though she dares not discover it to her for fear of her Husband's Resentment yet she endeavours to put her upon her Guard, and gives her such Advice as she thinks will render all his Schemes ineffectual.

Shakespeare calls this Woman *Emilia*, and makes her the Attendant and Friend of *Desdemona*; yet shews her stealing a Handkerchief from her which she gives her Husband, telling him at the same Time that the Lady will run mad when she misses it, therefore, if it is not for some Purpose of Importance that he wants it, desires him to return it to her again.

If her Husband wants it for any Purpose of Importance that Purpose cannot be very good. This Suspicion, however, never enters her Mind, but she gives it him only upon that very Condition which ought to have made her refuse it.

Yet this Woman is the first who perceives *Othello* to be jealous, and repeats this Observation to her Mistress upon hearing him so often demand the Handkerchief she had stolen, and fly into a Rage when he finds his Wife cannot produce it.

Emilia pronounces him jealous, perceives the Loss of that fatal Handkerchief, confirms some Suspicions he had entertained, and though she loves her Mistress to Excess chuses rather to let her suffer all the bad Consequences of his Jealousy than confess she had taken the Handkerchief, which might have set all right again. And yet this same Woman, who could act so base and cruel a Part against her Mistress, has no greater Care in dying than to be laid by her Side.[39] □

Taken out of the play in this way and considered apart, as one might be able to consider a character from a novel, Emilia does appear contradictory, or at least difficult to account for in terms of the sort of consistent psychological portrait one would expect to be able to offer for a character in a novel. Edmond Malone treats Emilia similarly:

■ It is remarkable that when she perceives Othello's fury on the loss of this token, though she is represented as affectionate to her mistress, she never attempts to relieve her from her distress; which she might easily have done by demanding the handkerchief from her husband, or divulging the story, if he refused to restore it. – But this would not have served the plot.[40] □

Johnson's remarks may be recalled at this point:

■ [T]he virtue of Emilia is such as we often find, worn loosely but not cast off, easy to commit small crimes but quickened and alarmed at atrocious villainies.[41] □

Johnson's comment may be greeted with a sense of relief: at last someone has been able to resolve the problem; she does not really think that
she is doing wrong when she steals the handkerchief and it does not
mean that she does not really love and respect Desdemona; we see what
she is truly made of when she sees at last what Iago is really like. Emilia
is not as intelligent as Charlotte Lennox; what Mrs Lennox would see
and take fright at Emilia cannot see. Thinking along these lines, however,
is looking beyond the play; it is treating the play as though there were
gaps that needed to be filled in. It has already been commented that
Charles Gildon's sturdy defence of the play against Rymer as early as
1694 employed the method of supplying by speculation what the play
did not actually rule out, and Rymer himself had suggested a few
improvements to the plot to make the play more what he thought it
should have been. All this imaginative activity encourages the reader to
think of the characters of the play as being like real people in a real
world, with choices and alternative possibilities, so that events could
have gone another way and people may have acted in another way.

All this is to ignore the fact that were it not for the play there would
be no Emilia to speculate about and that Emilia exists only as the play
presents her. The play does not give us a picture, a version, of Emilia;
there is no other picture or version that might be given of Emilia, there is
only Emilia as she is painted by the words Shakespeare gave the actor
playing her to speak and the freedom those words give the actor (perhaps more the director in a modern production) to play the character.

Here, perhaps, we glimpse the folly of pursuing this line of inquiry
too far. *Othello* is not a mere conglomeration of characters; no one would
produce a watchable *Othello* who only concentrated on getting each actor
to play their 'character'. There is only an Emilia because there is a plot in
which she figures.

Johnson's account is sometimes taken to be anti-theatrical and to
raise reading above theatregoing, but his objections seem to have more
to do with the expectations of contemporary theatregoers and their taste
for spectacle. His account of the effect of theatrical presentation is
commonsense:

■ Imitations produce pain or pleasure, not because they are mistaken
for realities, but because they bring realities to mind. When the imagination is recreated by a painted landscape, the trees are not supposed
capable to give us shade, or the fountains coolness; but we consider
how we should be pleased with such fountains playing beside us and
such woods waving over us.[42] □

This can usefully be compared with Edward Capell's note on the opening
scene of *The Tempest*:

■ No well advis'd poet will think, at this time of day, of bringing into his piece an action like to that of this scene; as, under every advantage that stages now derive from their scenery, or can ever derive were mechanism even push'd to the utmost, such action will want the power of imposing in that degree that we ourselves have made necessary. But this touch'd not Shakespeare, his imposing was not by eyes but by ears; the former his stage deny'd him, and therefore left him at liberty to fix upon any action that lik'd him, and that suited his plot. The other mode of imposing he has been at pains to provide for, by drawing his sea-characters justly, and by putting into their mouths the proper terms of their calling.[43] □

It will be clear from this note that Capell has in mind the technological developments that had begun with the pageants and displays at the Tudor courts and had infected dramatic practice with the development of the Masque in Ben Jonson's time and that continued to develop throughout the eighteenth and nineteenth centuries. Capell does not openly lament this development. However, there is a note of wistfulness perhaps in his recognition that this development has been deserved; no power of machinery can produce the effect 'in that degree that we ourselves have made necessary'.

Johnson and Capell are, in fact, distinguishing between different kinds of theatre; one seeks to produce an illusion and the other does not. It should be made clear at this point that by the word 'illusion' it is not meant that anything is mistaken for a reality, but that something appears to the eye if not to the reason to be a reality. A useful analogy is the stage magician's illusion; the reason does not believe that the lady has been sawn into two, but the eye perceives that she has been. Johnson's attack on the unities is aimed at the argument that theatre is supposed to produce illusion; Capell notes that Shakespeare could not produce illusion and did not try to. The argument is not in itself anti-theatrical in either case. Neither Johnson nor Capell allow one to conclude that reading a play is exactly the same as reading a novel. It is true that Johnson writes contemptuously of the contribution made by performance:

■ A dramatic exhibition is a book recited with concomitants that increase or diminish its effect. Familiar comedy is often more powerful on the theatre than in the page; imperial tragedy is always less. The humour of Petruchio may be heightened by grimace; but what voice or what gesture can hope to add dignity of force to the soliloquy of Cato?[44] □

This at least appears arguable; Capell notes the effectiveness of gesture in a note on *King Lear*, on Albany's 'Fall, and cease!' [V, iii, 262], which

Pope, Hanmer, Theobald and Warburton had all excised, even though it appears in both Quarto and Folio texts:

■ Albany's *'Fall, and cease!'* were made very intelligible by the action accompanying; the wide display of his hands and the lifting-up of his eye, both directed toward the heavens, would shew plain enough that it is they who are call'd upon to *fall*, and crush a world that is such a scene of calamity.[45] □

Johnson's point is more subtle perhaps; it is not that gesture is idle decoration, but that some speeches cannot be improved upon by accompanying gesture. That gets the balance just about right for a theatre whose time had long passed away to be replaced by spectacle and illusionism. Capell's point is that certain imaginative experiences are precluded by illusionism because the technology is not up to it, and, he thinks, cannot be. It is only the limitation that restricts the effort in Capell's account; paradoxically the stage has become conservative because it cannot produce convincing illusions outside a narrow confinement. Johnson argues that it is the same principle that has driven the insistence upon the unities and that lies behind (though he does not name him) Rymer's attack on *Othello*. Certainly *Othello* is in Johnson's mind:

■ As nothing is essential to the fable but unity of action, and as the unities of time and place arise evidently from false assumptions, and, by circumscribing the extent of the drama, lessen its variety, I cannot think it much to be lamented that they were not known by him, or not observed; nor, if such another poet could arise, should I very vehemently reproach him that his first act passed at Venice, and his next in Cyprus.[46] □

His note on *Othello* must be placed next to this:

■ Had the scene opened in Cyprus, and the preceding incidents been occasionally related, there had been little wanting to a drama of the most exact and scrupulous regularity.[47] □

This would have been, according to the *Preface*:

■ . . . the product of superfluous and ostentatious art, by which is shewn, rather what is possible, than what is necessary.[48] □

This may appear inconsistent and yet Johnson also says in the *Preface*, immediately after the phrase just quoted:

observed the great defect of the tragedy of *Othello* was, that it had
a moral; for that no man could resist the circumstances of suspicion
ch were artfully suggested to Othello's mind.

NSON. 'In the first place, Sir, we learn from *Othello* this very use-
oral, not to make an unequal match; in the second place, we learn
to yield too readily to suspicion. The handkerchief is merely a
, though a very pretty trick; but there are no other circumstances
asonable suspicion, except what is related by Iago of Cassio's
n expressions concerning Desdemona in his sleep; and that
nded entirely upon the assertion of one man. No, Sir, I think
o has more moral than almost any play.'[59] □

ay compare Rymer:

at ever rubs or difficulty may stick on the Bark, the Moral, sure,
Fable is very instructive.
st, This may be a caution to all Maidens of Quality how, without
arents consent, they run away with Blackamoors . . .
ondly, This may be a warning to all good Wives, that they look
their Linnen.
rdly, This may be a lesson to Husbands, that before their
sie be Tragical, the proofs may be Mathematical.[60] □

's objection had not deterred generations of playgoers; Johnson
es the play's meaning towards a congruence with a reasonable
; Rymer ridicules a very similar 'moral' as the first step in his
n the taste of the playgoers of his time. Very little has changed in
ears. These three views are incompatible with each other but not
play; each may be seen as a view of the play that is not out-
to reason. Boswell is not being silly; it is difficult to see a moral
ense widely accepted at the time of a useful picture of life.
is not twisting the play; such a useful picture of life can be seen,
ne may feel that the word 'unequal' is underplaying some of
concerns. Othello himself acknowledges that his 'colour', age
gnness may stand in the way of understanding. These things are
ies but the word itself suggests less glaring inequalities. The
nson uses links him directly with one of his greatest fans, Jane
The dreadful consequences of 'unequal matches' are made
her novels. Lieutenant Price of *Mansfield Park* is not Othello
y's mother is not smothered but there is an instructive com-
be drawn. Jane Austen is always careful not to stray too far in
on of *Wuthering Heights*, though, when it comes to inequality.
on in *Emma* whether Harriet Smith be suited to Mr Elton or to

■ He that, without diminution of any other excellence, shall preserve
all the unities unbroken deserves the like applause with the architect
who shall display all the orders of architecture in a citadel without any
deduction from its strength; but the principal beauty of a citadel is to
exclude the enemy, and the greatest graces of a play are to copy nature
and instruct life.[49] □

He does not say that accordance with the unities must not be attempted,
nor that the attempt successfully carried out is without beauty, for:

■ [T]hough they may sometimes conduce to pleasure, they are always
to be sacrificed to the nobler beauties of variety and instruction.[50] □

'They *may* sometimes conduce to pleasure'; surely his remark on *Othello*
means that their observance would have done so, with no detriment.
This view diminishes the importance of the opening scenes and relegates
them to the status of that which may without loss be 'occasionally related'.
This shows an insensitivity to their dramatic effectiveness, but there is no
need, in this instance, to tax Johnson with inconsistency.

Rymer, of course, did not take much notice of the play's infraction of
the unity of place:

■ For the *Second Act*, our Poet having dispatcht his affairs at *Venice*, shews
the Action next (I know not how many leagues off) in the Island of
Cyprus. The Audience must be there too: And yet our *Bays* had it never
in his head, to make any provision of Transport Ships for them.
    In the days that the *Old Testament* was Acted in *Clerkenwell*, by the
Parish Clerks of *London*, the Israelites might pass through the *Red sea*:
but, alass, at this time, we have no *Moses* to bid the Waters *make way*,
and to Usher us along. Well, the absurdities of this kind break no
Bones. They may make Fools of us; but do not hurt our Morals.[51] □

This last sentence is the most important for Rymer; he is not at all interested in illusionism. The irony of the situation is that Rymer had sought
to expose inconsistencies and absurdities not at all in the name of a realism attempting to mimic History, but in the name of what he thought
was the opposite of History, Philosophy. His objections are being taken
up by people the underlying assumptions of whose arguments tend in an
exactly opposite direction to that in which Rymer hoped to point critical
discussion. All this is happening, it should be said, quite without conscious direction. Rymer took a conscious and deliberate stand for what
he believed to be true and right, and he called that Nature and he said
that Philosophy guided you towards it and he held that History could not
guide you towards it. Perhaps he believed this because of what he had

seen around him. He was succeeded by people who did not hold as strongly as he did that History and Philosophy were irreconcilably opposed. Perhaps they did not because of what they saw around them. Perhaps it is not as simple as what they saw around them, but more a matter of what they hoped for and believed. Be that as it may be, people had become more interested in *John an Oaks* and *John a Stiles*, as Rymer puts it, and in the *higlety-piglety* of History. That had issued in the Novel and in a different way of looking at plays.

The situation is complicated by the third element, the persistence of spectacle. The illusionism against which Johnson is arguing is a form of spectacle. The convincing presentation of domestic reality is as much a matter of spectacle as the 'flyings' of the witches in *Macbeth* or the vanishing feasts in *The Tempest* recorded by John Downes in *Roscius Anglicanus*.[52] The significance of spectacle is that it has to be *seen*. It is diminished in imagination or in memory; it cannot be supplied in reading. Johnson goes too far, perhaps, in reducing the contribution of the actors, but it can be seen that he is doing this for the same reasons Capell is arguing for a similar view of Shakespeare's theatre and that is because their present age was, they thought, too taken up with spectacle. It can easily be seen that if a contest were waged between the Novel and the Theatre one clear distinction between the two could be spectacle. It would be a great pity (and Capell and Johnson both seem to have felt this) if that became the only distinction between the two. On the other hand, it can be thought that it was perhaps hopelessly unrealistic even to speculate that Shakespeare's theatre might be revived in that age.

Ironically, the theatre people had caught up with Rymer (or at least with Dennis and Gildon and the others) and were now preaching Neo-classicism in the theatre. Brian Vickers comments:

■ It is not without significance that what we might call the harder, purer Neo-classic attitudes in this period are largely to be found in theatrical circles, with actors such as Gentleman, Potter, and (in some respects at least, notably his defence of the Unities), Hiffernan. It is as if the theatre, immersed in its own activities and traditions, were a generation behind contemporary taste.[53] □

Johnson and Capell, taken together, might suggest another reason; that the illusionist ambitions of the theatre could only be protected by such an insistence.

Eighteenth-century theatre is not a simple phenomenon. For all the brash spectacle there was an intensely serious concern but on the other hand for all that Shakespeare's status grew vastly in this period it is associated with some of the brashest spectacle and none were so guilty as his greatest propagandist, Garrick. Brian Vickers writes:

■ As an adapter of Shakespeare Garrick has not him to posterity. His influence was pernicious, for ther the work of Tate and others but also, in his new and bad fashions which were to persist for m

Vickers points particularly to *The Faeries*, but it is p out Garrick; Purcell's *The Fairy Queen* (music to ar had been performed in London in 1692 and tal more liberties with Shakespeare's work. The que far an adaptation has to go from its original before other than an adaptation and owes so little to its o cannot be implicated any longer. How much ha away before the original is no longer a significant bound to bear upon the question of performance

G. W. Stone comments (perhaps wryly) that larity of a number of Shakespeare's plays lay in t

The plays were often followed by a dance ar 'new masquerade dance' that followed *Romeo* 1748 or the 'vocal parts and solemn dirge sung sion' for the January 1763 production.[56] Vicker

■ What we know of the taste of the mid-ei theatre audience hardly encourages us to rate crimination highly.[57] □

The taste for Shakespeare was for Shakespea worth noting that in terms of performanc feature. Stone lists performances of Shakesp and Covent Garden between 1747 and 1776

	Drury Lane
Romeo and Juliet	141
Hamlet	114
King Lear	82
Macbeth	76
Othello	

All had had song and dance pieces added way, with the exception of *Othello*.[58] The age. In order to try to summarise the rea it is worth recalling the conversation re 12 April:

Robert Martin seems to take the reader a long way away from the world of *Othello*. Johnson's reasonableness seems to play down some of the play's dangers and excitements; it makes the play less exotic, less extraordinary. The question is whether or not his view is a distortion.

Rymer is not exaggerating; Boswell is not being silly. It is difficult to see a moral in that useful sense of a useful picture of life in *Othello*. Johnson is not wrong; you can if you try. These three represent a circle of argument that continues unabated into our century and that must now be taken into the turbulent period at the end of the eighteenth century to which contemporary commentators gave the name 'Romantic Revival'.

CHAPTER THREE

The Nineteenth Century: Romantics to Victorians

■ Imitations produce pain or pleasure, not because they are mistaken for realities, but because they bring realities to mind.[1] □

Dr Johnson's words point to the central inadequacy of Neo-classical formulations about art such as Sir Philip Sidney's definition of the purpose of poetry that it is 'to teach and to delight', or as Martin Coyle puts it, the purpose of art is 'not only to entertain but also to instruct'. These formulations of Neo-classical principle are not at fault; that is really what critics of this persuasion think. What they reveal is that there is a fault-line in the thinking itself. 'To teach and to delight' does not say what the relationship between 'teaching' and 'delighting' is exactly. It allows the thought that the two are separate, parallel, aims. It allows the thought that a work might delight, but not teach and another work that teaches might not delight. The Neo-classical critic will say of the first of these possibilities that teaching is more important than delighting, but that cannot be known from the formulation itself. Art does both things at its best, but the formulation does not have any idea how the two things are related and it is not obvious.

How can these two goals be made compatible? Only if the delighting is carefully subordinated to the teaching. However, it can then be argued that the delighting is superfluous. Only if you can show that the delight is the means by which the teaching is accomplished and that the teaching could not be accomplished in any other way can you argue for the primacy of delight as a goal. Dr Johnson's formula offers a way to do this. He is talking about pain and pleasure, it is true, but if it can be shown that the realities brought to mind teach in a unique manner then the task is accomplished. This task will be left to the moralists to accomplish. Matthew Arnold will play a large part and in the twentieth century in Britain, F. R. Leavis. The work of the Novel, especially that of George

Eliot, will be important. What is being traced at the moment is the emergence of the conditions that will allow certain insights that will form the basis of the new view. None of the critics after Rymer can answer him; his total case has not been addressed, still less refuted. What has happened is that piecemeal dissatisfaction has opened up areas of the argument for discussion. The answer to Rymer is that the events and experiences portrayed by *Othello*, the realities that it brings to mind, are not extraordinary but ordinary; this is Nature.

Understandably perhaps, no one wants to say this, or perhaps can even imagine it, at least not yet. It is not that they are not used to appalling realities; Pepys witnesses the execution of a man in a manner our state of civilisation would find revolting and frightening and yet sees justice in it. Rymer's point is just that they are used to a vigorous marginalisation of the deviant; of its exposure to ridicule at Southwark Fair or its exposure to contempt at Charing Cross. *Othello* offers a terrible challenge, put quite clearly by Lodovico (described in the 'Willow Song' scene by Desdemona as 'a proper man'):

■ O thou, Othello, that wert once so good,
  Fallen in the practice of a damned slave,
  What should be said to thee? [V, ii, 288–90] □

(I am following *Quarto* and M.R. Ridley's *Arden*; Honigmann's *Arden* follows *Folio* and has 'cursed' instead of 'damned' in 289 and 'shall' instead of 'should' in 290.)

'What should be said to thee?' is the question put by the play. It is a question perhaps best answered by silence. The dramatic effect of Lodovico's question is to provoke silence. The mind does not leap in with a judgement that lies to hand. This, perhaps, is why Rymer thought it so important to set up the Rules and to throw down this play by their authority. What is happening after Rymer is the effect of a convergence of quite different responses towards a common centre. On the one hand is the persistence of a theatregoing tradition that recognised the power of the play in performance in spite of the critics' contempt. Their criterion was simply one of delight. On the other hand the critics' camp itself was far from unanimous. Though there might be some embarrassment at Rymer's outburst there was no real confidence that it could be seen off; the one good attempt at a refutation was made by a man who came to share Rymer's views sixteen years later. That might be accidental, but it does not inspire confidence. It looks as though the play continues to be popular with audiences who just do not care about deeper critical reflection.

There is a patchy development of responses to particular aspects of the criticisms; John Shebbeare, for example, offers a really good critical discussion of Act III, Scene iii – the scene Rymer had simply dismissed out of hand. Shebbeare takes his readers through the scene carefully, as a good critic should, going from text to explication and back to text. Here he is on Iago's subtlety at the beginning of the exchange between them:

■ The scene in the third act between Othello and Iago, where the latter first insinuates the idea of jealousy into the mind of the Moor, that timidity of accusing the innocent, that regard for the reputation of Desdemona, with the insinuation against her fidelity, are so artfully mixt that it is impossible but that Othello must have been insnared by his manner of conducting the conversation. How inimitable is his pretended love for Othello, his conjuring up the Moor's resolution to know his sentiments by distant hints and suggestions; and when Othello breaks out

I'll know thy thoughts [III, iii,164].

He answers

You cannot, if my heart were in your hand:
Nor shall not, whilst 'tis in my custody [III, iii, 165f.].

At this seemingly determined secrecy, the Moor pronouncing 'ha!', Iago with all possible art cries out

Oh! Beware, my lord, of jealousy;
It is a green-eyed monster, which doth mock
The meat it feeds on. That cuckold lives in bliss
Who, certain of his fate, loves not his wronger:
But oh! what damned minutes tell he o'er
Who doats yet doubts, suspects yet strongly loves? [III, iii, 167ff.]

This speech necessarily turns the thoughts of Othello on the idea of jealousy with all the appearance of nature and refined art; and then by proceeding in the same manner he leads him to examine the conduct of Desdemona, and creates a suspicion of her infidelity to the Moor from her having chosen him, and refused those

Of her own clime, complexion and degree [III, iii, 234].

From this he draws an inference which reflects on the character of Desdemona; this almost convinces the Moor of her being false to his bed, and he desires Iago to set his wife to watch Desdemona. In answer to this the subtle villain pretends to intreat Othello to think no more of what he had told him, to attempt discovering Desdemona's true disposition by the vehemence of her suit to him for restoring Cassio, and to believe his fears for his honour had been too importunate in the affair; with this he leaves him. In all this scene there appears nothing which can discover the Moor weaker than an honest, plain, brave man may be allowed to be; not one step carried beyond the truth in nature by Iago.² □

The quality of Shebbeare's essay is not in the originality of his discoveries but in his manner of discovering them. He makes his general statements, then he takes us through the passages showing in detail how the effect is produced.

Benjamin Victor's account of Barton Booth's Othello gives a good insight into how impressive the play must have been able to seem on the stage. He quotes III, iii, 256–83 and comments:

■ I look upon this Soliloquy to be the Touchstone for every New Actor. When *Iago* has left him, after a long Pause, the Eye kept looking after him, *Booth* spoke the following Remark in a low Tone of Voice:

> This fellow's of exceeding Honesty,
> And knows all Qualities with a learn'd Spirit
> Of human Dealings [III, iii, 262ff.].

Then a Pause; the Look starting into Anger.

> If I do find her Haggard,
> Though that her Jesses were my dear Heart-strings,
> I'd whistle her off, and let down the Wind
> To prey on Fortune! [III, iii, 264ff.]

A long Pause, as to ruminate.

> Haply, for I am black,
> And have not those soft Parts of Conversation
> That Chamberers have – Or, for I am declin'd
> Into the Vale of Years – Yet that's not much – [III, iii, 267ff.].

After a Pause the following Start of violent Passion.

> She's gone! I am abused! And my Relief
> Must be to loath her! O Curse of Marriage!
> That we can call these delicate Creatures ours,
> And not their Appetites! [III, iii, 271ff.]

What follows in a quicker, contemptuous Tone.

> I'd rather be a Toad,
> And live upon the Vapour of a Dungeon,
> Than keep a Corner in the Thing I love
> For other's Uses! [III, iii, 274ff.]

A Look of Amazement, seeing *Desdemona* coming.

> Look where she comes! [III, iii, 282]

A short Pause, the Countenance and Voice softened.

> If she be false, O then Heav'n mocks itself!
> I'll not believe it [III, iii, 283f.].

In this Soliloquy the Transitions are frequent and require such judicious Pauses, such Alteration of Tones and Attitudes, such corresponding Looks that no Actor since *Booth* has been quite compleat in it.

In the distressful Passages, at the heart-breaking Anguish of his Jealousy, I have seen all the Men susceptible of the tender Passions, in Tears.[3] □

This is an interesting, moving, careful account; Victor writes as an intelligent and sensitive theatregoer. It must be clear, though, that his attention is entirely upon Othello's feelings and the actor's portrayal of those feelings successfully evoking sympathetic response in the audience, an achievement that is far from negligible. However, his attention is not on the design as a whole, which might offer a slightly more complex perspective on what is happening immediately on stage. Tobias Smollett, writing of another part of Act III, Scene iii, makes a point that will be made again in the early twentieth century as part of a further important revision of critical opinion:

■ We find *Othello*, in the midst of those jealous conceptions which in a manner desolated his whole soul, breaking out into a puerile lamentation in which he recapitulates a number of idle circumstances as the objects of his regret.

> Farewell the neighing steed, and the shrill trump,
> The spirit stirring drum, th'ear-piercing fife,
> The royal banner, (*which by the bye he could not unfold in the service of Venice*) and all quality,
> Pride, pomp, and *circumstance* of glorious war!

And (*mark the prosopopeia*[4]) oh, you mortal engines whose rude
   throats
Th'immortal Jove's (*he was a Christian too*) dread clamours
   counterfeit,
Farewell! [III, iii, 354–60]

Let us only ask the candid reader, Whether or not this speech or excla-
mation has not all the air of an affected rhapsody; and if he does not
think it would have been more properly assigned to *Iago* when he
attempted to dissuade the simple *Roderigo* from returning to *Venice*?[5] ☐

Smollett's point is that, if any one has a right to lament the loss of opportunity to obtain glory, it is Iago, who has failed to secure the appointment
for which he hoped and which he thought his due. What is interesting is
that the sort of language (it is from the same scene) that Booth made the
instrument to move his auditors to tears is coolly dismissed by Smollett
as 'an affected rhapsody'. It is precisely this cool superiority to theatrical
effect that distinguishes the Neo-classical approach and defines criticism
for so long.
   Coleridge was no stranger to Neo-classical prejudice; his suggestion
that 'Nor Heav'n peep through the blanket of the dark' (*Macbeth*, I, v, 53)
should be amended to 'Nor Heav'n peep through the *blank height* of the
dark' is as ingenious almost to the same degree as it misses the point of
the image – another distinguishing mark of Neo-classicism's worst
excesses.[6] His remarks on *Othello* are fragmentary, being mainly recon-
structions by H. N. Coleridge from a manuscript set of notes for a
projected but never completed Study of the play, and some comments
from *Table Talk*. Nevertheless, they offer some useful views and show
what an important poet thought of the work.
   Coleridge puts *Othello* together with *King Lear* and *Hamlet* to the
advantage of *Othello*:

■ *Lear* is the most tremendous effort of Shakespeare as a poet; *Hamlet* as
a philosopher or meditator; and *Othello* is the union of the two. There is
something gigantic and unformed in the former two; but in the latter
everything assumes its due place and proportion, and the whole
mature powers of his mind are displayed in admirable equilibrium.[7] ☐

Coleridge's interest, to judge from the notes, is fixed first on Iago and
then on Othello. He begins by analysing closely the opening of the play,
as he does with others:

■ [I, i] The admirable preparation, so characteristic of Shakespeare, in
the introduction of Roderigo as the dupe on whom Iago first exercises

his art, and in so doing displays his own character. Roderigo is already fitted and predisposed [to be a dupe] by his own passions – being without any fixed principle or strength of character (the want of character and the power of the passions, like the wind loudest in empty houses, form his character) – but yet not without the moral notions and sympathies with honour which his rank and connexions had hung upon him. The very three first lines happily state the nature and foundation of the friendship – the purse – as well as showing the contrast of Roderigo's intemperance of mind with Iago's coolness, the coolness of a preconceiving *experimenter*. The mere language of protestation in –

> If ever I did dream of such a matter,
> Abhor me – [I, i, 4–5].

which, fixing the associative link that determines Roderigo's continuation of complaint –

> Thou told'st me
> Thou didst hold him in thy hate – [I, i, 5–6].

elicits a true feeling of Iago's – the dread of contempt habitual to those who encourage in themselves and have their keenest pleasure in the feeling and expression of contempt for others. His high self-opinion is seen here – and how a wicked man employs his real feelings as well as assumes those most alien from his own, as instruments of his purpose.[8] □

This is an excellent example of how the critical habit is developing of seeing in the words of the play the whole of the play's work. In this instance, Coleridge produces from a line and a half (at most) a vivid picture of a most important aspect of Iago's character that of course could not come from a first acquaintance with the first three lines of the play but must emerge at last from close and careful meditation on the whole of the play. But Coleridge is not wrong; it is clear, on reflection, how Iago's 'Abhor me' could well come from the mind of one of 'those who encourage in themselves and have their keenest pleasure in the feeling and expression of contempt for others'. He continues:

■ In what follows, let the reader feel how, by and through the glass of two passions, disappointed passion and envy, the very vices he is complaining of are made to act upon him as so many excellences, and the more appropriately because cunning is always admired and wished for by minds conscious of inward weakness. And yet it is but *half* – it acts like music on an inattentive auditor, *swelling* the thoughts which prevent him from listening to it.[9] □

It has to be clear that the kind of attention Coleridge is paying, and demanding from his reader, can only arise from reading; 'the reader' here refers not to the reader of Coleridge (these notes were for planned lectures – to be published surely but to be listened to first) but to the reader of Shakespeare. It is a fascinating insight (and surely right) that Iago sees his being outwitted as admirably clever (from his viewpoint as a villain, admiring the skill of others) at the same as he sees himself the victim and resents it. Coleridge's illustration shows the new strain entering the discussion of Shakespeare. The tension between the music and the thoughts of the inattentive listener is caught in the word *'swelling'*. This is not a process of thought, but of the emotional charging of thought. The thoughts distract from the music; the music *'swells'* the thought. Thus neither is resolved. Iago cannot let go his admiration for the cunning by which he has been outwitted nor of his resentment that he has been outwitted. Thus neither is resolved, nor can it be. The more he admires, the more he resents; the more he resents, the more he admires. The image of music reminds us, perhaps, of the effect of the West Wind on Shelley, or of the image of Xanadu on Coleridge himself; the state of tension is itself, if not desired, at least enjoyed. He moves on to discuss Othello, and is pure Rymer:

■ Roderigo turns off to Othello; and here comes the one if not the only justification of the blackamoor Othello, namely as a negro, who is not a *Moor* at all.

What a full fortune does the thick-lips owe,
If he can carry't thus! [I, i, 65–6]

Even if we supposed this an uninterrupted tradition of the theatre, and that Shakespeare himself, from want of scenes and the experience that nothing could be made too *marked* for the nerves of his audience, had sanctioned it, would this prove aught concerning his own intentions as a poet for all ages? Can we suppose him so utterly ignorant as to make a barbarous *negro* plead royal birth? Were negroes then known but as slaves; on the contrary were not the Moors the warriors, etc.?

Iago's speech to Brabantio implies merely that he was a *Moor*, i.e., black. Though I think the rivalry of Roderigo sufficient to account for his wilful confusion of Moor and negro – yet though compelled to give this up, I should yet think it only adapted for the then *acting*, and should complain of an enormity built only on one single word – in direct contradiction of Iago's 'Barbary' horse'. If we can in good earnest believe Shakespeare ignorant of the distinction, still why take one chance against ten – as Othello cannot be *both*?[10] ☐

In 1694 Charles Gildon had written:

■ Any Man that has convers'd with the best Travels, or read any thing of the History of those parts on the continent of *Africa* discover'd by the *Portugueze*, must be so far from robbing the *Negroes* of some Countrys there of *Humanity* that they must grant them not only greater Heroes, nicer observers of Honour and all the Moral Virtues that distinguish'd the old *Romans*, but also much better Christians (where Christianity is profess'd) than we of *Europe* generally are. They move by a nobler Principle, more open, free and generous, and not such slaves to sordid Interest.[11] ☐

It is true though that by 1710 he had changed his mind. There is a hint of Montaigne in the younger Gildon's thought; perhaps that is the explanation. Perhaps the slave trade had become too lucrative for any one in Britain to be too free with these opinions. Coleridge is right in line with Rymer and with Gildon in 1710; that has to be said. Jane Austen (whose enthusiasm for Shakespeare was not less than Coleridge's) was showing the dreadful Mrs Elton embarrassed by the insinuation she thinks she catches in *Emma* that her family are involved in the slave trade and Sir Thomas Bertram's excursions to Antigua in *Mansfield Park* are not merely diversions but imply a profound criticism of a man whose interests take him overseas when his interest should be engaged at home. Coleridge is unembarrassed. Clearly he sees no reason to be embarrassed. He returns to this theme in *Table Talk*:

■ Othello must not be conceived as a negro, but a high and chivalrous Moorish chief. Shakespeare learned the spirit of the character from the Spanish poetry which was prevalent in England in his time.[12] ☐

The unpleasantly confident pontificating tone, the hieratic tone to which it is so easy to take exception in Coleridge, is evident in this pronouncement. In the earlier notes there can be seen a man struggling to maintain a cherished view against the uncertainty that it might not be as he hopes it is; in *Table Talk* he is confidently pronouncing, it is so. 'Shakespeare learned the spirit of the character from the Spanish poetry which was prevalent in England in his time' irritates especially because of its throwaway note. Of course, this is so widely known that Coleridge needs to provide no evidence; nor has he any to offer other than the merely circumstantial to support what is nothing more than an objectionable prejudice – one that, moreover, it was obviously possible to challenge in

1694. Scott's picture of Saladin in *The Talisman* shows a similar generosity of spirit towards one who may not share one's religion exactly but who shares one's conception of chivalry. Such generosity of spirit is almost a Romantic convention. Aside from this, Coleridge is again and again good on the detail:

■ BRABANTIO Look to her, Moor, if thou hast eyes to see:
   She has deceived her father, and may thee.
   OTHELLO My life upon her faith! [I, iii. 293–5]

In real life how do we look back to little speeches, either as presentimental of, or most contrasted with, an affecting event. Shakespeare, as secure of being read over and over, of becoming a family friend, how he provides this for *his readers*, and leaves it to them.[13] □

Here again he treats Shakespeare as the property of *'his readers'*, though he is surely right to the extent that several acquaintances at least with the play performed would be needed to pick up such detail. It can be argued against this that the story will have become so well known that such detail will be easily available even on a first viewing, but surely Coleridge would have been aware of this if it were so. It is worth returning briefly to the note on I, i in this connection:

■ Even if we supposed this an uninterrupted tradition of the theatre, and that Shakespeare himself, from want of scenes and the experience that nothing could be made too *marked* for the nerves of his audience, had sanctioned it, would this prove aught concerning his own intentions as a poet for all ages?[14] □

He anticipates an argument that Shakespeare's age would not have been moved by the presentation of 'the blackamoor Othello' and counters with a notion at first sight hard to take in: 'would this prove aught concerning his own intentions as a poet for all ages?' This seems to mean that whatever Shakespeare felt about his own age's views he must have had an eye to the future. As Ben Jonson wrote of Shakespeare: 'He was not of an age, but for all time.'[15]

Coleridge cannot be quite sure of his ground because he goes on:

■ Can we suppose him so utterly ignorant as to make a barbarous *negro* plead royal birth?[16] □

This sort of argument only works if the astonished tone in which the question is asked is met by the reader's confident denial that what is asked could be true. It is not an argument, in other words, at all.

'Ignorant', to be fair, probably here means 'of future ages' taste and inclinations in this matter' and the expected answer is 'No, of course not'. Coleridge's guess about the future was not as good as he believed Shakespeare's must have been, so perhaps Shakespeare's guess was, in fact, better than Coleridge believed it was. Much more likely, he did not think much about the future at all. The famous passage on Iago is undoubtedly good:

■ IAGO Virtue! A fig! 'tis in ourselves that we are thus or thus [I, iii, 320].

Iago's passionless character, all *will* in intellect; therefore a bold partisan here of a truth, but yet of a truth converted into falsehood by absence of all the modifications which the frail nature of man would necessitate. And the *last sentiment* –

. . . our raging motions, our carnal stings, our unbitted lusts; whereof I take this, that you call love, to be a sect or scion [I, iii, 331–3]

– there lies the Iagoism of how many! And the repetition, 'Go make money!' – a pride in it, of an anticipated dupe, stronger than the love of lucre.

IAGO Go to, farewell, put money enough in your purse;
Thus do I ever make my fool my purse [I, iii, 381–2].

The triumph! Again, 'put money', after the effect has been fully produced. The last speech, Iago's soliloquy, shows the motive-hunting of motiveless malignity – how awful! In itself fiendish; while yet he was allowed to bear the divine image, it is too fiendish for his own steady view. He is a being next to devil, only *not* quite devil – and this Shakespeare has attempted – executed – without disgust, without scandal![17] □

Othello himself makes the point:

■ I look down towards his feet, but that's a fable.
If that thou be'st a devil, I cannot kill thee [V, ii, 283–4]. □

The picture of Iago had drawn some censure, from Rymer onwards. Rymer had complained:

■ The *Ordinary* of *New gate* never had the like Monster to pass under his examination. Can it be any diversion to see a Rogue beyond what the Devil ever finish'd? Or wou'd it be any instruction to an Audience?[18] □

And Lord Kames was worried:

■ Iago's character in the tragedy of *Othello* is insufferably monstrous and Satanical: not even Shakespeare's masterly hand can make the picture agreeable.[19] □

Mrs Lennox agreed:

■ [T]he Murder of *Desdemona* was such an Excess of wanton Cruelty that one can hardly conceive it possible that a Man could be so transcendently wicked.[20] □

Thomas Wilkes compared the play to Young's *Zanga*:

■ Iago prosecutes to destruction a noble unsuspecting officer for having preferred above him *one Michael Cassio*. He has no other real motive for his villainy. He, indeed, in the first scene of the Play mentions to Roderigo that he hates the general on another account, for, says he, 'He has, between my sheets, done me the unlawful office;' [I, iii, 386ff.] and again he declares he will not be easy 'till he is even with him wife for wife' [II, i, 297]. But from his deportment through the rest of the play he leaves us at liberty to judge that he has invented this story the better to help his designs on Roderigo, without whom it is impossible his schemes can work. He then proceeds to destroy an honest gallant soldier, an innocent beautiful woman, a well-beloved modest man, and a simple outwitted coxcomb. He completes a mean but barbarous revenge, excited by a very trifling disappointment; he levels every thing in his way, and spares neither age, sex, or condition. When his villanies are detected he deports himself with all the gloomy malice of a slave. 'What ye know, says he, ye know; seek no more of me, for from this hour I never will speak more [V, ii, 300f.].' In few words, he has neither the spirit to triumph in his vengeance, nor the least spark of refined feeling for having destroyed characters so amiable as Desdemona and Othello. How very different are the motives and deportment of Zanga! How intimately acquainted was the poet who drew the character with the manner both of his rank and country![21] □

It is interesting to note that hostility to a work can often produce more clear sight than partiality struggling to defend the indefensible. Wilkes's obvious preference for the clarity (not to say the obviousness) of *Zanga* produces a sharpness in the definition of his picture of Iago that is devastatingly accurate. The last three sentences apart, Wilkes could be building towards a revelation of wonder at the boldness of the character-isation of Iago but, instead, in the simplicity that leads him to prefer *Zanga*, he has left a horrifying portrait from which he turns in dislike but which may make the reader think what consequences follow from admitting the truth of this picture. That is what Coleridge is attempting to think out. Kames and Mrs Lennox take the Rymer view; Wilkes thinks the picture lacks spirit; Coleridge sees Iago in a few suggestive phrases as 'all *will* in intellect', praising Shakespeare's depiction of 'Iago's coolness, the coolness of a preconceiving *experimenter*' and of 'the motive-hunting of motiveless malignity'. The brilliant touch is the perception that Iago cannot bear to confront his own wickedness:

■ In itself fiendish; while yet he was allowed to bear the divine image, it is too fiendish for his own steady view.[22] □

Whether this view is accepted or not, it must be accepted that it accords with what is known and that it offers an exciting emotional depth that might not have been envisaged before Coleridge pointed it out. His com-ment on III, iii, 282–3 can be compared with Benjamin Victor's account of actor Barton Booth's Othello. Victor had said:

■ A Look of Amazement, seeing *Desdemona coming.*
     Look where she comes!
A short Pause, the Countenance and Voice softened.
     If she be false, O then Heav'n mocks itself!
     I'll not believe it.[23] □

Coleridge, typically, elaborates:

■ [III, iii, 282–3: The sight of Desdemona drives away Othello's suspi-cion.]

    If she be false, O then heaven mocks itself!
    I'll not believe it.

Divine! The effect of innocence and the better genius.[24] □

There is nothing illegitimate in elaborating the psychological implica-tions of the words in this way; it is a necessary part of understanding and interpreting. What must always be borne in mind is that the process of understanding *is* a process of interpretation and that the necessary elab-oration must not go beyond the warrant the words provide. This Guide has already shown how Gildon's enthusiastic rebuttal to Rymer depended upon an elaboration that supplied a great deal beyond the warrant given by the play, and how Johnson, Charlotte Lennox and Edmond Malone merely followed on and discussed the characters of the play as though they were separable from the play; the power of Coleridge's insight into Othello's psychological state at this moment must not make the reader forget that Coleridge is offering an interpretation of words supposed to be composed by Shakespeare, not an insight into a human being.

It will become increasingly important to insist upon this point, and increasingly difficult to resist the temptation to forget it as the nineteenth century progresses; William Hazlitt's lectures on Shakespeare were entitled *The Characters of Shakespeare's Plays*, and that is what we get. Before leaving Coleridge, however, his discussion of jealousy from *Table Talk* must be considered, because it is an important precursor to A.C. Bradley's detailed discussion of *Othello* at the end of this century.

■ Othello must not be conceived as a negro, but a high and chivalrous Moorish chief. Shakespeare learned the spirit of the character from the Spanish poetry which was prevalent in England in his time. Jealousy does not strike me as the point in his passion; I take it to be rather an agony that the creature whom he had believed angelic, with whom he had garnered up his heart and whom he could not help still loving, should be proved impure and worthless. It was the struggle *not* to love her. It was a moral indignation and regret that virtue should so fall: – 'But yet the *pity* of it, Iago! – O Iago! The *pity* of it, Iago! [IV, I, 192–3]' In addition to this, his honour was concerned: Iago would not have succeeded but by hinting that his honour was compromised. There is no ferocity in Othello; his mind is majestic and composed. He deliberately determines to die, and speaks his last speech with a view of showing his attachment to the Venetian State, though it had superseded him . . . I have often told you that I do not think there is any jealousy, properly so called, in the character of Othello. There is no predisposition to suspicion, which I take to be an essential term in the definition of the word. Desdemona very truly told Emilia that he was not jealous, that is, of a jealous habit, and he says so as truly of himself. Iago's suggestions, you see, are quite new to him; they do not correspond with anything of a like nature previously in his mind. If Desdemona had, in fact, been guilty, no one would have thought of calling Othello's conduct that of a jealous man. He could not act otherwise than he did with the lights he had: whereas jealousy can never be strictly right. See how utterly unlike Othello is to Leontes in *The Winter's Tale*, or even to Leonatus in *Cymbeline*! The jealousy of the first proceeds from an evident trifle, and something like hatred is mingled with it, and the conduct of Leonatus in accepting the wager and exposing his wife to the trial denotes a jealous temper already formed.[25] □

F.R. Leavis's strictures on this account will offer an opportunity to consider this point in more depth, but it is easy to imagine the response of a Thomas Rymer to such a picture. There is no warrant at all to speak of what is, or is not, in Othello's mind; properly speaking, there is no such thing as Othello's mind at all. This is not like, say, *Middlemarch* or *Emma*, in both of which we can quite properly speak of characters' minds, because they are presented. In the justly praised Chapter 16 of *Emma*, or in the important scene in *Middlemarch* in which Dorothea is deciding whether or not to wear an ornamented cross, the reader is presented with the characters' minds. In a poetic drama the audience or reader is only presented with what people say, and with what they do. Their minds exist only as an inference made by the member of the audience or by the reader from what they say and what they do, and it is important to remember this. This is not to say that such inferences must not be made; often they are essential. It is to say that the play must not be forgotten in the welter of inferences made in order to understand it.

Another point to be made at this juncture is that the sort of cosmic scheme within which Rymer insisted the play, and indeed all plays, must be seen, has entirely vanished from consideration. Either that or the scheme Rymer favoured has been replaced with another one in which the illogicality and absurdity of which he complained no longer appear as such. Coleridge has found a reason:

■ Jealousy does not strike me as the point in his passion; I take it to be rather an agony that the creature whom he had believed angelic, with whom he had garnered up his heart and whom he could not help still loving, should be proved impure and worthless. It was the struggle *not* to love her. It was a moral indignation and regret that virtue should so fall: – 'But yet the *pity* of it, Iago! – O Iago! The *pity* of it, Iago! [IV, I, 192–3]'[26] □

This goes much further than Johnson:

■ The fiery openness of Othello, magnanimous, artless, and credulous, boundless in his confidence, ardent in his affection, inflexible in his resolution, and obdurate in his revenge.[27] □

Thomas Wilkes's description of him as 'an honest gallant soldier' is much briefer but in the same line, and is found in many sympathetic discussions of the play. It is much less complex and, in some ways, less interesting as a description of a character, but consider again Thomas Wilkes's description of Iago's activities:

■ He then proceeds to destroy an honest gallant soldier, an innocent beautiful woman, a well-beloved modest man, and a simple outwitted coxcomb. He completes a mean but barbarous revenge, excited by a very trifling disappointment; he levels every thing in his way, and spares neither age, sex, or condition. When his villanies are detected he deports himself with all the gloomy malice of a slave. 'What ye know, says he, ye know; seek no more of me, for from this hour I never will speak more [V, ii, 300f.].' In few words, he has neither the spirit to triumph in his vengeance, nor the least spark of refined feeling for having destroyed characters so amiable as Desdemona and Othello.[28] □

Wilkes thinks the characterisation unsuccessful because he compares what Iago does with his motive and with his final behaviour and finds a disproportion, but he sums up the action of the play well and highlights the pattern of the work. That pattern depends upon such simple figures as 'an honest gallant soldier' and 'an innocent beautiful woman'. The terror of the play, from this point of view, is that it is all done relatively easily. That's why Rymer's question is so important: 'If this be our end, what boots it to be vertuous?' This sort of account finds the focus of interest in the pattern; Coleridge's sort of account finds the focus of interest in the characters.

Hazlitt displays the same sort of interest. In *Characters of Shakespear's Plays* he offers a picture of the play that has to do with the contrast of character:

■ The picturesque contrasts of character in this play are almost as remarkable as the depth of the passion. The Moor Othello, the gentle Desdemona, the villain Iago, the good-natured Cassio, the fool Roderigo, present a range and variety of character as striking and palpable as that produced by the opposition of costume in a picture. Their distinguishing qualities stand out to the mind's eye, so that even when we are not thinking of their actions or sentiments, the idea of their persons is still as present to us as ever. These characters and the images they stamp upon the mind are the farthest asunder possible, the distance between them is immense: yet the compass of knowledge and invention which the poet has shewn in embodying these extreme creations of his genius is only greater than the truth and felicity with which he has identified each character with itself, or blended their different qualities together in the same story.[29] □

Hazlitt's summary survey of the play is masterful:

■ The movement of the passion in Othello is exceedingly different from that of Macbeth. In Macbeth there is a violent struggle between opposite feelings, between ambition and the stings of conscience, almost from first to last: in Othello, the doubtful conflict between contrary passions, though dreadful, continues only for a short time, and the chief interest is excited by the alternate ascendancy of different passions, the entire and unforeseen change from the fondest love and most unbounded confidence to the tortures of jealousy and the madness of hatred. The revenge of Othello, after it has once taken thorough possession of his mind, never quits it, but grows stronger and stronger at every moment of its delay. The nature of the Moor is noble, confiding, tender, and generous; but his blood is of the most inflammable kind; and being once roused by a sense of his wrongs, he is stopped by no considerations of remorse or pity till he has given a loose to all the dictates of his rage and his despair. It is in working his noble nature up to this extremity through rapid but gradual transitions, in raising passion to its height from the smallest beginnings and in spite of all obstacles, in painting the expiring conflict between love and hatred, tenderness and resentment, jealousy and remorse, in unfolding the strength and the weaknesses of our nature, in uniting sublimity of thought with the anguish of the keenest woe, in putting in motion the various impulses that agitate this our mortal being, and at last blending them in that noble tide of deep and sustained passion, impetuous but majestic, that 'flows on to the Propontic, and knows no ebb', that Shakespear has shewn the mastery of his genius and of his power over the human heart. The third act of OTHELLO is his masterpiece, not of knowledge or passion separately, but of the two combined, of the knowledge of character with the expression of passion, of consummate art in the keeping up of appearances with the profound workings of nature, and the convulsive movements of uncontroulable agony, of the power of inflicting torture and of suffering it. Not only is the tumult of passion heaved up from the very bottom of the soul, but every the slightest undulation of feeling is seen on the surface as it arises from the impulses of imagination or the different probabilities maliciously suggested by Iago. The progressive preparation for the catastrophe is wonderfully managed from the Moor's first gallant recital of the story of his love, of 'the spells and witchcraft he had used', from his unlooked-for and romantic success, the fond satisfaction with which he dotes on his own happiness, the unreserved tenderness of Desdemona and her innocent importunities in favour of Cassio, irritating the suspicions instilled into her husband's mind by the perfidy of Iago, and rankling there to poison, till he loses all command of himself, and his rage can only be appeased by blood. She is introduced, just before Iago begins to put his scheme in practice, pleading for Cassio with all the thoughtless gaiety of friendship and winning confidence in the love of Othello.

'What! Michael Cassio?
That came a wooing with you, and so many a time,
When I have spoke of you dispraisingly,
Hath ta'en your part, to have so much to do
To bring him in? – Why this is not a boon:
'Tis as I should intreat you wear your gloves,
Or feed on nourishing meats, or keep you warm;
Or sue to you to do a peculiar profit
To your person. Nay, when I have a suit,
Wherein I mean to touch your love indeed,
It shall be full of poise, and fearful to be granted [III, iii, 70–83].'

Othello's confidence, at first only staggered by broken hints and insin-
uations, recovers itself at sight of Desdemona; and he exclaims

'If she be false, O then Heav'n mocks itself!
I'll not believe it [III, iii, 282–3].'

But presently after, on brooding over his suspicions by himself, and
yielding to his apprehensions of the worst, his smothered jealousy
breaks out into open fury, and he returns to demand satisfaction of
Iago like a wild beast stung with the envenomed shaft of the hunters.
'Look where he comes [III, iii, 333]', etc. In this state of exasperation
and violence, after the first paroxysms of his grief and tenderness have
had their vent in that passionate apostrophe, 'I felt not Cassio's kisses
on her lips [III, iii, 344]', Iago by false aspersions, and by presenting
the most revolting images to his mind [Hazlitt's footnote refers to the
passage beginning: 'It is impossible you should see this, were they prime
as goats' and so on – that is, III, iii, 405–11], easily turns the storm of
passion from himself against Desdemona, and works him up into a
trembling agony of doubt and fear, in which he abandons all his love
and hopes in a breath.

'Now do I see 'tis true. Look here, Iago,
All my fond love thus do I blow to Heav'n. 'Tis gone.
Arise black vengeance from the hollow hell;
Yield up, O love, thy crown and hearted throne
To tyrannous hate! Swell bosom with thy fraught;
For 'tis of aspick's tongues [III, iii, 447–53].'

From this time, his raging thoughts 'never look back, ne'er ebb to
humble love' [III, iii, 461], till his revenge is sure of its object, the
painful regrets and involuntary recollections of past circumstances
which cross his mind amidst the dim trances of passion, aggravating the

sense of his wrongs, but not shaking his purpose. Once indeed, where Iago shews him Cassio with the handkerchief in his hand, and making sport (as he thinks) of his misfortunes, the intolerable bitterness of his feelings, the extreme sense of shame, makes him fall to praising her accomplishments and relapse into a momentary fit of weakness, 'Yet, Oh the pity of it, Iago, the pity of it! [IV, I, 192–3]' This returning fondness however only serves, as it is managed by Iago, to whet his revenge, and set his heart more against her. In his conversations with Desdemona, the persuasion of her guilt and the immediate proofs of her duplicity seem to irritate his resentment and aversion to her; but in the scene immediately preceding her death, the recollection of his love returns upon him in all its tenderness and force; and after her death, he all at once forgets his wrongs in the sudden and irreparable sense of his loss.

> 'My wife! My wife! What wife? I have no wife.
> Oh insupportable! Oh heavy hour! [V, ii, 96–7]'

This happens before he is assured of her innocence; but afterwards his remorse is as dreadful as his revenge has been, and yields only to fixed and death-like despair. His farewel speech, before he kills himself, in which he conveys his reasons to the senate for the murder of his wife, is equal to the first speech in which he gave them an account of his courtship of her, and 'his whole course of love [I, iii, 92]'. Such an ending was alone worthy of such a commencement.[30] □

Hazlitt keeps a firm grasp of the whole shape of the play and guides the listener clearly through it; this is a long way from Rymer's contemptuous dismissal of this scene and, between them, Hazlitt and Coleridge have added considerably to Johnson's generous and measured depiction, but without fundamentally changing the view he put forward, with others who shared his estimation, in whole or in part. What gives Hazlitt's picture greater significance than many others is that he has a theory of tragedy, which he puts forward at the beginning of his lecture:

■ It has been said that tragedy purifies the affections by terror and pity. That is, it substitutes imaginary sympathy for mere selfishness. It gives us a high and permanent interest, beyond ourselves, in humanity as such. It raises the great, the remote, and the possible to an equality with the real, the little and the near. It makes man a partaker with his kind. It subdues and softens the stubbornness of his will. It teaches him that there are and have been others like himself, by shewing him as in a glass what they have felt, thought, and done. It opens the chambers of the human heart. It leaves nothing indifferent to us that can affect our common nature. It excites our sensibility by exhibiting the passions wound up to the utmost pitch by the power of imagination or the temptation of circumstances; and corrects their fatal excesses in ourselves by pointing to the greater extent of sufferings and of crimes to which they have led others. Tragedy creates a balance of the affections. It makes us thoughtful spectators in the lists of life. It is the refiner of the species; a discipline of humanity. The habitual study of poetry and works of imagination is one chief part of a well-grounded education. A taste for liberal art is necessary to complete the character of a gentleman. Science alone is hard and mechanical. It exercises the understanding upon things out of ourselves, while it leaves the affections unemployed, or engrossed with our own immediate, narrow interests.[31] □

This passage anticipates Matthew Arnold's famous remarks in 'The Study of Poetry' and 'The Function of Criticism at the Present Time' and can be usefully put alongside Wordsworth's *Preface* to *Lyrical Ballads*; it is of its time. It can also be compared with Johnson's remarks on the moral of *Othello*:

■ In the first place, Sir, we learn from *Othello* this very useful moral, not to make an unequal match; in the second place, we learn not to yield too readily to suspicion. The handkerchief is merely a trick, though a very pretty trick; but there are no other circumstances of reasonable suspicion, except what is related by Iago of Cassio's warm expressions concerning Desdemona in his sleep; and that depended entirely upon the assertion of one man. No, Sir, I think *Othello* has more moral than almost any play.[32] □

Is Hazlitt saying something so very different when he says of tragedy in general:

■ It excites our sensibility by exhibiting the passions wound up to the utmost pitch by the power of imagination or the temptation of circumstances; and corrects their fatal excesses in ourselves by pointing to the greater extent of sufferings and of crimes to which they have led?[33] □

The continuity is important, but to emphasise that is to ignore the tone of the remarks as a whole. The first paragraph of his lecture on *Othello* is a sustained gloss on his creative reading of Aristotle's theory of *catharsis* or 'purgation':

■ It has been said that tragedy purifies the affections by terror and pity. That is, it substitutes imaginary sympathy for mere selfishness.[34] □

'That is', here, meaning not 'in other words', because it plainly can not, but 'the way in which this works is . . .'. Hazlitt's humanism is founded upon the assumption that man is naturally selfish until educated into sympathy by acquaintance with the best that has been thought and written, to use Arnold's phrase. It is an eloquent plea for culture. The difference between Hazlitt and Johnson is *passion*; Johnson's remarks breathe a sober good sense and reflectiveness where Hazlitt's are wrung with agonised sympathy for failing humanity. More precisely, the difference is *in passion confessed and shown*. Johnson's remarks are not without passion; he just does not *show* that passion except by implication. Hazlitt shows emotion and Johnson does not. That does not mean that Johnson does not *express* emotion because he does, in a way. That 'in a way' is the entire difference between Hazlitt and Johnson, and between Coleridge and Johnson.

Getting the balance right in each case is not always easy. There is much about Hazlitt's lecture and about Coleridge's remarks that is 'Romantic' – for example, the enthusiastic affirmation of the strong emotional complex of the play, and their being so attracted to the figure of the hero of emotion, as it were, the man who feels so strongly. Comparison with eighteenth-century comments shows how this reaction was not uncommon in the earlier period, though more or less restrained by a reflective awareness that is less obvious if it is there at all in these later writers. In this context reflective awareness means an eye to the consequences for the rest of us of the heroic emotion of Othello; a consciousness of ethical responsibility, that is, of a responsibility to the community. It is possible to read Coleridge and Hazlitt and come away with the belief that a man of Othello's stature is beyond such responsibilities and must be judged by his own lights:

■ If Desdemona had, in fact, been guilty, no one would have thought of calling Othello's behaviour that of a jealous man. He could not act otherwise than he did with the lights he had: whereas jealousy can never be strictly right.[35] □

Had Coleridge had the opportunity to revise this remark for public delivery would he have amended it so as to remove entirely the opportunity for the listener or reader to make the inference that Coleridge is saying that there are circumstances in which what Othello does might be considered to be right? Hazlitt's comments on Desdemona draw out the contrast with Othello that is one of Hazlitt's themes:

■ The character of Desdemona is inimitable both in itself, and as it contrasts with Othello's groundless jealousy, and with the foul conspiracy of which she is the innocent victim. Her beauty and external graces are only indirectly glanced at: we see 'her visage in her mind'; her character every where predominates over her person.

'A maiden never bold:
Of spirit so still and quiet, that her motion
Blush'd at itself [I, iii, 95–7].'

There is one fine compliment paid to her by Cassio, who exclaims triumphantly when she comes ashore at Cyprus after the storm,

'Tempests themselves, high seas, and howling winds,
As having sense of beauty, do omit
Their mortal natures, letting safe go by
The divine Desdemona [II, i, 68–73].'

In general, as is the case with most of Shakespear's females, we lose sight of her personal charms in her attachment and devotedness to her husband. 'She is subdued even to the very quality of her lord [I, iii, 251–2]'; and to Othello's 'honours and his valiant parts her soul and fortunes consecrates [I, iii, 254–5]'. The lady protests so much herself, and she is as good as her word. The truth of conception, with which timidity and boldness are united in the same character, is marvellous. The extravagance of her resolutions, the pertinacity of her affections, may be said to arise out of the gentleness of her nature. They imply an unreserved reliance on the purity of her own intentions, an entire surrender of her fears to her love, a knitting of herself (heart and soul) to the fate of another. Bating the commencement of her passion, which is a little fantastical and headstrong (though even that may be perhaps consistently accounted for from her inability to resist a rising inclination) [. . .]

[Hazlitt's note to this parenthesis cites IV, i, 191–2, '*Iago.* Ay, too gentle./*Othello.* Nay, that's certain . . .']

[. . .] her whole character consists in having no will of her own, no prompter but her obedience. Her romantic turn is only a consequence of the domestic and practical part of her disposition; and instead of following Othello to the wars, she would gladly have 'remained at home a moth of peace', if her husband could have staid with her. Her resignation and angelic sweetness of temper do not desert her at the last. The scenes in which she laments and tries to account for Othello's estrangement from her are exquisitely beautiful. After he has struck her, and called her names, she says,

'– Alas, Iago,
What shall I do to win my lord again?

> Good friend, go to him; for by this light of heaven,
> I know not how I lost him. Here I kneel;
> If e'er my will did trespass 'gainst his love,
> Either in discourse, or thought, or actual deed,
> Or that mine eyes, mine ears, or any sense
> Delighted them on any other form;
> Or that I do not, and ever did,
> And ever will, though he do shake me off
> To beggarly divorcement, love him dearly,
> Comfort forswear me. Unkindness may do much,
> And his unkindness may defeat my life,
> But never taint my love.
>
> IAGO I pray you be content: 'tis but his humour.
> The business of the state does him offence.
>
> DESDEMONA If 'twere no other! [IV, ii, 150–69]'

The scene which follows with Æmilia and the song of the Willow, are equally beautiful, and shew the author's extreme power of varying the expression of passion, in all its moods and in all circumstances.

> 'ÆMILIA Would you had never seen him.
>
> DESDEMONA So would not I: my love do so approve him,
> That even his stubbornness, his checks, his frowns,
> Have grace and favour in them [IV, iii, 16–19]' etc.

Not the unjust suspicions of Othello, not Iago's treachery, place Desdemona in a more amiable or interesting light than the casual conversation (half earnest, half jest) between her and Æmilia on the common behaviour of women to their husbands. This dialogue takes place just before the last fatal scene. If Othello had overheard it, it would have prevented the whole catastrophe; but then it would have spoiled the play.[36] □

Many points in this picture need to be taken up in detailed discussion with close reference to the play; many are quite contentious (Hazlitt's dismissal of Desdemona's 'person' is quite wide of the mark). Hazlitt also tends to treat the quotation naively without placing it in its context: both 'A maiden never bold' and Cassio's extreme compliment need to be considered carefully in context and as part of the complex and tightly woven pattern of the play before being used; Desdemona's conversation with Emilia can not be dismissed as 'half earnest, half jest', especially given its placing, on which Hazlitt comments.

Hazlitt's final 'character' is Iago:

■ The character of Iago is one of the supererogations of Shakespear's genius. Some persons, more nice than wise, have thought this whole character unnatural, because his villainy is *without a sufficient motive.* Shakespear, who was as good a philosopher as he was a poet, thought otherwise. He knew that the love of power, which is another name for the love of mischief, is natural to man. He would know this as well or better than if it had been demonstrated to him by a logical diagram, merely from seeing children paddle in the dirt or kill flies for sport. Iago in fact belongs to a class of characters, common to Shakespear and at the same time peculiar to him; whose heads are as acute and active as their hearts are hard and callous. Iago is to be sure an extreme instance of the kind; that is to say, of diseased intellectual activity, with an almost perfect indifference to moral good or evil, or rather with a decided preference of the latter, because it falls more readily in with his favourite propensity, gives greater zest to his thoughts and scope to his actions. He is quite or nearly as indifferent to his own fate as to that of others; he runs all risks for a trifling and doubtful advantage; and is himself the dupe and victim of his ruling passion – an insatiable craving after action of the most difficult and dangerous kind. 'Our ancient' is a philosopher, who fancies that a lie that kills has more point in it than an alliteration or an antithesis; who thinks a fatal experiment on the peace of a family a better thing than watching the palpitations in the heart of a flea in a microscope; who plots the ruin of his friends as an exercise for his ingenuity, and stabs men in the dark to prevent *ennui.* His gaiety, such as it is, arises from the success of his treachery; his ease from the torture he has inflicted on others. He is an amateur of tragedy in real life; and instead of employing his invention on imaginary characters, or long-forgotten incidents, he takes the bolder and more desperate course of getting up his plot at home, casts the principal parts among his nearest friends and connections, and rehearses it in downright earnest, with steady nerves and unabated resolution.[37] □

The image of the perverted scientist recalls Coleridge's brilliant guess when he calls Iago an *'experimenter'*; it is of course at home with Hazlitt's sense of science expressed at the beginning of the lecture, with Wordsworth's comments in the *Preface* to *Lyrical Ballads* and with Mary Shelley's *Frankenstein*. The portrait of Iago is less sharp than that given by Thomas Wilkes, but it allows Hazlitt to develop a guess as remarkable as Coleridge's *'experimenter'*, Iago as 'amateur tragedian'. Hazlitt is wrestling with the triviality of Iago's resentment just as Wilkes is, and his answer is a good one: Iago's motive is his artfulness itself. Coleridge sees curiosity; Hazlitt sees delight in skill. Both could have been thinking of Shakespeare himself. The groundwork is being laid for the picture of the artist as Hero and Villain rolled into one that will haunt the romantic imagination of both the nineteenth and the twentieth centuries.

The next extracts are taken from Edward Dowden's study, *Shakspere: His Mind and Art*. Dowden is a liberal humanist in the Arnoldian manner; deeply read in and influenced by, continental, especially German, scholarship. Steeped at once in Idealist philosophy and a vivid sense of History he has an acute sense of Shakespeare – 'Shakspere' is Dowden's preferred spelling – as a man in his time as well as a man for all time. His discussion of *Othello* is part of a discussion of Shakespeare's tragedies:

■ Around the year 1600 are grouped some of the most mirthful comedies that Shakspere ever wrote. Then, a little later, as soon as Hamlet is completed, all changes. From 1604 to 1610 a show of tragic figures, like the kings who passed before Macbeth, filled the vision of Shakspere; until at last the desperate image of Timon rose before him; when, as though unable to endure or to conceive a more lamentable ruin of man, he turned for relief to the pastoral loves of Prince Florizel and Perdita; and as soon as the tone of his mind was restored, gave expression to its ultimate mood of grave serenity in The Tempest: and so ended.[38] □

Dowden's scholarly interest in the dating of the plays, to which he devotes some discussion in the Preface, is at the service of this deeper interest in the career of the poet. The full significance of the title, *Shakspere: His Mind and Art*, becomes clear: Dowden means to find the mind in the art. The artist as Hero and Villain, as *experiencer*, is beginning to take shape. The speculation to which so many critics resorted to fill in what they felt to be the gaps in the play, or the necessary background to a fuller understanding, is here being applied to Shakespeare himself, and the art being discussed, not as an expression of the man, but as his deepest engagement and as a clue to the man:

■ In these years the utmost imaginative susceptibility is united with the utmost self-control. Every portion of his being is at length engaged in the magnificent effort. At first in the career of most artists a portion of their nature holds aloof from art, and is ready for application to other service. They have a poetical side, and a side which is prosaic. Gradually, as they advance towards maturity, faculty after faculty is brought into fruitful relation with the art-instinct, until at length the entire nature of the artist is fused into one, and his work becomes the expression of a complete personality. This period had now arrived for Shakspere.[39] □

Dowden proceeds to outline his theory of the tragedies of this period:

■ Tragedy as conceived by Shakspere is concerned with the ruin or the restoration of the soul, and of the life of men. In other words its subject is the struggle of good and evil in the world. This strikes down upon the roots of things. The comedies of Shakspere had, in comparison, played upon the surface of life. The Histories, though very earnest, had not dealt with the deeper mysteries of being. Henry V., the ideal figure of the historical plays, has a real and firm grasp of the actual world; he has his religion, and he has his passion of love; but both are positive, practical, and limited . . . With a devout optimism, Henry perceives there is 'some soul of goodness in things evil [IV, I, 4]' . . . But such devout optimism was absolutely without avail for the spiritual needs of the man who had conceived Hamlet . . . And as comment upon such devout optimism, Shakspere produces Goneril and Regan, Iago, and the Witches in Macbeth.[40] □

'Shakspere' does not attempt explanations:

■ Here, upon the earth, evil *is* – such was Shakspere's declaration in the most emphatic accent. Iago actually exists. There is also in the earth a sacred passion of deliverance, a pure redeeming ardour. Cordelia exists. This Shakspere can tell for certain. But how Iago can be, and why Cordelia lies strangled across the breast of Lear – are these questions which you go on to ask? Something has already been said of the severity of Shakspere. It is a portion of his severity to decline all answers to such questions as these. Is Ignorance painful? Well, then, it is painful. Little solutions of your large difficulties can readily be obtained from priest or *philosophe*. Shakspere prefers to let you remain in the solemn presence of a mystery. He does not invite you into his little church or his little library brilliantly illuminated by philosophical or theological rushlights. You remain in the darkness. But you remain in the vital air. And the great night is overhead.[41] □

Dowden's style is excessively dramatic perhaps but the point made so emphatically was an important one to make in an age that took poets to be philosophers and imagined that it might find answers in Browning, for example, rather than questions. The morality is Stoical, and bracing; it is eagerly and enthusiastically proposed; one might find the eagerness and enthusiasm disturbing. It does, however, provide the beginnings of an answer to Rymer, who did, incidentally, ask why Iago can be and, by implication at least, why Cordelia lies strangled across the breast of Lear, and answered, because the poet had followed History and not Philosophy. Dowden is offering an alternative philosophy:

■ This period during which Shakspere was engaged upon his great tragedies was not, as it has been sometimes represented, a period of depression and of gloom in Shakspere's spiritual progress. True, he was now sounding the depths of evil as he had never sounded them before. But his faith in goodness had never been so strong and sure. Hitherto it had not been thoroughly tested . . . Now, with every fresh discovery of crime Shakspere made discovery of virtue which cannot suffer defeat. The knowledge of evil and of good grow together. While Shakspere moved gaily upon the surface of life, it was the play of intellect that stirred within him the liveliest sense of pleasure. The bright speech and unsubduable mirth, not disjoined from common sense and goodness of heart of a Rosalind or a Beatrice, filled him with a sense of quickened existence. Now that he had come to comprehend more of the sorrow and more of the evil of the earth – treachery, ingratitude, cruelty, lust – Shakspere found perhaps less to delight him in mere brightness of intellect; he certainly gave his heart away with more fervour of loyalty to human goodness, to fortitude, purity of heart, self-surrender, self-mastery – to every noble expression of character . . . If the sense of wrong sank deep into his soul, if life became harder and more grave, yet he surmounted all sense of personal wrong, and while life grew more severe, it grew more beautiful.[42] □

Dowden's very enthusiasm seems to suggest that he is not looking for a solution to a problem but a presentation of a mystery in the form of art. If we compare Dowden's view with Hazlitt's humanist account of the virtue of tragedy we see here a more extreme, but none the less consistent, development. Humanism became more extreme as the century went on. Dowden's summary of *Othello* is striking:

■ The tragedy of Othello is the tragedy of a free and lordly creature taken in the toils, and writhing to death. In one of his sonnets [23], Shakspere has spoken of

> Some fierce thing replete with too much rage
> Whose strength's abundance weakens his own heart.

Such a fierce thing, made weak by his very strength, is Othello. There is a barbaresque grandeur and simplicity about the movements of his soul. He sees things with a large and generous eye, not prying into the curious or the occult. He is a liberal accepter of life, and with a careless magnificence wears about him the ornament of strange experience; memories of

> Antres vast, and desarts idle,
> Rough quarries, rocks, and hills whose heads touch heaven
> [I, iii, 141–2],

memories of 'disastrous chances, of moving accidents by flood and field [I, iii, 135–6]'. There is something of grand innocence in his loyalty to Venice, by which Mr. Browning was not unaffected when he conceived his Moorish commander, Luria.[43] Othello, a stranger, with tawny skin and fierce traditions in his blood, is fascinated by the grave senate, the nobly ordered life (possessing a certain rich colouring of its own), and the astute intelligence of the City of the Sea. At his last moment, through the blinding sandstorm of his own passion, this feeling of disinterested loyalty recurs to Othello, and brings him a moment's joy and pride . . . [44] □

Dowden's account of Desdemona's falling in love with Othello is a model of his approach:

■ Desdemona, moving to and fro at her house-affairs, or listening with grave wonder, and eager, restrained sympathy to the story of his adventurous life, became to him, at first in an unconscious way, the type of beauty, gentleness, repose, and tender womanhood. And Desdemona, in her turn, brought up amidst the refinements and ceremonies of Venetian life, watching each day the same gondolas glide by, hearing her father's talk of some little new law of the Duke, found in the Moor strangeness and splendour of strong manhood, heroic simplicity, the charm of one who had suffered in solitude, and on whose history compassion might be lavished . . . In the love of each there was a romantic element; and romance is not the highest form of the service which imagination renders to love. For romance disguises certain facts, or sees them, as it were, through a luminous mist; but the highest service which the imagination can render to the heart is the discovery of every fact, the hard and bare as well as the beautiful; and, to effect this, like a clear north wind it blows all mists away. There was a certain side of Othello's nature which it were well that Desdemona had seen, though she trembled . . . The nature of Othello is free and open; he looks on men with a gaze too large and royal to suspect them of malignity and fraud . . . He has, however, a sense of his own inefficiency in dealing with the complex and subtle conditions of life in his adopted country. Where all is plain and broad, he relies upon his own judgment and energy. He is a master of simple, commanding action . . . But for curious inquiry into complex facts he has no faculty; he loses his bearings; 'being wrought upon' he is 'perplexed in the extreme' [V, ii, 343–4]. Then, too, his hot Mauritanian blood mounts quickly to the point of boiling. If he be infected, the poison hurries through his veins, and he rages in his agony.[45] □

His inability to suspect men of 'malignity and fraud' and the image of becoming infected and poisoned lead Dowden to offer a picture of Iago as a serpent whose poisonous bite Othello could not have foreseen, nor even seen, and the infection of which is his undoing. He makes a good point about Desdemona's courage:

■ When she could stand by Othello's side, Desdemona was able to confront her father.[46] □

Now she is on her own:

■ What will her refined feminine accomplishments avail her then – her delicacy with her needle, the admirable music with which she 'will sing the savageness out of a bear [IV, I, 186]'.[47] □

He deals with the handkerchief effectively:

■ The handkerchief which she has lost becomes terrible to her, when Othello with oriental rapture into the marvellous describes its virtue . . . For Desdemona, with her smooth, intelligible girl's life in Venice, having at largest its little pathetic romance of her maid Barbara, with her song of 'Willow', here flowed in romance too stupendous, too torrid, and alien to be other than dreadful. Shall we wonder that in her disturbance of mind she trembles to declare to her husband that this talisman could not be found.[48] □

His discussion of Iago adds little to Hazlitt and Coleridge who themselves have been anticipated to some extent by earlier critics; weightings and emphases differ but there is not a revolution in the portrait. What makes the difference is the evaluation of the total picture, and Dowden's final comments are compelling:

■ Of the tragic story what is the final issue? The central point of its spiritual import lies in the contrast between the two men, Iago and his victim. Iago, with keen intellectual faculties and manifold culture in Italian vice, lives and thrives after his fashion in a world from which all virtue and all beauty are absent. Othello with his barbaric inno-cence and regal magnificence of soul must cease to live the moment he ceases to retain faith in the purity and goodness which were to him the highest and most real things upon earth. Or if he live, life must become to him a cruel agony. Shakspere compels us to acknowledge that self-slaughter is a rapturous energy – that such prolonged agony is joy in comparison with the earthly life-in-death of such a soul as that of Iago. The noble nature is taken in the toils because it is noble . . . To die as Othello dies is indeed grievous. But to live as Iago lives, devouring the dust and stinging – this is more appalling.[49] □

Dowden sometimes writes as though he were summarising a story that contained far more detail than the play does. He speaks of Desdemona, for example, in this way:

■ Desdemona . . . brought up amidst the refinements and ceremonies of Venetian life, watching each day the same gondolas glide by, hearing her father's talk of some little new law of the Duke.[50] □

This is surmise; it fills out the picture quite consistently with what the audience or reader knows but it exceeds what they know. It offers a picture of Desdemona that resembles the picture of her life that a narrative would have given. The reader of a narrative has a different experience from that enjoyed by the member of an audience at a dramatic performance. A dramatic performance can affect a member of an audience in ways a narrative cannot because a dramatic performance has resources a narrative has not. When Dowden comes to consider the final impression left by the play he does not make this distinction sufficiently clear:

■ We look upon 'the tragic loading of the bed [V, ii, 361]', and we see Iago in presence of the ruin he has wrought. We are not compelled to seek for any resolution of these apparent discords in any alleged life to come. That may also be; we shall accept it, if it be. But looking sternly and strictly at what is now actual and present to our sight, we yet rise above despair. Desdemona's adhesion to her husband and to love survived the ultimate trial. Othello dies 'upon a kiss [V, ii, 357]'. He perceives his own calamitous error, and he recognizes Desdemona pure and loyal as she was. Goodness is justified of her child. It is evil which suffers defeat. It is Iago whose whole existence has been most blind, purposeless, and miserable – a struggle against the virtuous powers of the world, by which at last he stands convicted and condemned.[51] □

The high point of this tendency in critical appreciation of Shakespeare's plays to read them as though they were novels and to see in them the sort of reflective moral view that affirms humanist heroism is reached in the work of A. C. Bradley. The following extract is extensive; it must be read as a single argument. Bradley's method is simple, but subtle. He pursues the play minutely, teasing out implications and weaving together suggestions to create almost a new text. Again and again it may be argued that Bradley has gone too far but when Shakespeare's text is checked it is found that almost all of it is there, if not in one place at one time. It is true that there are things that are not there in the plays at all, when Bradley's intense imaginative evocation of the scene has betrayed him, but this does not happen as often as his detractors say and it is often at least as defensible as the enthusiastic supplying of background that has been already noted in several critical accounts:

■ Othello is, in one sense of the word, by far the most romantic figure among Shakespeare's heroes; and he is so partly from the strange life of war and adventure which he has lived from childhood. He does not belong to our world, and he seems to enter it we know not whence – almost as if from wonderland. There is something mysterious in his descent from men of royal siege; in his wanderings in vast deserts and among marvellous peoples; in his tales of magic handkerchiefs and prophetic Sybils; in the sudden vague glimpses we get of numberless battles and sieges in which he has played the hero and has borne a charmed life; even in chance references to his baptism, his being sold to slavery, his sojourn in Aleppo.

And he is not merely a romantic figure; his own nature is romantic. He has not, indeed, the meditative or speculative imagination of Hamlet; but in the strictest sense of the word he is more poetic than Hamlet. Indeed, if one recalls Othello's most famous speeches – those that begin. 'Her father loved me [I, iii, 129ff.]', 'O now for ever [III, iii, 350ff.]', 'Never, Iago [III, iii, 456ff.]', 'Had it pleased Heaven [IV, ii, 48ff.]', 'It is the cause [V, ii, 1ff.]', 'Behold, I have a weapon [V, ii, 257ff.]', 'Soft you, a word or two before you go [V, ii, 336ff.]' – and if one places side by side with these speeches an equal number by any other hero, one will not doubt that Othello is the greatest poet of them all. There is the same poetry in his casual phrases – like 'These nine moons wasted [I, iii, 85]', 'Keep up your bright swords, for the dew will rust them [I, ii, 59]', 'You chaste stars [V, ii, 2]', 'It is a sword of Spain, the ice-brook's temper [V, ii, 251]', 'It is the very error of the moon [V, ii, 107]' – and in those brief expressions of intense feeling which ever since have been taken as the absolute expression, like

> If it were now to die,
> 'Twere now to be most happy; for, I fear,
> My soul hath her content so absolute
> That not another comfort like to this
> Succeeds in unknown fate [II, i, 187–91],

or

> If she be false, O then Heaven mocks itself.
> I'll not believe it [III, iii, 282–3];

or

No, my heart is turned to stone; I strike it, and it hurts my hand
[IV, i,179–80],

or

But yet the pity of it, Iago! O Iago, the pity of it, Iago! [IV, I, 192–3]

or

> O thou weed
> Who art so lovely fair and smell'st so sweet
> That the sense aches at thee, would thou hast ne'er been born
> [IV, ii, 68–70].

And this imagination, we feel, has accompanied his whole life. He has watched with a poet's eye the Arabian trees dropping their med'cinable gum, and the Indian throwing away his chance-found pearl; and has gazed in a fascinated dream at the Pontic sea rushing, never to return, to the Propontic and the Hellespont; and has felt as no other man ever felt (for he speaks of it as none other ever did) the poetry of the pride, pomp, and circumstance of glorious war.

So he comes before us, dark and grand, with a light upon him from the sun where he was born; but no longer young, and now grave, self-controlled, steeled by the experience of countless perils, hardships and vicissitudes, at once simple and stately in bearing and in speech, a great man naturally modest but fully conscious of his worth, proud of his services to the State, unawed by dignitaries and unelated by honours, secure, it would seem, against all dangers from without and all rebellion from within. And he comes to have his life crowned with the final glory of love, a love as strange, adventurous and romantic as any passage of his eventful history, filling his heart with tenderness and his imagination with ecstasy. For there is no love, not that of Romeo in his youth, more steeped in imagination than Othello's.

The sources of danger in this character are revealed but too clearly by the story. In the first place, Othello's mind, for all its poetry, is very simple. He is not observant. His nature tends outward. He is quite free from introspection, and is not given to reflection. Emotion excites his imagination, but it confuses and dulls his intellect. On this side he is the very opposite of Hamlet, with whom, however, he shares a great openness and trustfulness of nature. In addition, he has little experience of the corrupt products of civilised life, and is ignorant of European women.

In the second place, for all his dignity and massive calm (and he has greater dignity than any other of Shakespeare's men), he is by nature full of the most vehement passion. Shakespeare emphasizes his self-control, not only by the wonderful pictures of the First Act, but by references to the past. Lodovico, amazed at his violence, exclaims:

> Is this the noble Moor whom our full Senate
> Call all in all sufficient? Is this the nature
> Whom passion could not shake? whose solid virtue
> The shot of accident nor dart of chance
> Could neither graze nor pierce? [IV, I, 264–9]

Iago, who has here no motive for lying, asks:

> Can he be angry? I have seen the cannon
> When it hath blown his ranks into the air,
> And, like the devil, from his very arm
> Puffed his own brother – and can he be angry? [III, iv, 135–8]

This, and other aspects of his character, are best exhibited by a single line – one of Shakespeare's miracles – the words by which Othello silences in a moment the night-brawl between his attendants and those of Brabantio:

> Keep up your bright swords, for the dew will rust them [I, ii, 59].

And the same self-control is strikingly shown where Othello endeavours to elicit some explanation of the fight between Cassio and Montano. Here, however, there occur ominous words, which make us feel how necessary was this self-control, and make us admire it the more:

> Now, by heaven,
> My blood begins my safer guides to rule,
> And passion, having my best judgment collied,
> Assays to lead the way [II, iii, 200–203].

We remember these words later, when the sun of reason is 'collied', blackened and blotted out in total eclipse.

Lastly, Othello's nature is all of one piece. His trust, where he trusts, is absolute. Hesitation is almost impossible to him. He is extremely self-reliant, and decides and acts instantaneously. If stirred to indignation, as 'in Aleppo once', he answers with one lightning stroke. Love, if he loves, must be to him the heaven where either he must live or bear no life. If such a passion as jealousy seizes him, it will swell into a well-nigh uncontrollable flood. He will press for immediate conviction or immediate relief. Convinced, he will act with the authority of a judge and the swiftness of a man in mortal pain. Undeceived, he will do like execution on himself.

This character is so noble, Othello's feelings and actions follow so inevitably from it and from the forces brought to bear on it, and his sufferings are so heart-rending, that he stirs, I believe, in most readers a passion of mingled love and pity which they feel for no other hero in Shakespeare, and to which not even Mr Swinburne can do more than justice.[52] Yet there are some critics and not a few readers who cherish a grudge against him. They do not merely think that in the later stages of his temptation he showed a certain obtuseness, and that, to speak pedantically, he acted with unjustifiable precipitance and violence; no one, I suppose, denies that. But, even when they admit that he was not of a jealous temper, they consider that he *was* 'easily jealous'; they seem to think that it was inexcusable in him to feel any suspicion of his wife at all; and they blame him for never suspecting Iago or asking him for evidence. I refer to this attitude of mind chiefly in order to draw attention to certain points in the story. It comes partly from mere inattention (for Othello did suspect Iago and did ask him for evidence); partly from a misconstruction of the text which makes Othello appear jealous long before he really is so; and partly from failure to realize certain essential facts. I will begin with these.

(1) Othello, we have seen, was trustful, and thorough in his trust. He put entire confidence in the honesty of Iago, who had not only been his companion in arms, but, as he believed, had just proved his faithfulness in the matter of the marriage. This confidence was misplaced, and we happen to know it; but it was no sign of stupidity in Othello. For his opinion of Iago was the opinion of practically everyone who knew him: and that opinion was that Iago was before all things 'honest', his very faults being those of excess in honesty. This being so, even if Othello had not been trustful and simple, it would have been quite unnatural in him to be unmoved by the warnings of so honest a friend, warnings offered with extreme reluctance and manifestly from a sense of a friend's duty. *Any* husband would have been troubled by them.

(2) Iago does not bring these warnings to a husband who had lived with a wife for months and years and knew her like his sister or his bosom-friend. Nor is there any ground in Othello's character for supposing that, if he had been such a man, he would have felt and acted as he does in the play. But he was newly married; in the circumstances he cannot have known much of Desdemona before his marriage; and further he was conscious of being under the spell of a feeling which can give glory to the truth but can also give it to a dream.

(3) This consciousness in any imaginative man is enough, in such circumstances, to destroy his confidence in his powers of perception. In Othello's case, after a long and most artful preparation, there now comes, to reinforce its effect, the suggestions that he is not an Italian, not even a European; that he is totally ignorant of the thoughts and the customary morality of Venetian women; that he had himself seen in

Desdemona's deception of her father how perfect an actress she could be. As he listens in horror, for a moment at least the past is revealed to him in a new and dreadful light, and the ground seems to sink under his feet. These suggestions are followed by a tentative but hideous and humiliating insinuation of what his honest and much-experienced friend fears may be the true explanation of Desdemona's rejection of acceptable suitors, and of her strange, and naturally temporary, preference for a black man. Here Iago goes too far. He sees something in Othello's face that frightens him, and he breaks off. Nor does this idea take any hold of Othello's mind. But it is not surprising that his utter power-lessness to repel it on the ground of knowledge of his wife, or even of that instinctive interpretation of character which is possible between persons of the same race, should complete his misery, so that he feels he can bear no more, and abruptly dismisses his friend [III, iii, 238].

Now I repeat that *any* man situated as Othello was would have been disturbed by Iago's communications, and I add that many men would have been made wildly jealous. But up to this point, where Iago is dismissed, Othello, I must maintain, does not show jealousy. His confidence is shaken, he is confused and deeply troubled, he feels even horror; but he is not yet jealous in the proper sense of that word. In his soliloquy [III, iii, 258ff.] the beginning of this passion may be traced; but it is only after an interval of solitude, when he has had time to dwell on the idea presented to him, and especially after statements of fact, not mere general grounds of suspicion, are offered, that the passion lays hold of him. Even then, however, and indeed to the very end, he is quite unlike the essentially jealous man, quite unlike Leontes. No doubt the thought of another man's possessing the woman he loves is intolerable to him; no doubt the sense of insult and the impulse of revenge are at times most violent; and these are the feelings of jealousy proper. But these are not the chief or the deepest source of Othello's suffering. It is the wreck of his faith and his love. It is the feeling,

If she be false, oh then Heaven mocks itself [III, iii, 282];

the feeling

O Iago, the pity of it, Iago! [IV, I, 193]

the feeling

But there where I have garner'd up my heart,
Where either I must live, or bear no life;
The fountain from the which my current runs,
Or else dries up – to be discarded thence [IV, ii, 58–61] . . .

You will find nothing like this in Leontes.

Up to this point, it appears to me, there is not a syllable to be said against Othello. But the play is a tragedy, and from this point we may abandon the ungrateful and undramatic task of awarding praise and blame. When Othello, after a brief interval, re-enters [III, iii, 332], we see at once that the poison has been at work and 'burns like the mines of sulphur'.

> Look where he comes! Not poppy, nor mandragora,
> Nor all the drowsy syrups of the world,
> Shall ever medicine thee to that sweet sleep
> Which thou owedst yesterday [III, iii, 333–6].

He is 'on the rack', in an agony so unbearable that he cannot endure the sight of Iago. Anticipating the probability that Iago has spared him the whole truth, he feels that in that case his life is over and his 'occupation gone' with all its glories. But he has not abandoned hope. The bare possibility that his friend is deliberately deceiving him – though such a deception would be a thing so monstrously wicked that he can hardly conceive it credible – is a kind of hope. He furiously demands proof, ocular proof. And when he is compelled to see that he is demanding an impossibility he still demands evidence. He forces it from the unwilling witness, and hears the maddening tale of Cassio's dream. It is enough. And if it were not enough, has he not sometimes seen a handkerchief spotted with strawberries in his wife's hand? Yes, it was his first gift to her.

> I know not that; but such a handkerchief –
> I am sure it was your wife's – did I today
> See Cassio wipe his beard with [III, iii, 440–2].

'If it be that,' he answers – but what need to test the fact? The 'madness of revenge' is in his blood, and hesitation is a thing he never knew. He passes judgment, and controls himself only to make his sentence a solemn vow.

The Othello of the Fourth Act is Othello in his fall. His fall is never complete, but he is much changed. Towards the close of the temptation-scene he becomes at times most terrible, but his grandeur remains almost undiminished. Even in the following scene [III, iv], where he goes to test Desdemona in the matter of the handkerchief, and receives a fatal confirmation of her guilt, our sympathy with him is hardly touched by any feeling of humiliation. But in the Fourth Act 'Chaos has come'. A slight interval of time may be admitted here. It is but slight; for it was necessary for Iago to hurry on, and terribly dangerous to leave a chance for a meeting of Cassio with Othello; and his insight into Othello's nature taught him that his plan was to deliver blow on blow, and never allow his victim to recover from the confusion of the first shock. Still there is a slight interval; and when Othello re-appears we see at a glance that he is a changed man. He is physically exhausted, and his mind is dazed. He sees everything blurred through a mist of blood and tears. He has actually forgotten the incident of the hand-kerchief, and has to be reminded of it. When Iago, perceiving that he can now risk almost any lie, tells him that Cassio has confessed his guilt, Othello, the hero who has seemed to us only second to Coriolanus in physical power, trembles all over; he mutters disjointed words; a blackness suddenly intervenes between his eyes and the world; he takes it for the shuddering testimony of nature to the horror he has just heard, and he falls senseless to the ground. When he recovers it is to watch Cassio, as he imagines, laughing over his shame. It is an imposition so gross, and should have been one so perilous, that Iago would never have ventured it before. But he is safe now. The sight only adds to the confusion of intellect the madness of rage; and a ravenous thirst for revenge, contending with motions of infinite long-ing and regret, conquers them. The delay till nightfall is torture to him. His self-control has wholly deserted him, and he strikes his wife in the presence of the Venetian envoy. He is so lost to all sense of reality that he never asks himself what will follow the deaths of Cassio and his wife. An ineradicable instinct of justice, rather than any last quiver of hope, leads him to question Emilia; but nothing could convince him now, and there follows the dreadful scene of accusation; and then, to allow us the relief of burning hatred and burning tears, the interview of Desdemona with Iago, and that last talk of hers with Emilia, and her last song.

But before the end there is again a change. The supposed death of Cassio [V, i] satiates the thirst for vengeance. The Othello who enters the bedchamber with the words,

> It is the cause, it is the cause, my soul [V, ii, 1],

is not the man of the Fourth Act. The deed he is bound to do is no mur-der, but a sacrifice. He is to save Desdemona from herself, not in hate but in honour; in honour, and also in love. His anger has passed; a boundless sorrow has taken its place; and

> this sorrow's heavenly:
> It strikes where it doth love [V, ii, 21–2].

Even when, at the sight of her apparent obduracy, and at the hearing of words which by a crowning fatality can only reconvince him of her guilt, these feelings give way to others, it is to righteous indignation they give way, not to rage; and, terribly painful as this scene is, there is almost nothing here to diminish the admiration and love which heighten pity. And pity itself vanishes, and love and admiration alone remain, in the majestic dignity and sovereign ascendancy of the close. Chaos has come and gone; and the Othello of the Council Chamber and the quay of Cyprus has returned, or a greater and nobler Othello still. As he speaks those final words in which all the glory and agony of his life – long ago in India and Arabia and Aleppo, and afterwards in Venice, and now in Cyprus – seem to pass before us, like the pictures that flash before the eyes of a drowning man, a triumphant scorn for the fetters of the flesh and the littleness of all the lives that must survive him sweeps our grief away, and when he dies upon a kiss the most painful of all tragedies leaves us for the moment free from pain, and exulting in the power of 'love and man's unconquerable mind'.[53] □

Bradley's picture of Othello and of the play as a whole tends to dictate a view of other characters, notably of Desdemona and Iago. Desdemona emerges, unsurprisingly, as an innocent victim:

■ She appears passive and defenceless, and can oppose to wrong nothing but the infinite endurance and forgiveness of a love that knows not how to resist or resent. She thus becomes at once the most beautiful example of this love, and the most pathetic heroine in Shakespeare's world.[54] □

But he goes on to say:

■ Of course this later impression of Desdemona is perfectly right, but it must be carried back and united with the earlier before we can see what Shakespeare imagined. Evidently, we are to understand, innocence, gentleness, sweetness, lovingness were the salient and, in a sense, the principal traits in Desdemona's character. She was, as her father supposed her to be,

> a maiden never bold,
> Of spirit so still and quiet that her motion
> Blushed at herself [I, iii, 95–7].

But suddenly there appeared something quite different – something which could never have appeared, for example, in Ophelia – a love not only full of romance but showing a strange freedom and energy of spirit, and leading to a most unusual boldness of action; and this action was carried through with a confidence and decision worthy of Juliet or Cordelia. Desdemona does not shrink before the Senate; and her language to her father, though deeply respectful, is firm enough to stir in us some sympathy with the old man who could not survive his daughter's loss.[55] □

When Bradley makes, very beautifully, his point about Othello the poet, he quietly adds a detail:

■ And this imagination, we feel, has accompanied his whole life. He has watched with a poet's eye the Arabian trees dropping their med'cinable gum, and the Indian throwing away his chance-found pearl; and has gazed in a fascinated dream at the Pontic sea rushing, never to return, to the Propontic and the Hellespont; and has felt as no other man ever felt (for he speaks of it as none other ever did) the poetry of the pride, pomp, and circumstance of glorious war.[56] □

Othello does not say 'chance-found' of the pearl that appears in his image of his situation:

■   of one whose hand,
   Like the base Indian, threw a pearl away
   Richer than all his tribe [V, ii, 344–6]. □

Nor does he claim ever to have seen the Pontic Sea, for that matter.

The point is that Bradley and Dowden, and the quite long tradition of which they are the full flowering, diminish the distinction between play and novel in filling out the detail. They thus diminish the specific capacities of each form. Bradley is as conscious as Capell and Johnson were that Shakespeare's stage is irrecoverable. He is marvellously acute on the question of Othello's colour, for example, making the point that Coleridge's argument (and, hence, all the arguments that take this form) is self-defeating: it is precisely the *disproportion* between Othello and Desdemona that so excites Brabantio and on which Iago is able to play; for Rymer and the others to argue that the match is disproportionate is for them to underline the significance of this element in the play's construction. Therefore, Othello must have been a 'negro' in Shakespeare's imagination. In a note Bradley then says:

■ I will not discuss the further question whether, granted that to Shakespeare Othello was a black, he should be represented as a black in our theatres now. I dare say not. We do not like the real Shakespeare.[57] □

He is right. In his answer to Rymer, John Dennis pointed out that the Athenian theatre was irrecoverable, being of a piece with the religion, politics and even climate of its time; the same is true for Shakespeare's theatre and our own time.[58] Bradley uses the category 'drama' to distinguish what he is discussing from 'theatre'. He had no high opinion of the theatre of his day. Speaking of the battle scenes Shakespeare often introduces, he remarks:

■ It is a curious comment on the futility of our spectacular effects that in our theatre these scenes, in which we strive after an 'illusion' of which the Elizabethans never dreamt, produce comparatively little excitement, and to many spectators are even somewhat distasteful.[59] □

Unfortunately perhaps his category, freed from 'theatre', allows him to drift too closely towards 'novel'. Forewarned, and ready to check if we need, we can learn prodigiously from Bradley, however. Of Iago, though he does go very much round about his point, he produces an entirely original and utterly compelling account:

■ [W]hat is clear is that Iago is keenly sensitive to anything that touches his pride or self-esteem. It would be most unjust to call him vain, but he has a high opinion of himself and a great contempt for others. He is quite aware of his superiority to them in certain respects; and he either disbelieves in or despises the qualities in which they are superior to him. Whatever disturbs or wounds his sense of superiority irritates him at once; and in *that* sense he is highly competitive. This is why the appointment of Cassio provokes him. This is why Cassio's scientific attainments provoke him. This is the reason of his jealousy of Emilia. He does not care for his wife; but the fear of another man's getting the better of him, and exposing him to pity or derision as an unfortunate husband, is wormwood to him; and as he is sure that no woman is virtuous at heart, this fear is ever with him. For much the same reason he has a spite against goodness in men (for it is characteristic that he is less blind to its existence in men, the stronger, than in women, the weaker). He has a spite against it, not from any love of evil for evil's sake, but partly because it annoys his intellect as a stupidity; partly (though he hardly knows this) because it weakens his satisfaction with himself, and disturbs his faith that egoism is the right and proper thing; partly because, the world being such a fool, goodness is popular and prospers. But he, a man ten times as able as Cassio or even Othello, does not greatly prosper. Somehow, for all the stupidity of these open and generous people, they get on better than the 'fellow of some soul'. And this, though he is not particularly eager to get on, wounds his pride. Goodness therefore annoys him. He is always ready to scoff at it, and would like to strike at it. In ordinary circumstances these feelings of irritation are not vivid in Iago – *no* feeling is so – but they are constantly present.[60] □

He sees, with striking insight, that 'the tragedy of *Othello* is in a sense his tragedy too':

■ It shows us not a violent man, like Richard, who spends his life in murder, but a thoroughly bad, *cold* man, who is at last tempted to let loose the forces within him, and is at once destroyed.[61] □

Everyone thinks Iago 'honest'; he is not an unpleasant man:

■ [O]n the contrary, he had a superficial good-nature, the kind of good-nature that wins popularity and is often taken as the sign, not of a good digestion, but of a good heart.[62] □

In Bradley's picture of him Iago does not clearly see in advance what he wants to achieve; he is drawn by temptation towards it quite gradually, until it is too late. Bradley takes up Swinburne's hint that Iago has 'the instinct of what Mr Carlyle would call an inarticulate poet'[63] and completes what Coleridge and Hazlitt had begun. He observes:

■ [T]he curious analogy between the early stages of dramatic composition and those soliloquies in which Iago broods over his plot, drawing at first only an outline, puzzled how to fix more than the main idea, and gradually seeing it develop and clarify as he works upon it or lets it work. Here at any rate Shakespeare put a good deal of himself into Iago. But the tragedian in real life was not the equal of the tragic poet. His psychology, as we shall see, was at fault at a critical point, as Shakespeare's never was. And so his catastrophe came out wrong, and his piece was ruined.[64] □

Iago dismissed his wife as beneath his notice as a mere pawn in the plot, and that was his undoing.

On the meaning of the play Bradley is less good: his opening lecture on Shakespeare's tragic sense is a masterpiece of exposition and explanation but fails to satisfy because it can offer in the end no more than the type of humanist heroism offered by Dowden. This is not a *bad* view in any way, it just seems to fall short. Bradley goes further than Dowden, offering a Hegelian view of a cosmic order in conflict with itself, bringing forth both good and evil and striving to overcome evil.[65] There is no evolutionary dimension to Bradley's account, and the struggle is not triumphant; evil is overcome and good is affirmed but the cost is high.

His view of Iago reflects this:

■ Iago is not merely negative or evil – far from it. Those very forces that moved him and made his fate – sense of power, delight in performing a difficult and dangerous action, delight in the exercise of artistic skill – are not at all evil things.[66] □

The sense is of waste; great beauty and power going to waste. Rymer's words are apposite: 'If this be our end, what boots it to be vertuous?' It is far from certain that Bradley's account of the ending of *Othello*, moving though it undoubtedly is, will provide an answer:

■ As he speaks those final words in which all the glory and agony of his life – long ago in India and Arabia and Aleppo, and afterwards in Venice, and now in Cyprus – seem to pass before us, like the pictures that flash before the eyes of a drowning man, a triumphant scorn for the fetters of the flesh and the littleness of all the lives that must survive him sweeps our grief away, and when he dies upon a kiss the most painful of all tragedies leaves us for the moment free from pain, and exulting in the power of 'love and man's unconquerable mind'.[67] □

Certainly two influential Modernist critics found this picture far from convincing, and it is to them that the following chapter turns.

CHAPTER FOUR

The Moderns: The Ghost of Rymer

T.S. ELIOT is the twentieth century's Coleridge, formidably distinguished both as a poet and as a critic as perhaps no other writer of the past one hundred years has been. He fared no better than Coleridge, however, if the yardstick is to be an account of the play commensurate with the complex responses the play arouses. Eliot offered some remarks in an essay that invoked other dramatic heroes of the period:

■ I want to be quite definite in my notion of the possible influence of Seneca on Shakespeare. I think it is quite likely that Shakespeare read some of Seneca's tragedies at school. I think it quite unlikely that Shakespeare knew anything of that extraordinarily dull and uninteresting body of Seneca's prose, which was translated by Lodge and printed in 1612. So far as Shakespeare was influenced by Seneca, it was by his memories of school conning and through the influence of the Senecan tragedy of the day, through Kyd and Peele, but chiefly Kyd. That Shakespeare deliberately took a 'view of life' from Seneca there seems to be no evidence whatever.

Nevertheless, there is, in some of the great tragedies of Shakespeare, a new attitude. It is not the attitude of Seneca, but is derived from Seneca; it is slightly different from anything that can be found in French tragedy, in Corneille or in Racine; it is modern, and it culminates, if there is ever any culmination, in the attitude of Nietzsche. I cannot say that it is Shakespeare's 'philosophy'. Yet many people have lived by it; though it may only have been Shakespeare's instinctive recognition of something of theatrical utility. It is the attitude of self-dramatization assumed by some of Shakespeare's heroes at moments of tragic intensity. It is not peculiar to Shakespeare; it is conspicuous in Chapman: Bussy, Clermont and Biron, all die in this way. Marston – one of the most interesting and least explored of all the Elizabethans – uses it; and Marston and Chapman were particularly Senecan. But Shakespeare, of course, does it very much better than any of the others, and makes it somehow more integral with the human nature of his characters. It is less verbal, more real. I have always felt that I have never read a more terrible exposure of human weakness – of universal human weakness – than the last great speech of Othello. (I am ignorant whether anyone else has ever adopted this view, and it may appear subjective and fantastic in the extreme.) It is usually taken on its face value, as expressing the greatness in defeat of a noble but erring nature.

> Soft you; a word or two before you go.
> I have done the state some service, and they know't.
> No more of that. I pray you, in your letters,
> When you shall these unlucky deeds relate,
> Speak of me as I am. Nothing extentuate,
> Nor set down aught in malice: then must you speak
> Of one that loved not wisely, but too well;
> Of one not easily jealous, but, being wrought,
> Perplex'd in the extreme; of one whose hand,
> Like the base Indian, threw a pearl away
> Richer than all his tribe; of one whose subdued eyes,
> Albeit unused to the melting mood,
> Drop tears as fast as the Arabian trees
> Their medicinal gum. Set you down this;
> And say, besides, that in Aleppo once,
> Where a malignant and a turban'd Turk
> Beat a Venetian and traduced the state,
> I took by the throat the circumcised dog
> And smote him, thus. [V, ii, 336–53]

What Othello seems to me to be doing in making this speech is *cheering himself up*. He is endeavouring to escape reality, he has ceased to think about Desdemona, and is thinking about himself. Humility is the most difficult of all virtues to achieve; nothing dies harder than the desire to think well of oneself. Othello succeeds in turning himself into a pathetic figure, by adopting an *aesthetic* rather than a moral attitude, dramatizing himself against his environment. He takes in the spectator, but the human motive is primarily to take in himself. I do not believe that any writer has ever exposed this *bovarysme*, the human will to see things as they are not, more clearly than Shakespeare.

If you compare the deaths of several of Shakespeare's heroes – I do not say *all*, for there are very few generalizations that can be applied to the whole of Shakespeare's work – but notably Othello, Coriolanus and Antony – with the deaths of heroes of dramatists such as Marston and Chapman, consciously under Senecan influence, you will find a strong similarity – except only that Shakespeare does it both more poetically and more lifelike.[1] □

This rather supercilious disdain for the character may be at least in part a strategic distancing from the enthusiasm of the Romantics of the previous century. Modernism was marking out its own territory and doing so, at least partly, by deliberately rejecting the sentiments (and the sentimentality, as they saw it) of the previous century. This does not at all mean that the views expressed are not felt; only that part of the motivation of the feeling may be looked for in the desire to reject the established view.

   G. Wilson Knight's approach shows in a different way how twentieth-century critics tried to move away from the domination of the Novel by exploring new emphases. Wilson Knight is famous for his deliberate attentiveness to the poetic effects of the plays, especially where the possibilities of symbolism are to be found. *Othello* did not quite fit in: '*Othello* is a story of intrigue rather than a visionary statement.' The following passage shows Knight's characteristic method in action:

■ *Othello* is dominated by its protagonist. Its supremely beautiful effects of style are all expressions of Othello's personal passion. Thus, in first analysing Othello's poetry, we shall lay the basis for an understanding of the play's symbolism: this matter of style is, indeed, crucial, and I shall now indicate those qualities which clearly distinguish it from other Shakespearian poetry. It holds a rich music all its own, and possesses a unique solidity and precision of picturesque phrase or image, a peculiar chastity and serenity of thought. It is, as a rule, barren of direct metaphysical content. Its thought does not mesh with the reader's: rather it is always outside us, aloof. This aloofness is the resultant of an inward aloofness of image from image, word from word. The dominant quality is separation, not, as is more usual in Shakespeare, cohesion. Consider these exquisite poetic movements:

> O heavy hour!
> Methinks it should be now a huge eclipse
> Of sun and moon, and that the affrighted globe
> Should yawn at alteration [V, ii, 97–100].

Or,

> It is the very error of the moon;
> She comes more near the earth than she was wont,
> And makes men mad [V, ii, 108–10].

These are solid gems of poetry which lose little by divorce from their context: wherein they differ from the finest passages of *King Lear* or

Macbeth, which are as wild flowers not to be uptorn from their rooted soil if they are to live. In these two quotations we should note how the human drama is thrown into sudden contrast and vivid, unexpected relation with the tremendous concrete machinery of the universe, which is thought of in terms of individual heavenly bodies: 'sun' and 'moon'. The same effect is apparent in:

> Nay, had she been true,
> If Heaven would make me such another world
> Of one entire and perfect chrysolite,
> I'd not have sold her for it [V, ii, 139–42].

Notice the single word 'chrysolite' with its outstanding and remote beauty: this is typical of *Othello*.

The effect in such passages is primarily one of contrast. The vastness of the night sky, and its moving planets, or the earth itself – here conceived objectively as a solid, round, visualized object – these things, though thrown momentarily into sensible relation with the passions of man, yet remain vast, distant, separate, seen but not apprehended; something against which the dramatic movement may be silhouetted, but with which it cannot be merged. This poetic use of heavenly bodies serves to elevate the theme, to raise issues infinite and unknowable. Those bodies are not, however, implicit symbols of man's spirit, as in *King Lear*: they remain distinct, isolated phenomena, sublimely decorative to the play. In *Macbeth* and *King Lear* man commands the elements and the stars: they are part of him. Compare the above quotations from *Othello* with this from *King Lear*:

> You nimble lightnings, dart your blinding flames
> Into her scornful eyes! Infect her beauty,
> You fen-suck'd fogs, drawn by the powerful sun,
> To fall and blast her pride [II, ii, 354–67].

This is typical: natural images are given a human value. They are insignificant, visually: their value is only that which they bring to the human passion which cries out to them. Their aesthetic grandeur, in and for themselves, is not relevant to the *King Lear* universe. So, too, Macbeth cries

> Stars, hide your fires;
> Let not light see my black and deep desires [I, iv, 50–1].

And Lady Macbeth:

> Come, thick night,
> And pall thee in the dunnest smoke of Hell,
> That my keen knife see not the wound it makes,
> Nor Heaven peep through the blanket of the dark,
> To cry 'Hold, hold! [I, v, 50–4].

Here, and in the *King Lear* extract, there is no clear visual effect as in *Othello*: tremendous images and suggestions are evoked only to be blurred as images by the more powerful passion which calls them into being. Images in *Macbeth* are thus continually vague, mastered by passion; apprehended, but not seen. In Othello's poetry they are concrete, detached; seen but not apprehended. We meet the same effect in:

> Like to the Pontic sea,
> Whose icy current and compulsive course
> Ne'er feels retiring ebb, but keeps due on
> To the Propontic and the Hellespont,
> Even so my bloody thoughts, with violent pace,
> Shall ne'er look back, ne'er ebb to humble love,
> Till that a capable and wide revenge
> Swallow them up. Now, by yond marble heaven,
> In the due reverence of a sacred vow
> I here engage my words [III, iii, 456–65].

This is a strongly typical speech. The long comparison, explicitly made, where in *King Lear* or *Macbeth* a series of swiftly evolving metaphors would be more characteristic, is another example of the separateness obtaining throughout *Othello*. There is no fusing of word with word, rather a careful juxtaposition of one word or image with another. And there are again the grand single words, 'Propontic', 'Hellespont', with their sharp, clear, consonant sounds, constituting defined aural solids typical of the *Othello* music: indeed, fine single words, especially proper names, are a characteristic of this play – Anthropophagi, Ottomites, Arabian trees, 'the base Indian', the Egyptian, Palestine, Mauretania, the Sagittary, Olympus, Mandragora, Othello, Desdemona. This is a rough assortment, not all used by Othello, but it points the Othello quality of rich, often expressly con-sonantal, outstanding words. Now Othello's prayer, with its 'marble heaven', is most typical and illustrative. One watches the figure of Othello silhouetted against a flat, solid, moveless sky: there is a plas-tic, static suggestion about the image. Compare it with a similar *King Lear* prayer:

> O heavens,
> If you do love old men, if your sweet sway
> Allow obedience, if yourselves are old,
> Make it your cause; send down and take my part! [II, ii, 378–81]

Here we do not watch Lear: 'We are Lear'. There is no visual effect, no rigid subject-object relation between Lear and the 'heavens', nor any contrast, but an absolute unspatial unity of spirit. The heavens blend with Lear's prayer, each is part of the other. There is an intimate inter-dependence, not a mere juxtaposition. Lear thus identifies himself in kind with the heavens to which he addresses himself directly: Othello speaks of 'yond marble heaven', in the third person, and swears by it, does not pray to it. It is conceived as outside his interests.[2] ☐

Knight detects a fracturing of this style under pressure:

■ At the most agonizing moments of Othello's story, however, there is apparent weakness: we find an exaggerated, false rhetoric.

There is a speech in *Othello* that begins in the typical restrained manner, but degenerates finally to what might almost be called bombast. It starts:

> Where should Othello go?
> Now, how dost thou look now? O ill-starr'd wench!
> Pale as thy smock! When we shall meet at compt,
> This look of thine will hurl my soul from Heaven,
> And fiends will snatch at it. Cold, cold, my girl!
> Even like thy chastity [V, ii, 269–74].

Here we have the perfection of the *Othello* style. Concrete, visual, detached. Compare it with Lear's, 'Thou art a soul in bliss . . .', where the effect, though perhaps more powerful and immediate, is yet vague, intangible, spiritualized. Now this speech, started in a style that can in its own way challenge that of *King Lear*, rapidly degenerates as Othello's mind is represented as collapsing under the extreme of anguish:

> O cursed, cursed slave! Whip me, ye devils,
> From the possession of this heavenly sight!
> Blow me about in winds! roast me in sulphur!
> Wash me in steep-down gulfs of liquid fire!
> O Desdemona! Desdemona! dead!
> Oh! Oh! Oh! [V, ii, 274–9]

There is a sudden reversal of poetic beauty: these lines lack cogency because they exaggerate rather than concentrate the emotion.[3] ☐

In this Knight sees the meaning of the play:

■ This is the primary fact of Othello and therefore of the play: something of solid beauty is undermined, wedged open so that it exposes an extreme ugliness.[4] ☐

Knight relates the characteristic speech of Othello to literary history:

■ Othello's speech is nearer the style of the aftermath of Elizabethan literature, the settled lava of that fiery eruption, which gave us the solid image of Marvell and the 'marmoreal phrase' of Browne: it is the most Miltonic thing in Shakespeare.[5] ☐

This fascinating suggestion allows a link to be made between Knight's discussion of *Othello* and Eliot's remark about a 'dissociation of sensibility' having taken place 'at some time in the seventeenth century'. Milton was a force to be overcome as far as Eliot was concerned if English poetry were to be put back on track. When it is recalled that Wordsworth claimed Milton as the most potent influence on him it can be seen that the task Eliot set himself is not inconsiderable.

Knight takes his perception about the meaning of the play into an attempt to read the play's symbolism:

■ *Othello* is eminently a domestic tragedy. But this element in the play is yet to be related to another more universal element. Othello is concretely human, so is Desdemona. Othello is very much the typical middle-aged bachelor entering matrimony late in life, but he is also, to transpose a phrase of Iago's, a symbol of human – especially masculine – 'purpose, courage, and valour' [IV, ii, 216], and, in a final judgement, is seen to represent the idea of human faith and value in a very wide sense. Now Desdemona, also very human, with an individual domestic feminine charm and simplicity, is yet also a symbol of woman in general daring the unknown seas of marriage with the mystery of man. Beyond this, in the far flight of a transcendental interpretation, it is clear that she becomes a symbol of man's ideal, the supreme value of love. At the limit of the series of wider and wider suggestions which appear from imaginative contemplation of a poetic symbol she is to be equated with the divine principle.[6] ☐

Knight identifies the theme of the play as 'the cynical intellect pitted against a lovable humanity transfigured by qualities of grace and heroism' and sees Iago as 'cynicism incarnate and projected into action' and as 'utterly devilish'. My final extract is his summary of what he believes he has done in the essay:

■ In this essay I have attempted to expose the underlying thought of the play. Interpretation here is not easy, nor wholly satisfactory. As all within *Othello* – save the Iago-theme – is separated, differentiated, solidified, so the play itself seems at first to be divorced from wider issues, a lone thing of meaningless beauty in the Shakespearian universe, solitary, separate, unyielding and chaste as the moon. It is unapproachable, yields itself to no easy mating with our minds. Its thought does not readily mesh with our thought. We can visualize it, admire its concrete felicities of phrase and image, the mosaic of its language, the sculptural outline of its effects, the precision and chastity of its form. But one cannot be lost in it, subdued to it, enveloped by it, as one is drenched and refreshed by the elemental cataracts of *King Lear*; one cannot be intoxicated by it as by the rich wine of *Antony and Cleopatra*. *Othello* is essentially outside us, beautiful with a lustrous, planetary beauty. Yet the Iago-conception is of a different kind from the rest of the play. This conception alone, if no other reason existed, would point the necessity of an intellectual interpretation. So we see the Iago-spirit gnawing at the root of all the *Othello* values, the *Othello* beauties; he eats into the core and heart of this romantic world, worms his way into its solidity, rotting it, poisoning it. Once this is clear, the whole play begins to have meaning. On the plane of dramatic humanity, we see a story of the cynic intriguing to ruin the soldier and his love. On the plane of poetic conception, in matters of technique, style, personification – there we see a spirit of negation, colourless, and undefined, attempting to make chaos of a world of stately, architectural, and exquisitely coloured forms. The two styles of Othello's speech illustrate this. Thus the different technique of the Othello and Iago conceptions is intrinsic with the plot of the play: in them we have the spirit of negation set against the spirit of creation. That is why Iago is undefined, devisualized, inhuman, in a play of consummate skill in concrete imagery and vivid human delineation. He is a colourless and ugly thing in a world of colour and harmony. His failure lies in this: in the final scene, at the moment of his complete triumph, Emilia dies for her mistress to the words of Desdemona's willow-song, and the *Othello* music itself sounds with a nobler cadence, a richer flood of harmonies, a more selfless and universalized flight of the imagination than before. The beauties of the *Othello* world are not finally disintegrated: they make 'a swan-like end, fading in music'.[7] □

A useful stylistic contrast may be drawn between this essay and Bradley's lectures, for where Bradley is at pains to clarify and to explain, Knight seems to be piling word upon word to gain his meaning. This exploratory, almost mystical, certainly, to use his word, 'poetic' method is just right for the adventure upon which Knight takes us. His method is not as successful with *Othello* as it is with *King Lear* as he says himself, but it does remind us that the plays are poetic dramas and that poetry is not exhausted in psychological presentation but may have a life, as it were, of its own independently of its speakers. Also, Knight points towards the vast resource of what Philip Larkin was to deride as 'the myth-kitty': the imaginative world of archetypes and hidden forces. The link between this element in Knight's work and his (albeit fleeting) interest in literary-historical discussions connects him with Bradley too: this is the world of Hegelian philosophy, of the Spirit becoming itself through History. 'The spirit of negation set against the spirit of creation' recalls Carlyle's 'Everlasting Nay!' and 'Everlasting Yea!' of *Sartor Resartus* so a range can be seen of attempted alternatives to Humanism and Realism and the Novel culminating in Knight's work, and that is its strength. Its weakness is obvious: the symbolism, though not really deniable, does not very much compel agreement.

William Empson's essay 'Honest in *Othello*' (1951) reflects an emphasis on language that may also be found in the influence of I. A. Richards and the movement to 'Practical Criticism' and, more widely, in a changing attitude to the way in which language was being conceived of and treated across Europe during the twentieth century. Empson's work is subtle and does not yield its main points straight away or straightforwardly, so some prior summary is necessary.

Empson believes that the character of Iago is a puzzle. This is not a new view, but Empson's treatment of Iago as a puzzle is, to a certain extent, strategic. That is, he treats Iago as a puzzle because that enables him to develop an argument he wishes to develop. Put briefly, Empson says that he believes that Bradley's picture is correct (he calls it 'A. C. Bradley's magnificent analysis'[8]) but that 'Shakespeare, and the audience he had, and the audience he wanted, saw the thing in rather different proportions'. He believes that:

■ Many of the audience were old soldiers disbanded without pension; they would dislike Cassio as the new type of officer, the boy who can displace men of experience merely because he knows enough mathematics to work the new guns. The tragedy plays into their hands by making Cassio a young fool who can't keep his mistress from causing scandals and can't drink.[9] □

He speaks of a 'confusion of moral theory in the audience' and says that this confusion 'would make them begin by approving of Iago' because he is 'ready to blow the gaff' and 'frank to (himself) about (his) own desires'.[10] The result is that 'more force was needed to make Shakespeare's audience hate Iago than to make them accept the obviously intolerable Macbeth as a tragic hero'.[11] Empson's interest is historical: he is interested in mutations of the word 'honest' that led to 'the Restoration use'[12] in which is implied a frank heartiness about natural desires and a generous fidelity to friendship. Shakespeare's interest in the word, Empson speculates, is that 'the flat hearty use bored him; it was a blank space where one might have had a bit of word play',[13] but the conception of the figure implied by its use was a false one, which he exposed. He puts his finger on an important point when he says that:

■ Most people would agree with what Bradley, for example, implied, that the way everybody calls Iago honest amounts to a criticism of the word itself; that is, Shakespeare means 'a bluff forthright manner, and amusing talk, which get a man called honest, may go with extreme dishonesty'. Or indeed that this is treated as normal, and the satire is on our nature not on language. But they would probably maintain that Iago is not honest and does not think himself so, and only calls himself so as a lie or an irony. It seems to me, if you leave the matter there, that there is much to be said for what the despised Rymer decided, when the implications of the hearty use of *honest* had become simpler and more clear-cut. He said that the play is ridiculous, because that sort of villain (silly-clever, full of secret schemes, miscalculating about people) does not get mistaken for that sort of honest man. This if true is of course a plain fault, whatever you think about 'character-analysis'. It is no use taking short cuts in these things, and I should fancy that what Rymer said had a large truth when he said it, and also that Iago was a plausible enough figure in his own time.[14] □

Thus Bradley has not met Rymer's argument at all: the outward appearance suggested by 'honest' is not at all compatible with the inward reality of a conscious schemer *unless* there has been a change in the meaning of 'honest'. The argument is complex and there are some problems with it. Rymer's objection to Iago is this:

■ *Shakespear* knew his Character of *Jago* was inconsistent. In this very Play he pronounces,

If thou dost deliver more or less than Truth,
Thou are no Souldier . . . [II, iii, 215–16].

This he knew, but to entertain the Audience with something new and surprising, against common sense, and Nature, he would pass upon us a close, dissembling, false, insinuating rascal, instead of an open-hearted, frank, plain-dealing Souldier, a character constantly worn by them for some thousands of years in the World.[15] ☐

He found as well a good many more reasons than this to find the play ridiculous. It is in fact not true that Rymer said that 'the play is ridiculous, because that sort of villain (silly-clever, full of secret schemes, miscalculating about people) does not get mistaken for that sort of honest man'. It might, of course, be true that 'that sort of villain (silly-clever, full of secret schemes, miscalculating about people) does not get mistaken for that sort of honest man'. If it is true, then the play does display 'a plain fault, whatever you think of "character-analysis"'. This last phrase leads on to Bradley. It may be questioned whether Bradley's portrait of Iago really does amount to 'silly-clever, full of secret schemes, miscalculating about people'.

What is happening is that Rymer and Bradley are both being misrepresented in the interests of designing a picture that will promote a puzzle – a very real puzzle. If Iago is 'silly-clever, full of secret schemes, miscalculating about people' but is widely regarded as 'honest', how can that apparent contradiction be accounted for? Empson says, in two ways, but there are actually three. The first is that the word in Shakespeare's time means nothing more than 'a bluff forthright manner, and amusing talk, which get a man called honest'; the second is that this is often only what is meant by the word 'honest'; the third is that appearances are too easily trusted. The first two will serve Empson's purpose while the third will not. He discounts the third implicitly by adducing Rymer's argument that Iago's kind of villain (as defined by Bradley's 'magnificent analysis') is never mistaken for the kind of honest man implied by 'a bluff forthright manner, and amusing talk, which get a man called honest', and that to represent the mistake makes the play ridiculous. This is not Rymer's argument and it is not Bradley's picture. The third option will stand after all and it will fit very easily with Bradley's picture of Iago.

Empson often tries to get too much into one argument. At one point he is discussing the difference between Iago's use of the word 'honest' and 'the Restoration use':

■ Certainly one cannot simply treat his version of *honest* as the Restoration one – indeed, the part of the snarling critic involves a rather Puritanical view, at any rate towards other people. It is the two notions of being ready to blow the gaff on other people and frank to yourself about your own desires that seem to me crucial about Iago; they grow on their own, independently of the hearty feeling that would normally humanize them; though he can be a good companion as well.[16] ☐

It is a great mistake to attempt to associate Iago with Puritanism. Empson is on safer ground with the later suggestion that:

■ The resentment of the lower classes towards the graces of the upper really has been known to take ugly forms, and Shakespeare with his new coat of arms was ready to go out of his way to reprove it.[17] □

The picture of the Stratford *bourgeois* using his plays as the Jacobean equivalent of a popular newspaper column is not unbelievable, and it is a corrective at least to some of the more inflated pictures, but it needs more justification than it is given here. The irony is perhaps that Shakespeare's intention may well have been nearer to Rymer's picture of the Soldier, 'an open-hearted, frank, plain-dealing Souldier', whose very open-heartedness and frankness are not at all deceitfully put on but confront a world he has become convinced is made worthless by the hypocrisy of the powerful: this is surely the force of Empson's observation that 'the resentment of the lower classes towards the graces of the upper really has been known to take ugly forms'. His resentment against Cassio – 'He has a daily beauty in his life,/Which makes me ugly' [V, I, 19–20] – is then easily explained: he wishes to see these graces as concealment for the same desires he feels and deprecates in himself. Iago's dominant emotion is rage against hypocrisy – not against immorality shrouded by hypocrisy. He speaks for open-heartedness and frankness about one's natural desires (Empson is surely right about this) not for pious renunciation. 'The snarling critic' (Thersites from *Troilus and Cressida* most obviously) is not quite right either; Iago gets involved.

Getting down to analysis, Empson makes some sharp points. He sees that the first use of the word in the opening scene ('whip me such honest knaves [I, i, 48]') 'can only mean that Iago has a different idea of honesty from the one that these knaves have'.[18] The last use in that scene occurs in the lines: 'The Moor is of a free and open nature,/And thinks men honest that but seem to be so [I, iii, 398–9]'.

Empson comments:

■ [H]e is enumerating the conditions of his problem, and the dramatic purpose, one may say, is to make certain that nobody in the audience has missed the broad point. The act then closes with 'I have it' and the triumphant claim that he has invented the plot. Even here, I think, there is room for an ironical tone in Iago's use of *honest*; he can imply that Othello's notion of honesty is crude as well as his judgements about which people exemplify it. For that matter, Iago may simply be speaking about Cassio, not about himself. He has just said that Cassio is framed to make women false, and he certainly regards the virtues of Cassio as part of his superficial and over-rewarded charm of manner.

But I think that, even so, Iago has himself somewhere in view; to claim that he did not would be overstraining my argument.[19] □

This is the way to do it – careful, speculative; recognising that the analysis is a line of hypothesis in pursuit of the proof of an argument, the proof of which will be the reader's acceptance that the hypothesis advanced as an argument matches completely at all points the hypothesis advanced as analysis. The difference from Bradley could not be more marked: where Bradley had Iago's 'inside' in view, Empson is aware at all points that all he is suggesting is a way of imagining a character from the evidence we have in the words given to him and to others to speak when actors portray them.

In the following extract, Empson discusses the extraordinary quibbling with the word 'honest' at Act III, Scene iii, 102ff.

■ I think a queer kind of honesty is maintained in Iago through all the puzzles he contrives; his emotions are always expressed directly, and it is only because they are clearly genuine ('These stops of thine', Othello tells him, 'are close relations, working from the heart') that he can mislead Othello as to their cause.

OTHELLO *Is he not honest?* (Faithful, etc.)

IAGO *Honest, my lord?* (Not stealing, etc. Shocked.)

OTHELLO *Ay, honest.* ('Why repeat? The word is clear enough'.)

IAGO *My Lord, for aught I know . . .* ('In some sense'.)

IAGO *For Michael Cassio*
I dare be sworn I think that he is honest.

OTHELLO *I think so too.*

IAGO *Men should be what they seem,*
Or, those that be not, would they might seem none.

OTHELLO *Certain, men should be what they seem.*

IAGO *Why, then, I think that Cassio's an honest man*

[III, iii, 102–6; 127–32.].

Othello has just said that Cassio 'went between them very oft', so Iago now learns that Cassio lied to him in front of Brabantio's house when he pretended to know nothing about the marriage. Iago feels he has been snubbed, as too coarse to be trusted in such a manner, and he takes immediate advantage of his discomposure. The point of his riddles is to get 'not hypocritical' – 'frank about his own nature' accepted as the relevant sense; Iago will readily call him honest on that basis, and Othello cannot be reassured. 'Chaste' (the sense normally used of women) Cassio is not, but he is 'not a hypocrite' about Bianca. Iago indeed, despises him for letting her make a fool of him in public; for that and for other reasons (Cassio is young and without experience) Iago can put a contemptuous tone into the word; the feeling is genuine, but not the sense it may imply. This gives room for a hint that Cassio has been 'frank' to Iago in private about more things than may honestly be told. I fancy too, that the idea of 'not being men' gives an extra twist. Iago does not think Cassio manly nor that it is specially manly to be chaste; this allows him to agree that Cassio may be honest in the female sense about Desdemona and still keep a tone which seems to deny it – if he is, after so much encouragement, he must be 'effeminate' (there is a strong idea of 'manly' in *honest*, and an irony on that gives its opposite). Anyway, Iago can hide what reservations he makes but show that he makes reservations; this suggests an embarrassed defence – 'Taking a broad view, with the world as it is, and Cassio my friend, I can decently call him honest'. This forces home the Restoration idea – 'an honest dog of a fellow, straightforward about women', and completes the suspicion. It is a bad piece of writing unless you are keyed up for the shifts of the word.

The play with the feminine version is doubtful here, but he certainly does it the other way round about Desdemona, where it had more point; in the best case it is for his own amusement when alone.

> And what's he then that says I play the villain?
> When this advice is free I give and honest,
> Probal to thinking, and indeed the course
> To win the Moor again? For 'tis most easy
> The inclining Desdemona to subdue
> In any honest suit. She's framed as fruitful
> As the free elements [II, iii, 331–7].

Easy, inclining, fruitful, free all push the word the same way, from 'chaste' to 'flat, frank, and natural'; all turn the ironical admission of her virtue into a positive insult against her. The delight in juggling with the word here is close to the Machiavellian interest in plots for their own sake, which Iago could not resist and allowed to destroy him. But a good deal of the 'motive-hunting' of the soliloquies must, I think, be seen as part of Iago's 'honesty'; he is quite open to his own motives or preferences and interested to find out what they are.[20] □

Brilliant speculation, to none of which the reader need consent, any more than to any speculation of Bradley's. The only principle of judgement in these cases is whether or not the sense made of the play by the speculative analysis may be borne by the play and whether or not, if it may be, it makes good sense. All depends upon our understanding of 'good'. Bradley may have made the play sound too much like a novel but Empson is doing almost the same here; the difference is in what we might call density. As Bradley weaves the spell of his subtly persuasive and above all clear and reasonable exposition it seems inevitable and true, and nothing in a poetic drama can be inevitable and true and nor can it in the most densely-realised realist novel for that matter. Empson weaves less densely than does Bradley.

In this next extract Empson discusses the repetition of the word 'honest' in Act V, Scene ii, 150:

■ In the nightmare scene where Othello clings to the word to justify himself he comes near accepting Iago's use of it.

EMILIA	*My husband!*
OTHELLO	*Ay, twas he that told me first:*
	An honest man he is, and hates the slime
	That sticks on filthy deeds . . .
EMILIA	*My husband say that she was false?*
OTHELLO	*He, woman;*
	I say thy husband: dost understand the word?
	My friend, thy husband, honest, honest Iago.

From the sound of the last line it seems as bitter and concentrated as the previous question; to the audience it is. Yet Othello means no irony against Iago, and it is hard to invent a reason for the repetition of *honest*. He may feel it painful that the coarse Iago, not Desdemona or Cassio, should be the only honest creature, or Iago's honesty may suggest the truth he told; or indeed you may call it a trick on the audience, to wind up the irony to its highest degree before Iago is exposed. Yet Iago would agree that one reason why he was honest was that he hated the slime. The same slime would be produced, by Desdemona as well as by Othello one would hope, if the act of love were of the most rigidly faithful character; the disgust in the metaphor is disgust at all sexuality. Iago playing 'honest' as prude is the rat who stands up for the ideal; as soon as Othello agrees he is finely cheated; Iago is left with his pleasures and Othello's happiness is destroyed. Iago has always despised his pleasures, always treated sex without fuss, like the lavatory; it is by this that he manages to combine the 'honest dog' tone with honesty as Puritanism. The twist of irony here is that Othello now feels humbled before such clarity. It is a purity he has failed to attain, and he accepts it as a form of honour. The hearty use and the horror of it are united in this appalling line.[21] □

The test of any speculation is how it stands up to others; Empson's fine reasoning must be judged against all the alternatives. The distinctly Bradleyan notes are cause for concern: 'always' is a worrying word where a play is concerned. But Empson is right, surely; intuitively right. The problem is proving it. He is as good on Emilia's final use of 'fool':

■ EMILIA	*He begged of me to steal it.*	
IAGO		*Villainous whore!*
EMILIA	*She give it Cassio! No, alas; I found it,*	
	And I did give't my husband.	
IAGO		*Filth, thou liest!*
EMILIA	*By heaven, I do not, I do not, gentlemen.*	
	O murderous coxcomb, what should such a fool	
	Do with so good a wife? [V, ii, 227–31]	
		(Iago stabs Emilia and escapes.)

On the face of it she praises herself to rebut his insults, which are given because she is not a 'good wife' in the sense of loyal to his interests. But her previous speech takes for granted that 'she' means Desdemona, and we go straight on to Emilia's death-scene, which is entirely selfless and praises Desdemona only. I think she is meant to turn and upbraid Othello, so that she praises Desdemona in this sentence: it would be a convenience in acting, as it explains why she does not notice Iago's sword . . . as her death-scene goes on the interpretation which the producer should reject is I think meant to come back into our minds; the real murderous coxcomb, the clown who did kill merely out of vanity, was Iago. The cynic had always hated to be treated as a harmless joker, and what finally roused him into stabbing her was perhaps that he thought she had called him a clown . . . It is perhaps an unnecessarily elaborate interpretation (the reference to Iago is much the more important one) but I think it is needed for our feelings about Emilia that she should not deliberately give herself the praise which we none the less come to feel she deserves.[22] □

Empson's method increasingly comes to seem to be the provision of a perverse inversion or distortion followed by an analysis that straightens out that initial inversion or distortion in order to establish what may have been obvious as a new discovery. Of course Emilia is addressing Othello and referring to Desdemona! But to put it Empson's way is to allow the introduction of a very useful additional meaning that the obvious would overlook. There is no ambiguity; but if one is perversely insisted upon, a new, and profitable, view becomes possible. Empson's point about Emilia is true. Yes, it is true that Iago is a clown – though 'coxcomb' means, more immediately, a man priding himself upon his

masculinity; yes, a clown too, but that is a secondary, derivative meaning, so the word really obviously refers to Othello. It is as though the
text's unconscious had intruded. All the devices whereby meaning slips
between the images presented to us in dreams, for example, as Freud
had discussed those processes, seem to be on parade at such moments. To
take one example, a clown (a country person but also a fool and sometimes a word used for a professional Fool) is not necessarily a coxcomb (a
reference to the professional Fool's regalia), though a coxcomb (a young
– usually – man priding himself on his masculinity) may be a clown (a
fool – not a professional Fool); a coxcomb (a Fool) is not necessarily a
fool and a Fool is not necessarily a clown, and so on, apparently *ad infini-
tum*. Empson's point is to use these words drastically to make us see the
ruptures and sutures that are taking place in the *Maelstrom* of meaning
(Wilson Knight's metaphor was a volcanic eruption) occurring in the
Elizabethan/Jacobean era.

He calls his approach 'verbalist' and his meaning can be seen in a
passage in which he discusses Othello's 'why should honour outlive
honesty?/Let it go all [V, ii, 243–4]':

■ The straightforward meaning, I take it (though commentators have
disagreed a good deal), is something like 'I have lost my civilian reputation, because the killing of my wife has turned out unjust; why then
should I care about my military reputation, which depends on keeping my sword?' But the poetic or dramatic effect clearly means a great
deal more. The question indeed so sums up the play that it involves
nearly all of both words; it seems finally to shatter the concept of
honesty whose connecting links the play has patiently removed. There
are thirteen other uses of *honour* (and *honourable*); four of them by
Othello about himself and five by others about Othello. The effect has
been to make Othello the personification of honour; if honour does not
survive some test of the idea nor could Othello. And to him *honest* is
'honourable', from which it was derived; a test of one is a test of the
other. Outlive Desdemona's chastity, which he now admits, outlive
Desdemona herself, the personification of chastity (lying again, as he
insisted, with her last breath), outlive decent behaviour in, public
respect for, self respect in, Othello – all these are honour, not honesty;
there is no question whether Othello outlives them. But they are not
tests of an idea; what has been tested is a special sense of *honest*. Iago
has been the personification of honesty, not merely to Othello but to
his world; why should honour, the father of the word, live on and talk
about itself; honesty, that obscure bundle of assumptions, the play has
destroyed. I can see no other way to explain the force of the question
here.[23] □

This is an important and difficult passage: Empson is surely right to attempt to tackle the word 'honest' at the level at which he is attempting to discuss it, but there are confusions that get in the way of clarity. Does Empson, for example, by talking about 'the word', thoughout this essay, mean anything more than 'the meaning of the word'? If he does not then 'concept' and 'idea' in this passage mean only 'the meaning of the word'. If so, the confusion vanishes to be replaced by the important but much clearer meaning that what people meant when they said 'honest' was not a simple matter and it was changing. Thus Othello means 'But why should what I and others mean by the word "honour"' ('word' here meaning not 'the set of sounds' – in this instance – that denotes the idea or concept 'honour' but the idea or concept 'honour') 'outlive what I and others mean by the word "honesty"?' However, this cannot be what Empson means, for he says of the tests to which what he calls 'the words' have been subjected:

■ But they are not tests of an idea; what has been tested is a special sense of *honest*.[24] □

The 'sense' of a word is an idea; it is present to the mind, not to the senses. Empson means to distinguish between two senses of the word. We can distinguish between 'word' meaning the set of sounds or marks that denote the idea that is the sense, or the ideas that are the senses, of the word, and the idea or ideas themselves, but we shall get into trouble if we try to distinguish between the meaning of a word and an idea.

The question, 'What is Empson gaining by talking about "words"?' (adopting a verbalist approach, he says) is an important one because it comes to influence critical thinking very significantly in the course of the century. He means to link his discussion all the way through to the present day, and especially to identify Bradley's position in the historical process of change:

■ There seems a linguistic difference between what Shakespeare meant by Iago and what the nineteenth-century critics saw in him. They took him as an abstract term 'Evil'; he is a critique on an unconscious pun. This is seen more clearly in their own personifications of their abstract word; e.g. *The Turn of the Screw* and *Dr Jekyll and Mr Hyde*. Henry James got a great triumph over some critic who said that his villains were sexual perverts (if the story meant anything they could hardly be anything else). He said: 'Ah, you have been letting yourself have fancies about Evil; I kept it right out of my mind.' That indeed is what the story is about. Stevenson rightly made clear that *Dr Jekyll* is about hypocrisy. You can only consider Evil as all things that destroy the good life; this has no unity; for instance, Hyde could not be both the miser and the spendthrift and whichever he was would destroy Jekyll without further accident. Evil here is merely the daydream of a respectable man, and only left vague so that respectable readers may equate it unshocked to their own daydreams. Iago may not be a 'personality', but he is better than these; he is the product of a more actual interest in a word.[25] □

Once again it has been asked what Empson can mean by 'a linguistic difference between what Shakespeare meant by Iago and what the nineteenth-century critics saw in him'. All he goes on to say is that they interpreted the character differently, because it is quite clear that they did not take him 'as an abstract term "Evil"' at all, or as any other 'term'; they interpreted the character as they saw and read the play. Moreover, does he mean to go on: '(whereas) he is a critique on an unconscious pun' or '(that is to say) he is a critique on an unconscious pun'? Are the two stories he cites 'personifications of their abstract word' in the intention of their authors or in his interpretation of the stories? Is it possible to disagree with his interpretation (not of what the stories *mean*, it should be stressed, but of what they *are*) or is this given to us as matter of fact? In what sense is 'evil' *their* abstract word? Or is 'Evil' with a capital initial letter *their* abstract word and 'evil' without is ours? Which one was Shakespeare's? Another one perhaps? The Henry James story is a typical Pronouncement of the Great Man but its relevance is not made clear; 'That indeed is what the story is about' makes different senses depending upon what you take 'that' to refer to; 'You can only consider Evil as all things that destroy the good life; this has no unity' does not make it clear what 'this' refers to; 'daydream' is used idiosyncratically and not explained; the last sentence is suggestive but not very clear.

Yet this essay is important; its matter is significant. It is such a great pity that he wrote it incoherently. This difficult work repays attention; though it is not always right it is always interesting, and it is very often right. He is right here about evil, and fascinating too. Perhaps evil does not merely threaten to bring about incoherence but is itself incoherent because any activity will suit it that brings about its end. His example here is good. Hyde is in fact a spendthrift but if he were to be the opposite, a miser, he would still achieve his aim of degrading Dr Jekyll's reputation. Unfortunately it is not clear what point Empson means to make by adducing these two anyway, unless he means to suggest that the nineteenth-century critics (what – all of them?) thought Iago connected with supernatural evil; in that case the final sentence has a thoroughly materialist resonance and 'actual interest in a word' is meant to sweep away all flannel about Evil. In fact Empson does not want to mean 'the nineteenth-century critics':

■ Bradley opposes what seems to have been a common Victorian view that Iago had 'a general disinterested love of evil', and says that if he had a 'motiveless malignity' (Coleridge) it was only in the more narrow but more psychologically plausible way that Bradley has defined.[26] □

Bradley's picture is not 'more narrow but more psychologically plausible'; he has not sacrificed 'breadth' (what is that?) for plausibility. He has given a subtle and complex and new picture of Iago that dispenses with supernatural evil entirely. His weakness Empson fairly identifies:

■ [T]he character of Iago must have been intended to seem coherent to the first-night audience; therefore the solution cannot be reached by learned deductions from hints in the text about his previous biography, for instance; if the character is puzzling nowadays, the answer must be a matter of recalling the assumptions of the audience and the way the character was put across.[27] □

As long, that is, as we can assume that it was not puzzling then. Rymer did not find Iago puzzling, but then he did not want to: he simply wanted to find him inconsistent with what he should be, and he did.

The next extract displays all the difficulties that face an attempt to replace Bradley's picture of Iago with one that will answer the problem Empson has raised. How can everyone call Iago 'honest' and he himself call himself 'honest' without contradiction, lying or irony on Iago's part, or the hypothesis that Iago has concealed himself with unusual cunning. If the problem has the whiff of contrivance about it that is because Empson has contrived his problem to suit his analysis of the history of the word 'honest', about which, none the less, he has important things to say.

■ All this I think is true, and satisfies the condition about the first-night audience. The thwarted sense of superiority in Iago is thrust on them in the first scene, and they are expected to feel a good deal of sympathy for it; at the end of the first Act they are to appreciate the triumph with which he conceives the plot. However the question 'why does he do it?' would hardly present itself as a problem; obviously the play required a villain; the only question likely to arise is 'why does everybody take the villain for a good man?' Bradley of course recognises this question but he deals with it in terms of an ethical theory supposed to be held only by Iago, whereas you clearly need to consider how it was understood by the audience; and the effect of this twist is to take Bradley some way back towards the idea that Iago embodies Pure Evil.

He says that Iago has 'a spite against goodness in men as a thing not only stupid but, both in its nature and by its success, contrary to Iago's nature and irritating to his pride'. Not only that, but 'His creed – for he is no sceptic, he has a definite creed – is that absolute egoism is the only rational and proper attitude, and that conscience or honour or any kind of regard for others is an absurdity.' Bradley therefore finds it contradictory and somewhat pathetic when Iago shouts 'villainous whore' at his wife, or implies that since Cassio would like to be an adulterer it is not so bad to say he is one. This, he says, shows that Iago has a 'secret subjection to morality', an 'inability to live up to his creed'; also the soliloquies betray a desire to convince himself, so that his natural egoism is not perfect. Perfection is attained, however, in the way he hides his ethical theory from other people; when we consider his past life, says Bradley, 'the inference, which is accompanied with a thrill of admiration, (is) that Iago's power of dissimulation and of self-control must have been prodigious'. Since a thrill about his past life is not properly part of the play, this amounts to an admission that the stage character is not consistent. In effect, Bradley is agreeing with Rymer here.

It seems clear that Iago was not meant as a secret theoretician of this sort, and that the audience would not be misled into thinking him one. His opinions, so far as he has got them clear, are shared by many people around him, and he boasts about them freely. To be sure, he could not afford to do this if they were not very confused, but even the confusion is shared by his neighbours. When Iago expounds his egotism to Roderigo in the first scene of the play, he is not so much admitting a weak criminal to his secrets as making his usual claim to Sturdy Independence in a rather coarser form. He is not subservient to the interests of the men in power who employ him, he says; he can stand up for himself, as they do. No doubt an Elizabethan employer, no less than Professor Bradley, would think this a shocking sentiment; but it does not involve Pure Egotism, and I do not even see that it involves Machiavelli. It has the air of a spontaneous line of sentiment among the lower classes, whereas Machiavelli was interested in the deceptions necessary for a ruler. Certainly it does not imply that the Independent man will betray his friends (as apart from his employer), because if it did he would not boast about it to them. This of course is the answer to the critics who have said that Roderigo could not have gone on handing all his money to a self-confessed knave. And, in the same way, when it turns out that Iago does mean to betray Roderigo, he has only to tell the audience that this fool is not one of his real friends; indeed he goes on to claim that it would be *wrong* to treat him as one. I do not mean to deny there is a paradox about the whole cult of the Independent Man (it is somehow felt that his selfishness makes him more valuable as a friend); but the paradox was already floating in the minds of the audience. No doubt Shakespeare thought that the conception was a false one, and gave a resounding demonstration of it, but one need not suppose that he did this by inventing a unique psychology for Iago, or even by making Iago unusually conscious of the problem at issue.[28] □

This final extract reveals the confusions about the word 'word' that have dogged the whole essay:

■ When opinion had become more settled or conventionalized, and the word had itself followed this movement by becoming simpler, there were of course two grounds for finding a puzzle in the character; but, of the two, I should say that failure to appreciate the complexity of the word was the more important ground, because after all the complexity of moral judgement had not become so difficult – what people had lost was the verbal pointer directing them to it. I think indeed that the Victorians were not ready enough to approve the good qualities of being 'ready to blow the gaff' and 'frank to yourself about your own desires'; and it is not likely that any analysis of one word would have altered their opinions.[29] □

It is difficult to make sense of the notion that 'the word itself' has 'followed' the movement of 'opinion'. It appears that Empson means that the meaning changed. During the change it was difficult to decide its meaning from time to time and from place to place. Then it all settled down. The next difficulty is the separation of the 'word' from 'moral judgement' and the notion of the 'verbal pointer' that directs people towards moral judgements. The complexity in the word is the complexity of people's attitudes to the range of behaviour indicated by the word; the complexity of their moral judgements. What has been lost is a moment in the meaning of the word when the meanings 'ready to blow the gaff' and 'frank to yourself about your own desires' existed at the same time as the meanings 'too stupid to be bad' and 'saying what you think and not saying what you do not think', and so on. Empson is right. It is a complex word. That is because it denotes behaviour that can be evaluated in a number of ways, not all of them consistent with all the others. The difficulties that stand in the way of the use of the word are the consequences of the difficulties that arise from the attempt to consider the behaviour and also from people's determination to use words to mean different things. But the word has no existence apart from the behaviour and the usage, and to talk as though it did is to risk confusion. The confusion is not fatal, but it is misleading. The deeper disagreements that arise in a consideration of Empson's serious and challenging argument, from which much may be learnt, may never come to light if the confusion gets in the way.

F. R. Leavis's approach to the Bradley problem was to attack it openly. In an essay ironically entitled 'Diabolic Intellect and the Noble Hero: A Note on *Othello*',[30] Leavis coolly mocks Bradley's approach and the picture it generates. The play, he suggests, 'suffers in current appreciation an essential and denaturing falsification'.[31] He says the play 'lends itself as no other of them does to the approach classically associated with Bradley's name',[32] but goes on to say:

■ It would, that is, have lent itself uniquely well to Bradley's approach if Bradley had made his approach consistently and with moderate intelligence. Actually, however, the section on *Othello* in *Shakespearian Tragedy* is more extravagant in misdirected scrupulosity than any of the others; it is, with a concentration of Bradley's comical solemnity, completely wrongheaded – grossly and palpably false to the evidence it offers to weigh.[33] □

His summary of Bradley is sharp:

■ According to the version of *Othello* elaborated by Bradley the tragedy is the undoing of the noble Moor by the devilish cunning of Iago. Othello we are to see as a nearly faultless hero whose strength and virtue are turned against him. Othello and Desdemona, so far as their fate depended on their characters and untampered-with mutual relations, had every ground for expecting the happiness that romantic courtship had promised. It was external evil, the malice of the demi-devil, that turned a happy story of romantic love – of romantic lovers who were qualified to live happily ever after, so to speak – into a tragedy. This – it is the traditional version of *Othello* and has, moreover, the support of Coleridge – is to sentimentalize Shakespeare's tragedy and to displace its centre.[34] □

Leavis maintains that far too much attention is usually paid to the character of Iago:

■ The plain fact that has to be asserted in the face of this sustained and sanctioned perversity is that in Shakespeare's tragedy of *Othello* Othello is the chief personage – the chief personage in such a sense that the tragedy may fairly be said to be Othello's character in action. Iago is subordinate and merely ancillary. He is not much more than a necessary piece of dramatic mechanism – that at any rate is a fit reply to the view of Othello as necessary material and provocation for a display of Iago's fiendish intellectual superiority. Iago, of course, is sufficiently convincing as a person; he could not perform his dramatic function otherwise. But something has gone wrong when we make him interesting in this kind of way:

> His fate – which is himself – has completely mastered him: so that, in the later scenes, where the improbability of the entire success of a design built on so many different falsehoods forces itself upon the reader, Iago appears for moments not as a consummate schemer, but as a man absolutely infatuated and delivered over to certain destruction.

We ought not, in reading those scenes, to be paying so much attention to the intrinsic personal qualities of Iago as to attribute to him tragic interest of that kind.[35] □

The misreading (for that is what it amounts to) is the more inexplicable because:

■ [T]he text was there for Coleridge, and Bradley accompanies his argument with constant particular reference to it. It is as extraordinary a history of triumphant sentimental perversity as literary history can show.[36] □

This claim is not merely rhetorical and it is not wrong, but it is exaggerated. Leavis can demonstrate an alternative view that does not on the face of it sit comfortably with Bradley's, but he cannot prove his case; his view remains a view. He has not exposed critical misconduct after all.

The view is an important corrective; it reminds us that there are other ways to look at the play. Insisting on reducing Iago's role as far as he can, Leavis offers this summary of the play's action:

■ Iago's power, in fact, in the temptation-scene is that he represents something that is in Othello – in Othello the husband of Desdemona: the essential traitor is within the gates. For if Shakespeare's Othello too is simple-minded, he is nevertheless more complex than Bradley's. Bradley's Othello is, rather, Othello's; it being an essential datum regarding the Shakespearean Othello that he has an ideal conception of himself.

The tragedy is inherent in the Othello-Desdemona relation, and Iago is a mechanism necessary for precipitating tragedy in a dramatic action.[37] □

Leavis's account of Othello's 'ideal conception of himself' is given in the following extract: having quoted Bradley's view that Othello is 'of a great openness and trustfulness of nature', Leavis comments that 'it would be putting it more to the point to say that he has great consciousness of worth and confidence of respect'. He continues:

■ The worth is really and solidly there; he is truly impressive, a noble product of the life of action – of

> The big wars
> That make ambition virtue [III, iii, 352–3].

'That make ambition virtue' – this phrase of his is a key one: his virtues are, in general, of that kind; they have, characteristically, something of the quality suggested. Othello, in his magnanimous way, is egotistic. He really is, beyond any question, the nobly massive man of action, the captain of men, he sees himself as being, but he does very much see himself:

> Keep up your bright swords, for the dew will rust them [I, ii, 59].

In short, a habit of self-approving self-dramatization is an essential element in Othello's make-up, and remains so at the very end.

It is, at the best, the impressive manifestation of a noble egotism. But, in the new marital situation, this egotism isn't going to be the less dangerous for its nobility. This self-centredness doesn't mean self-knowledge: that is a virtue which Othello, as soldier of fortune, hasn't had much need of. He has been well provided by nature to meet all the trials a life of action has exposed him to. The trials facing him now that he has married this Venetian girl with whom he's 'in love' so imaginatively (we're told) as to outdo Romeo and who is so many years younger than himself (his colour, whether or not 'colour-feeling' existed among the Elizabethans, we are certainly to take as emphasizing the disparity of the match) – the trials facing him now are of a different order.

And here we have the significance of the storm, which puts so great a distance between Venice and Cyprus, between the old life and the new, and makes the change seem so complete and so momentous. The storm is rendered in that characteristic heroic mode of the play which Professor Wilson Knight calls the 'Othello music':

> For do but stand upon the foaming shore,
> The chidden billows seem to chide the clouds;
> The wind-shaked surge, with high and monstrous mane,
> Seems to cast water on the burning bear,
> And quench the guards of the ever-fixed pole:
> I never did like molestation view
> On the enchafed flood [II, i, 11–17].

This mode (Professor Wilson Knight, in his own way, describes it well) gives the effect of a comparatively simple magnificence; the characteristic verse of *Othello* is firm, regular in outline, buoyant and sonorous. It is in an important sense Othello's own verse, the 'large-mouthed utterance' of the noble man of action. Bradley's way of putting it is that Othello, though he 'has not, indeed, the meditative or speculative imagination of Hamlet', is 'in the strictest sense of the word' 'more poetic than Hamlet'. We need not ask Bradley what the 'strictest sense of the word' is, or stop to dispute with him whether or not Othello is 'the greatest poet' of all Shakespeare's heroes. If characters in poetic drama speak poetry we ought to be able to notice the fact without concluding that they are poets. In *Othello*, which is poetic drama, Shakespeare works by poetic means: it is through the characteristic noble verse described above that, very largely, we get our sense of the noble Othello. If the impression made by Othello's own utterance is often poetical as well as poetic, that is Shakespeare's way, not of representing him as a poet, but of conveying the romantic glamour that, for Othello himself and others, invests Othello and what he stands for.

'For Othello himself' – it might be said that to express Othello's sense of himself and make us share it is the essential function of this verse, the 'Othello music'. But, of course, there are distinctions to be noted. The description of the storm quoted above, though it belongs to the general heroic mode of the play, cannot be said to exhibit the element of self-dramatization that is characteristic of Othello's own utterances. On the other hand, the self-dramatizing trick commands subtle modulations and various stops. It is not always as assertive as in

Behold, I have a weapon [V, ii, 257]

or the closing speech. In these speeches, not only is it explicit, it clearly involves, we may note, an attitude *towards* the emotion expressed – an attitude of a kind we are familiar with in the analysis of sentimentality.

The storm, within the idealizing mode, is at the other extreme from sentimentality; it serves to bring out the reality of the heroic Othello and what he represents. For his heroic quality, realized in this verse (here the utterance of others) is a real thing, though it is not, as Othello takes it to be, the whole of the reality. Another way of making the point would be to say that the distinctive style under discussion, the style that lends itself to Othello's self-dramatization and conveys in general the tone and ideal import of this, goes, in its confident and magnificent buoyancy, essentially with the outer storm that both the lovers, in their voyage to Cyprus, triumphantly outride.

With that kind of external stress the noble Othello is well qualified to deal (if he went down – and we know he won't – he would go down magnificently). But it is not that kind of stress he has to fear in the new life beginning at Cyprus. The stresses of the spiritual climate are concentrated by Iago (with his deflating, unbeglamouring, brutally realistic mode of speech) into something immediately apprehensible in drama and comparable with the storm. In this testing, Othello's inner timbers begin to part at once, the stuff of which he is made begins at once to deteriorate and show itself unfit. There is even a symbolic foundering when, breaking into incoherent ejaculations, he 'falls in a trance' [IV, i, 43 s.d.].[38] □

The strength of this approach is its determination to see the play as a *fiction*; as a poetic, dramatic construct. The key difference between Leavis and Bradley is their different conceptions of the proper relationship between art and reality. For Leavis art must not part company with reality ('Iago, of course, is sufficiently convincing as a person; he could not perform his dramatic function otherwise') but it has its own organising principle. Leavis is often tantalising on this point, at least apparently. He tends to use figures of speech that suggest that art has an 'organic' integrity that is the effect of the quality of imaginative grasp expressed in the procedures of art. This model allows him to deal with 'unrealistic' art particularly well because his attention is not on the parallel between the work and reality in any direct way, but on the quality of imaginative grasp that can be inferred from a detailed examination of the work. This allows direct comparison of 'realistic' and 'unrealistic' works through a comparison of the quality of imaginative grasp that can be inferred from each. A comparison of 'realistic' works and 'unrealistic' works with the world inevitably tends to favour the 'realistic' because we can see the world in them more easily. Leavis (and Wilson Knight, and Empson) tend to be better on the poetry than Bradley because Bradley sees the poetry as something spoken by the characters while the others realise from the beginning that without the poetry there are no characters. This perspective enables Leavis to tackle Bradley head-on:

■ Bradley, however, his knowledge of Othello coinciding virtually with Othello's, sees nothing but the nobility. At the cost of denaturing Shakespeare's tragedy, he insistently idealizes. The 'feelings of jealousy proper', he says, 'are not the chief or deepest source of Othello's suffering. It is the feeling, "If she be false, oh then Heaven mocks itself;" the feeling, "O Iago, the pity of it, Iago!"' It is Shakespeare's tragedy of Othello that the man who exclaims this can exclaim three lines later, when he next speaks:

I will chop her into messes. Cuckold me! [IV, i, 197]

Again, three lines further on he says:

Get me some poison, Iago; this night. I'll not expostulate with her, lest her body and beauty unprovide my mind again: this night, Iago [IV, i, 201–3].

This surely has some bearing on the nature of 'the pity of it': to equate Bradley's knowledge of Othello with Othello's own was perhaps unfair to Othello.

In any case, this association of strong sensuality with ugly vindictive jealousy is insistent in Shakespeare's play:

Now he tells how she plucked him to my chamber. O, I see that nose of yours, but not that dog I shall throw it to [IV, i, 140].

I would have him nine years a-killing. A fine woman! A fair woman! A sweet woman! [IV, i, 175]

'O Iago, the pity of it, Iago!': it is plain here that 'fine', 'fair' and 'sweet' apply, not to Desdemona as a complete person (the immediate provocation is Iago's remark, 'she gave it him and he hath given it [the handkerchief] his whore'), but to her person in abstraction from the character of the owner, whom Othello hardly, at this point, respects. And the nature of this regret, this tragically expressed regret, bears an essential relation to the nature of the love with which Othello, however imaginatively and Romeo-like, loved Desdemona. That romantic idealizing love could be as dubiously grounded in reality as this is an essential condition of the tragedy. But Bradley's own idealizing is invincible. He can even say:

An ineradicable instinct of justice, rather than any last quiver of hope, leads him to question Emilia.

That's no doubt how Othello would have put it; but for the reader – the unidealizing reader – what the questioning of Emilia [IV, ii] shows in brutal, resolute, unrestricted predominance is the antithesis of any instinct of justice.[39] □

The criticism is surely right; Bradley is expressing the play as Othello sees it. Yet Bradley is equally right to insist that the mainspring of the tragedy is the way Othello sees what is going on. The implication of Bradley's view is, by what authority can Othello's way of seeing things be denounced? He is wrong, from other people's point of view – the audience's and the reader's as well as other characters' – but he is so sunk in his conviction that it is almost beside the point that he is wrong. Desdemona's hopeless yielding suggests that she sees this too and feels only 'the pity of it' too. Looked at in this way the play seems to suggest that his being wrong is only part of his tragedy, deepening it rather than undermining it. How Othello *feels* is the whole of the play, but it is not what is really going on. Leavis's difficulty is that he has to insist that:

■ By the time he becomes the jealous husband it has been made plain beyond any possibility of doubt or reversal that we are to take him, in the dramatic critic's sense, seriously – at any rate, such a habit of expectation has been set up with regard to him (and he is well established as the main focus of attention) that no development will be acceptable unless the behaviour it imposes on him is reconcilable with our notions of ordinary psychological consistency. Other characters in the play can be 'convincing' on easier terms; we needn't inquire into the consistency of Emilia's behaviour – we accept her as a datum, and not even about Iago are we – or need we be – so psychologically exacting. His combination of honest seeming with devilish actuality we accept as, at least partly, a matter of tacit convention; convention acceptable because of the convincingly handled tragic theme to which it is ancillary.[40] □

And we cannot reconcile any idea of nobility fuller than that offered in the phrase 'the noble man of action' with 'I will chop her into messes. Cuckold me!' That indeed is a difficulty. Leavis's solution of the difficulty is to say that he is not any more noble than to the degree implied by the phrase 'the noble man of action'. Bradley, the argument continues, stands at the near end of a long tradition of sentimental idealisation of Othello that has made necessary the corollary figure of a demonic Iago as the only figure subtle and powerful enough to corrupt such a noble man.

Leavis's contempt for the man of action is clear ('This self-centredness doesn't mean self-knowledge: that is a virtue which Othello, *as a soldier of fortune*, hasn't had much need of' – my italics) as is his contempt for a love that does not acknowledge the need for clear self-scrutiny. This last extract follows the key scenes in the last act. He begins with Othello's speech at the beginning of Act V, Scene ii:

■ It opens with the accent of a contained holy revulsion, the containing power appearing as inexorable, impersonal justice:

It is the cause, it is the cause, my soul!
Let me not name it to you, you chaste stars!
It is the cause [V, ii, 1–3].

Now comes a shrinking back from the deed:

> Yet I'll not shed her blood,
> Nor scar that whiter skin of hers than snow
> And smooth as monumental alabaster [V, ii, 3–5].

Tenderness here quite clearly is that characteristic voluptuousness of Othello's which, since it is unassociated with any real interest in Desdemona as a person, slips so readily into possessive jealousy. Now the accent of impersonal justice is heard again:

> Yet she must die, else she'll betray more men [V, ii, 6]

– but the accent is so clearly unrelated to any effectual motive in Othello that the concern for justice, the self-bracing to noble sacrifice, appears as self-deception. Next come misgivings over the finality of the deed:

> Put out the light, and then put out the light;
> If I quench thee, thou flaming minister,
> I can again thy former light restore,
> Should I repent me: but once put out thy light,
> Thou cunning'st pattern of excelling nature,
> I know not where is that Promethean heat
> That can thy light relume. When I have pluck'd the rose
> I cannot give it vital growth again,
> It must needs wither: I'll smell it on the tree [V, ii, 7–15].

Tenderness here is less specifically voluptuous sensuality than it was earlier, but we nevertheless remember:

> Get me some poison, Iago; this night. I'll not expostulate with her, lest her body and beauty unprovide my mind again: this night, Iago [IV, i, 201–3].

And there is in Othello a curious and characteristic effect of self-preoccupation, of preoccupation with his emotions rather than with Desdemona in her own right:

> O balmy breath, that almost dost persuade
> Justice herself to break her sword! One more, one more:
> Be thus when thou art dead, and I will kill thee,
> And love thee after: one more, and this the last.
> So sweet was ne'er so fatal. I must weep,

> But they are cruel tears: this sorrow's heavenly;
> It strikes where it doth love. She wakes [V, ii, 16–22].

When she is awake and so is no longer a mere body, but a person, it is not sorrowful love or noble self-bracing to a sacrifice that she becomes aware of in Othello:

> Alas, why gnaw you so your nether lip?
> Some bloody passion shakes your very frame:
> These are portents [V, ii, 43–5].

Moreover, though Othello says

> I would not kill thy unprepared spirit [V, ii, 31],

actually he refuses her the time to say one prayer.

When he discovers his mistake, his reaction is an intolerably intensified form of the common 'I could kick myself':

> Whip me, ye devils
> From the possession of this heavenly sight!
> Blow me about in winds! roast me in sulphur!
> Wash me in steep-down gulfs of liquid fire!
> O Desdemona! Desdemona! dead!
> Oh! Oh! Oh! [V, ii, 275–9]

But he remains the same Othello; he has discovered his mistake, but there is no tragic self-discovery. The speech closing with the words just quoted is that beginning

> Behold, I have a weapon [V, ii, 257],

one of the finest examples in the play of the self-dramatizing trick. The noble Othello is now seen as tragically pathetic, and he sees himself as pathetic too:

> Man but a rush against Othello's breast,
> And he retires. Where shall Othello go [V, ii, 268–9]?

He is ruined, but he is the same Othello in whose essential make-up the tragedy lay: the tragedy doesn't involve the idea of the hero's learning through suffering. The fact that Othello tends to sentimentalize should be the reverse of a reason for our sentimentalizing too.

For even, or rather especially, in that magnificent last speech of his

Othello does tend to sentimentalize, though to say that and no more would convey a false impression, for the speech conveys something like the full complexity of Othello's simple nature, and in the total effect the simplicity is tragic and grand. The quiet beginning gives us the man of action with his habit of effortless authority:

> Soft you; a word or two before you go.
> I have done the State some service, and they know't.
> No more of that. I pray you in your letters,
> When you shall these unlucky deeds relate,
> Speak of me as I am; nothing extenuate,
> Nor set down aught in malice [V, ii, 336–41] ...

Othello really is, we cannot doubt, the stoic-captain whose few words know their full sufficiency: up to this point we cannot say he drama-tizes himself, he simply *is*. But then, in a marvellous way (if we consider Shakespeare's art), the emotion works itself up until in less than half-a-dozen lines the stoic of few words is eloquently weeping. With

> Then must you speak
> Of one that loved not wisely but too well [V, ii, 341–2],

the epigrammatic terseness of the dispatch, the dictated dispatch, begins to quiver. Then, with a rising emotional swell, description becomes unmistakably self-dramatization – self-dramatization as un-self-comprehending as before:

> Of one not easily jealous, but being wrought,
> Perplex'd in the extreme; of one whose hand,
> Like the base Indian, threw a pearl away
> Richer than all his tribe; of one whose subdued eyes,
> Albeit unused to the melting mood,
> Drop tears as fast as the Arabian trees
> Their medicinal gum [V, ii, 343–9].

Contemplating the spectacle of himself, Othello is overcome with the pathos of it. But this is not the part to die in: drawing himself proudly up, he speaks his last words as the stern soldier who recalls, and re-enacts, his supreme moment of deliberate courage:

> Set you down this;
> And say besides, that in Aleppo once,
> Where a malignant and a turban'd Turk

Beat a Venetian and traduced the state,
I took by the throat the circumcised dog
And smote him, thus. (Stabs himself.) [V, ii, 349–53]

It is a superb *coup de théâtre*.

As, with that double force, a *coup de théâtre*, it is a peculiarly right ending to the tragedy of Othello. The theme of the tragedy is concentrated in it – concentrated in the final speech and action as it could not have been had Othello 'learnt through suffering'. That he should die acting his ideal part is all in the part: the part is manifested here in its rightness and solidity, and the actor as inseparably the man of action. The final blow is as real as the blow it re-enacts, and the histrionic intent symbolically affirms the reality: Othello dies belonging to the world of action in which his true part lay.

That so many readers – Coleridge, Swinburne, Bradley, for instance – not belonging to that world should have found Othello's part irresistibly attractive, in the sense that they have preferred to see the play through Othello's eyes rather than Shakespeare's, is perhaps not after all surprising. It may be suggested that the cult of T. E. Lawrence has some relevance here. And Othello is not merely a glamorous man of action who dominates all companies, he is (as we have all been) cruelly and tragically wronged – a victim of relentless intrigue, and, while remaining noble and heroic, is allowed to appreciate the pathos of his own fate. He has, in fact, all the advantages of that last speech, where the invitation to identify oneself with him is indeed hardly resistible. Who does not (in some moments) readily see himself as the hero of such a *coup de théâtre*?[41] □

This naturally leads Leavis to a consideration of Iago:

■ What but supremely subtle villainy could have brought to this kind of ruin the hero whose perfect nobility we admire and love?[42] □

But he is less than that:

■ Considered as a comprehensibly villainous person, he represents a not uncommon kind of grudging, cynical malice (and he's given, at least in suggestion, enough in the way of grievance and motive). But in order to perform his function as dramatic machinery he has to put on such an appearance of invincibly cunning devilry as to provide Coleridge and the rest with some excuse for their awe, and to leave others wondering, in critical reflection, whether he isn't a rather clumsy mechanism.[43] □

The reader can take away the impression from some of these passages that Leavis is building up a psychological portrait in just the same manner as Bradley, though the picture is different. He may have escaped the spell but his scorn for the figure leads him to construct just as solid an image as Bradley's. It is an interesting figure, and it makes much sense of the last speech, though there is no need to degrade Iago quite as much as he does. The hypothesis of devilish cunning is not needed to explain the corruption of nobility; but nor do you have to mock nobility as self-regarding self-dramatization to expose its limitations.

Shakespeare Survey 21 for 1968 is devoted to *Othello*; in it Helen Gardner surveyed the first half-century of *Othello* criticism under the title '*Othello*: A Retrospect, 1900–1967'. In the course of this essay Gardner suggests an interesting reason why the play's central character may have been received coolly by some critics:

■ The stigmatizing of Othello as 'unaware' had an obvious relation to the appalling catastrophe of the First World War, and the blow that the image of the professional soldier received from the senseless carnage in Flanders. It became axiomatic in the twenties and thirties that professional soldiers were stupid. Even Wyndham Lewis, who sympathized with the Lion against the Fox, saw Othello as a kind of dazed, unhappy bull with Iago as a clever matador dancing round him.[44] □

Gardner evidently does not believe that all professional soldiers are stupid but she clearly understands what motivated such hostility to the figure of the man of action as is evident in Leavis's reference to 'the cult of T. E. Lawrence'. The next chapter will address the views of *Othello* that emerged as the century progressed.

CHAPTER FIVE

The Mid-Century: Revaluation

THIS GUIDE began by pointing to Terry Eagleton's claim that criticism was a function of an unusually intimate social circle in the early eighteenth century – the *milieu* of the coffee shop. This is a simplification but it points in turn to an important fact about criticism, historically speaking; it was not an exclusively professional concern. Criticism was the concern of all concerned. The early twentieth century in Britain saw an attempt to demarcate a group that would lead critical activity, an attempt that was not without success; the late twentieth century has seen a rapid expansion of English studies in schools and in further and higher education, a 'mass' education that one English writer condemned in a famous phrase: 'more will mean worse'.[1] The social *milieu* of criticism has changed beyond recognition. Demarcations can not easily be made; a *spectrum* of activities must be proposed, stretching from the reviews in newspapers to the most erudite essay and beyond, to conversations about books and to the investments of publishing companies. The most hermetically professional pronouncements co-exist with unashamed self-publicisation; academics have unprecedented access to the news media and can, on rare occasions, 'star'; the 'popular' has become fashionable but the 'élite' has not disappeared; the most intensely private and the most openly public are sometimes indistinguishable. A particular understanding of democracy and the developing technology of mass communications have between them enabled these developments and they are not altogether unwelcome. The coffee shop has extended its boundaries. It remains to be seen whether or not it has managed to assimilate *Othello*.

Helen Gardner begins her retrospect with reference to Bradley:

■ Much of the criticism of *Othello* in this century has been marked by an uneasiness which was first voiced by Bradley. This was partly a consequence of his endeavour to discover and define the 'substance' of a Shakespearian Tragedy. Unable to deny that *Othello* was a masterpiece, and that if we are to distinguish certain of Shakespeare's tragedies as 'the great tragedies' we must place *Othello* among them, he had in honesty to recognize that the vision of the world given by *Othello* did not conform to his conception of the vision of the world that the great tragedies present. It is really impossible to see in the destruction of Othello and Desdemona 'a world travailing for perfection, but bringing to birth, together with glorious good, an evil which it is able to overcome only by self-torture and self-waste'; and Bradley made no attempt to persuade himself or us that at the end of *Othello* we are presented with a world that has, though at a fearful cost, purged itself of evil. On the contrary, he came very near to saying that the impression the course of the play makes on us is of a very different vision of the universe, suggesting that if there are powers outside the wills of men that shape human destinies then these powers are on the side of Iago. Shying away rapidly from this painful notion, he attempted to analyse why 'some readers', while acknowledging the play's power, and even owning that dramatically it is perhaps Shakespeare's greatest triumph, still 'regard it with a certain distaste', or 'hardly allow it a place in their minds beside *Hamlet, King Lear*, and *Macbeth*'. The distaste he ascribed to the repulsiveness of the subject of sexual jealousy 'treated with Elizabethan fulness and frankness', and to the violence and brutality to which his jealousy drives Othello. The reservation over the play's claim to supreme greatness he ascribed to the 'comparative confinement of the imaginative atmosphere'. '*Othello* has not . . . the power of dilating the imagination by vague suggestions of huge universal powers working in the world of individual fate and passion.' Compared with the other three 'great tragedies', 'it is, in a sense, less "symbolic"'. It leaves us with the impression that we are not 'in contact with the whole of Shakespeare'; and 'it is perhaps significant in this respect that the hero himself strikes us as having, probably, less of the poet's personality in him than many characters far inferior both as dramatic creations and as men'.[2] □

Her survey strikes this key note again and again, that the play has not sat easily with twentieth-century critics, at least not in the first half of that century, any more than it had done with some of the most generous and thoughtful minds of the preceding centuries.

Helen Gardner's own essay, 'The Noble Moor' (British Academy Shakespeare lecture for 1955), opens with a clear rebuff to Leavis's interpretation:

■ Among the tragedies of Shakespeare *Othello* is supreme in one quality: beauty. Much of its poetry, in imagery, perfection of phrase, and steadiness of rhythm, soaring yet firm, enchants the sensuous imagination. This kind of beauty *Othello* shares with *Romeo and Juliet* and *Antony and Cleopatra*; it is a corollary of the theme which it shares with them. But *Othello* is also remarkable for another kind of beauty. Except for one trivial scene with the clown, all is immediately relevant to the central issue; no scene requires critical justification. The play has a rare intellectual beauty, satisfying the desire of the imagination for order and harmony between the parts and the whole. Finally, the play has intense moral beauty. It makes an immediate appeal to the moral imagination, in its presentation in the figure of Desdemona of a love which does not alter 'when it alteration finds', but 'bears it out even to the edge of doom'. These three kinds of beauty are interdependent, since all arise from the nature of the hero. Othello's vision of the world expresses itself in what Mr. Wilson Knight has called the 'Othello music'; the 'compulsive course' of his nature dominates the action, driving it straight on to its conclusion; Othello arouses in Desdemona unshakeable love. I am unable, therefore, to accept some recent attempts to find meaning in a play, which has to more than one critic seemed to lack meaning, in its progressive revelation of the inadequacy of the hero's nobility. Such an interpretation disregards the play's most distinctive quality. It contradicts that immediate and overwhelming first impression to which it is a prime rule of literary criticism that all further analysis must conform.[3] □

Gardner's discussion of critical responses to the play in her own time leads her to an interesting and novel view of *Othello*:

■ There are various reasons why *Othello* should seem more remote from us than the other tragedies. A feature of Shakespearian studies in the last twenty years has been the interest in the Histories and the comparative neglect of the Comedies. The social and political ideas of the Elizabethans: the Tudor conception of history as the realm of providential judgements, the ideas of natural order, the chain of being, and 'degree, priority and place', obviously relevant to the Histories, have also some relevance to *Hamlet, King Lear*, and *Macbeth*. They throw some light there, though perhaps rather a 'dim religious one', and on the periphery rather than on the centre. They cast no light upon *Othello*, whose affinities are with the Comedies. We must shut up the *Book of Homilies* and *The Mirror for Magistrates* and open the love poets for a change.[4] □

This is a clear challenge to Leavis's entire outlook and to the assumptions that lie behind that outlook. Her invocation of 'the love poets', and her placing the *Book of Homilies* and *The Mirror for Magistrates* together with the Histories and in opposition to the Comedies and 'the love poets' creates a tension between what we might loosely call the 'real' world and whatever we are going to call the world created by the Comedies. *Othello*, according to Gardner, lies in that other world and not in the real world at all.

This procedure startlingly reminds the reader that Leavis's account has much of Bradley in it; the subtle psychology of Leavis's picture of Othello is as realistic as is Bradley's, in the sense that it fills out for the reader a sense of Othello as a real person. Brian Vickers's comment on Johnson's criticism may be recalled: Johnson evaluates behaviour as he would in real life.[5]

Why should he not? The answer is simply because it may not always be appropriate to do so. It may be that to do so is to misrepresent what you are trying to judge. How can we evaluate Puck or Ariel as we would in real life? Or Caliban? The interesting point is that it *can* be done, but only if a strong sense of the unnaturalness and paradoxical grotesqueness of the procedure is retained: that is part of its delight and even perhaps of the intention of the dramatist. To see resemblances between one's own life and theirs; to note relevancies to one's life in theirs; this is to perceive the touching of two worlds, one of romance and the other one's own, real, world. If Gardner is right, *Othello* should be seen in this way too. Gardner boldly sees Othello as 'heroic':

■ But the fundamental reason, I think, for *Othello*'s appearing of limited interest to many critics today is our distaste for the heroic, which has found little expression in our literature in this century, with the splendid exception of the poetry of Yeats. In *Othello* the heroic, as distinct from the exemplary and the typical: what calls out admiration and sympathy in contrast to what is to be imitated or avoided, the extraordinary in contrast to the representative, directly challenges the imagination.[6] □

She contrasts *Othello* with *Hamlet*: Hamlet is bound by circumstances beyond his control:

■ To this vision of man bound *Othello* presents a vision of man free. The past, whose claim upon the present is at the heart of *Hamlet*, is in *Othello* a country which the hero has passed through and left behind, the scene of his 'travels' history'. The ancestors of royal siege, the father and mother, between whom the handkerchief passed and from whom it came to him, have no claim upon him. His status in Venice is contractual. The Senate are his 'very noble and approv'd good masters' because he and they have chosen it should be so. His loyalties are not the tangle of inherited loyalties, but the few and simple loyalties of choice. His duties are not the duties of his station, but the duties of his profession. Othello is free as intensely as Hamlet is unfree, and the relation which fails to establish itself in *Hamlet* is the one relation which counts here, the free relation of love. It is presented in its most extreme, that is in heroic, form, as a relation between individuals, owing nothing to, and indeed triumphing over, circumstances and natural inclination. The universality of the play lies here, in its presentation of man as freely choosing and expressing choice by acts: Desdemona crossing the Senate floor to take her place beside her husband, Othello slaying her and slaying himself, Emilia crying out the truth at the cost of her life. *Othello* is particularly concerned with that deep, instinctive level where we feel ourselves to be free, with the religious aspect of our nature, in its most general sense. (This is why a theological interpretation seems so improper.) Othello's nobility lies in his capacity to worship: to feel wonder and give service.[7] □

His freedom, that is, to make the point general, lies in his choice of service. The subtlety of Gardner's final point in this extract being that Othello freely chooses romantic love as a fulfilment of 'the religious aspect of our nature, in its most general sense', only to find the responsibility of that choice overwhelming. Gardner comments:

■ The love between Othello and Desdemona is a great venture of faith. He is free; she achieves her freedom, and at a great cost.[8] □

Gardner sees the tragic experience of the play as the loss of faith induced by the insinuation, not of doubt positively, but of the uncertainty of knowledge. That very uncertainty is the essence of faith: 'for what man hopes for what he knows?' as St. Paul said. Romantic love fascinated the poets of the time as Gardner reminds her readers, and it fascinated the poet-dramatist of the Comedies. The significance of the Sonnets may be suggested at this point: Shakespeare's own venture into love poetry explores the dreams and agonies of this same venture even more vividly than do his Comedies and in more exacting detail. The parallels, paradoxes, and daring and even impudent substitutions of the Metaphysicals explore the relationships between romantic love and religious faith as alternatives. Faith was a matter keenly investigated by the age. If the attempt is made to view the play as a lesson in faith it should be remembered that the play is a drama presenting the consequences for persons of this crisis of faith as an object of interest in itself, not as an illustration of a moral. That does not mean, of course, that the moral can not be drawn.

Gardner sees the murder of Desdemona as having upon it 'the stamp of the heroic':

■ It has what Yeats saw in the Easter Rising,[9] which neither his moral nor his political judgement approved, and one of whose leaders he had disliked and despised: a 'terrible beauty', contrasting with the 'casual comedy' of daily life.

The act is heroic because Othello acts from inner necessity. Although the thought of social dishonour plays a part in his agony, it has no place in this final scene. He kills her because he can not 'digest the poison of her flesh' [Gardner refers us to Adriana in *The Comedy of Errors* II, ii, 144–8:

> I am possess'd with an adulterate blot;
> My blood is mingled with the crime of lust:
> For if we two be one and thou play false,
> I do digest the poison of thy flesh,
> Being strumpeted by thy contagion]

and also to save her from herself, to restore meaning to her beauty. The act is also heroic in its absoluteness, disinterestedness, and finality. Othello does not look beyond it. It must be done. The tragic hero usurps the functions of the gods and attempts to remake the world. This *hubris*,[10] which arouses awe and terror, appears in an extreme form in Othello's assumption of the role of a god who chastises where he loves, and of a priest who must present a perfect victim. He tries to confess her, so that in her last moment she may be true, and suffering the death of the body as expiation may escape the death of the soul. Her persistence in what he believes to be a lie and her tears at the news of Cassio's death turn the priest into the murderer. The heroic is rooted in reality here: the godlike is mingled with the brutal, which Aristotle saw as its true opposite, and Desdemona, love's martyr, dies like a frightened child, pleading for 'but half an hour' more of life.

'I am glad I have ended my revisal of this dreadful scene. It is not to be endured', said Johnson. And yet, this terrible act has wonderful tragic rightness. Only by it can the tragic situation be finally resolved, and in tragedy it is the peace of finality which we look for. Living, Desdemona can never prove her innocence. There is nothing she can do to 'win her lord again'. She could, of course, save herself, and in so doing save her husband from crime, dishonour, and death. She could leave this terrifying monster and ask for the protection of her own countrymen, the messengers of Venice. This sensible solution never crosses her mind. She remains with the man her 'love approves', and since

There is a comfort in the strength of love,

for all her bewilderment and distress she falls asleep, to wake to find her faith rewarded by death. But in death she does 'win her lord again'.[11] □

Later Gardner says:

■ Yet in this terrible end there is so solemn a sense of completeness that it might well be called the most beautiful end in Shakespearian tragedy.[12] □

She sees *Othello* as a 'tragedy of fortune' and contrasts it further with the other tragedies:

■ The design of the tragedy of fortune has a very different effect from the design of what may be called the tragedy of dilemma, in which, as in *Hamlet*, the hero is presented to us in circumstances not of his own making, confronted with another's crime; or from the design of the tragedy of error, where the hero's initial act releases evil forces and brings enormous suffering, or from that of the tragedy of crime and retribution. We never see Hamlet prosperous. Lear's rash and cruel act opens the action. Macbeth is no sooner before us than he is in temptation, 'rapt' in inner struggle. In plays with these designs, the conclusions have something of the nature of solutions: the end answers the beginning.[13] □

This version of the play echoes closely Othello's image of himself as the 'base Indian' who 'threw a pearl away/Richer than all his tribe (V, ii, 345–6)': it offers the image of the man of fortune throwing that fortune away. Her sense of the completeness of the ending, and of its beauty, derives from this picture.

John Bayley, in *The Characters of Love*, offers a view similarly sympathetic to the heroic, but one that leads in a different direction altogether. Bayley thinks the play very like a novel and talks about it in a way that suggests Proust, though he rejects the comparison explicitly:

■ I may seem here to be seeing Shakespeare through the spectacles of Proust, for whom A can never love B but only his idea of B, and *vice versa*, with confusing and depressing results. But though one would expect the two writers to corroborate each other's vision at some points, Proust's dogmatic authority, reposing as it does on methods of analysis copied from science and philosophy, is foreign to Shakespeare, and its illuminations are of a quite different order to those of *Othello*. In the enclosed world of Proust the idea of freedom depends on the universality of error: people and their emotions seem endless because of the infinite number of ways one can get them wrong. As a hypothesis about love 'Proust's Law' is abstract and rigid: it admits no outlet, while Shakespeare's poetry not only indicates with extraordinary compression and subtlety comparable facts about love but also celebrates its infinite potentiality, a freedom based not on error but on the absence of definition. Confined in their separate visions, the lovers do not 'place' each other; their incomprehension is, paradoxically, a form of spaciousness, and it is this which Shakespeare manifests as a positive glory. Nothing is fixed and fated, because of the largeness of love's world, the sheer quality of room it makes available.[14] □

This repeats some of Gardner's insistence on seeing *Othello* in terms of the Comedies, and her reminder of the significance of the love poets. Bayley's premise is a challenge to previous critical accounts:

■ The initial fallacy of much *Othello* criticism is the assumption that it is a simple clear-cut affair, and that the task of the critic is to determine what kind of simplicity, so to speak, is involved. For Wilson Knight it is the simplicity of intrigue; for Leavis, that of a special kind of character study; for Bradley (whose approach is less narrowly perspicacious and therefore less inadequate), the more exciting simplicity of a fathomless evil corrupting, though not eclipsing, good. The strong feelings aroused are all directed to one of these particular ends. But if we rather assume, from the nature of the subject and of the response we give to it, that the play is likely to be a very complex affair, with a Shakespearean variety of perceptions and significances, then we shall cease to be merely pro- or anti-Othello, or under the spell of a *coup de théâtre*, and instead be more receptive to its totality of effect.[15] □

He then argues the resemblance of the play to the kind of approach familiar in the novel:

■ In claiming for the play a far greater degree of complexity than is generally assumed, I am not saying that it closely resembles Shakespeare's other great plays, or that it works in the same way as they do. *Othello* is a tragedy of incomprehension, not at the level of intrigue but at the very deepest level of human dealings. And one would expect that the effect of such a tragedy would be significantly different from those in which a kind of understanding links the actors ever more closely as they suffer or inflict suffering; that it would be, in fact, more like that of a great novel. No one in *Othello* comes to understand himself or anyone else. None of them realize their situation. At the centre, between the poles of the play, Desdemona, Cassio, and Emilia show common sense and humanity, but it is more a matter of good instinct than illumination. Iago maintains to the end the dreadful integrity of his own ignorance, and in spite of – or perhaps because of – the revelation of Desdemona's innocence, Othello retains to the end his agonized incomprehension which is so moving an aspect of tragedy in sexual love. His love for Desdemona was to him a marvellous revelation of himself rather than a real knowledge of her. And the proof of her innocence is no substitute for such an awareness. This is the final tragic separation, intensified by the conviction that she is going to heaven and he is going to hell. But although the characters never achieve understanding, and although our response to them – as theirs to each other – shifts with the successive and conflicting pulls of emotion and analysis, so that we see Othello through his own eyes and Iago's as well as with our own, yet if we wait for the fullness of what the play has to offer we do reach a state of tragic comprehension; we are left with a greater insight into the passions and the will, and how they operate to cut us off from each other and from ourselves.[16] □

This seems to confirm Leavis rather than to be an attempt to refute his arguments, but Bayley's point is that no one of the ways of seeing any of the characters stays still for long enough to be seen to be the definitive view of the play. Successive views of the characters show audiences and readers that different ways of seeing are the norm in this world, and he says, quite rightly, that this is more like the world of the novel, the world of social observation, than it is like the world of poetic drama. His view of Othello's tragedy confirms this point:

■ The tragic atmosphere offers none of that harmonious and formal communion in sorrow which plays at the end of *King Lear*, or the participation in *Macbeth* at the re-establishment of spiritual order. Othello's tragedy is personal, ending in a total loneliness of spirit, and our recognition of it can only be correspondingly solitary. A parallel with the essentially private revelation of the novel form is always making itself felt.[17] □

Bayley is not talking about the *form* of the play: he is talking about its matter. Modern criticism has looked in poetic drama, he says, for 'levels' but *Othello* reveals itself not at different levels at the same time, but successively, as the action unfolds:

■ [T]he whole tendency of *Othello* is to make us partisan, to underline the incommensurability of opposed emotional stances. Just as Desdemona can never see Othello as Iago does, or Iago as does Desdemona, so our own succession of responses follows and reflects the partial and solipsistic attitudes of the protagonists. We are in the bafflingly relative world of social observation, where our own passions and prejudices distort reality as much as those of the people we are watching; and where our discernment of an unconscious motive or a comical lack of awareness . . . also reveals our own nature and desires to others who may themselves be noting our unawareness of the fact.[18] □

Love sets all this in motion in *Othello* because:

■ [L]ove is of all forces in society the most confusing and the most revealing; it stands both for the frightful difficulty of knowing other people and for the possibility of that knowledge.[19] □

Thus, love is the focus in the play both for people trying to get to know one another and for people deceiving one another and themselves. Poetry has a special place in *Othello* because:

■ [It] has a great deal more to do here than in the more organically conceived tragedies, the more so because it is not so native to the world of Othello as to the court of Lear and the castle of Macbeth . . . The verse must celebrate in heroic terms a domestic situation too realistic even for comedy.[20] □

This is an important insight: *Othello* concerns itself with what happens after most works dealing with love have ended; with the domestic situation that succeeds marriage. Thus *Othello* is 'domestic', and also 'social' in the sense in which the word is meant in the term 'social comedy'. It is about people interacting in society, socialising even.

The two extracts that follow show how effectively this theoretical framework offers insights into the play. The first concerns Act II, Scene i:

■ Act II, Scene i illustrates these points in detail. First Montano and the Gentleman celebrate in the language of love the storm at sea, that 'storm of fortunes' which the lovers expected and surmounted with such triumphant confidence.

> For do but stand upon the foaming shore,
> The chiding billow seems to pelt the clouds;
> The wind-shaked surge, with high and monstrous mane,
> Seems to cast water on the burning bear,
> And quench the guards of the ever-fixed pole:
> I never did like molestation view
> On the enchafed flood [II, i, 11–17].

In Cinthio's story the couple arrive 'on a perfectly tranquil sea', a detail only too much in keeping with the humdrum setting and the harmony of their previous conjugal life. Shakespeare's contrasting storm brings in the powers of love and danger – the latter in both its new and old senses. Cassio now arrives and thanks the previous speakers.

> *Thanks, you the valiant of this warlike isle,*
> *That so approve the Moor! O, let the heavens*
> *Give him defence against the elements,*
> *For I have lost him on a dangerous sea* [II, i, 43–6].

Valiancy and love are connected, their language the same: and with the entry of Cassio the chorus swells to include Desdemona in a paean of praise.

> *. . . he hath achieved a maid*
> *That paragons description and wild fame;*
> *One that excels the quirks of blazoning pens,*
> *And in the essential vesture of creation*
> *Does tire the ingener* [II, i, 61–4].

The storm is emphasized once more:

> *Tempests themselves, high seas and howling winds,*
> *The gutter'd rocks and congregated sands –*
> *Traitors ensteept to enclog the guiltless keel –*
> *As having sense of beauty, do omit*
> *Their mortal natures, letting go safely by*
> *The divine Desdemona* [II, i, 68–73].

And the power of love is invoked for all its votaries:

> *Great Jove, Othello guard,*
> *And swell his sail with thine own powerful breath,*
> *That he may bless this bay with his tall ship,*
> *Make love's quick pants in Desdemona's arms,*
> *Give renew'd fire to our extinguished spirits*
> *And bring all Cyprus comfort!* [II, i, 77–82]

The paean reaches its climax with the appearance of Desdemona herself,

> *O, behold,*
> *The riches of this ship is come on shore!*

> *Ye men of Cyprus, let her have your knees.*
> *Hail to thee, lady, and the grace of heaven*
> *Before, behind thee, and on every hand,*
> *Enwheel thee round!* [II, i, 82–7]

It is then abruptly checked and reversed by the presence of Iago. The whole atmosphere of the scene changes at once. Cassio, the noble and enthusiastic leader of the chorus, now appears almost absurd as he administers a gallant peck to the cheek of Emilia, observing

> *'tis my breeding*
> *That gives me this bold show of courtesy* [II, i, 98–9].

The little fatuity is endearing enough in its way, but with Iago there Cassio appears in a different light: we see him to some extent through Iago's eyes. We also realize that Cassio has an idea of himself as a well-bred person which can appear fitting and noble or as something a bit vulgar and even – in a comical way – calculating. Conscious as we are of ideas about personal identity, the *persona* and so forth, we should recognize the swiftness and accuracy with which Shakespeare makes his point about them here and connects it, *via* the realistic and operatic contrasts of the scene, with the enthusiasm and the poetry of love. Love, we might say, brings to a head this problem of identity, and also makes it seem to those in the grip of love a problem to which the answer must instantly be found. Our awareness of Cassio in this scene foreshadows the sense of him that Othello will soon come to have, and furthermore our mixed impression of Cassio as the celebrant of love foreshadows our impressions of Othello himself.[21] □

The second extract examines a later portion of the same scene:

■ As her speech before the senate shows, Desdemona's way of being in love is as clearly revealed as that of Othello. The love-duet in Act II, Scene i adds further touches of significance.

OTHELLO	*O my fair warrior!*
DESDEMONA	*My dear Othello!*
OTHELLO	*It gives me wonder great as my content*
	To see you here before me. O, my soul's joy,
	If after every tempest come such calms
	May the winds blow till they have wakened death!
	And let the labouring bark climb hills of seas
	Olympus-high, and duck again as low
	As hell's from heaven! If it were now to die

> 'Twere now to be most happy, for I fear
> My soul hath her content so absolute
> That not another comfort like to this
> Succeeds in unknown fate.
>
> DESDEMONA The heavens forbid
> But that our loves and comforts should increase
> Even as our days do grow!
>
> OTHELLO Amen to that, sweet powers!
> I cannot speak enough of this content,
> It stops me here, it is too much of joy:
> And this, and this, the greatest discords be (kissing her)
> That e'er our hearts shall make! [II, i, 179–97]

Two different kinds of love are movingly displayed here. Othello's is the masculine and romantic: his opening hyperbole invokes the romantic commonplace – 'Love calls to war' – and also receives Desdemona into his wholly martial personality, just as she had wished in refusing to remain a 'moth of peace'. The glory of the achievement is carried buoyantly on in the image of the ship riding the waves. What battles and dangers wouldn't they undergo for this? But then with the imagined calm a note of brooding appears; the tone changes and deepens; 'If it were now to die . . .' Othello has withdrawn his delighted gaze from Desdemona and is addressing himself and his own vision of love. And in the romantic context that vision has an alarming familiarity. Having achieved his desire, Othello turns naturally to the idea of the *Liebestod*, death as the only fit and comparable peer of love. How can the tension otherwise be kept up and the lover remain at the summit of his happiness? Unknowingly Othello is applying this fatal romantic logic, which will not compromise possession with the trivialities of domesticity. And it is of course as a possession, a marvellous and unexpected conquest, that he sees Desdemona. He has won her like a fortune or a battle.

> If heaven had made me such another jewel,
> One whole entire and perfect chrysolite,
> I'd not have changed her for it [V, ii, 140–41].

This attitude earns him the disapproval of Eliot and Leavis; but so far from singling out Othello as a type of the ignorant and ungentle lover, Shakespeare portrays him as epitomizing the positive glory of love, which like the glory of war includes and assumes the fact of suffering and injustice. Both love and war are summed up in the image of storm, a manifestation both glorious and terrifying. Yet, as we are finding, there is more in the love-duet than the poetic symbol of the storm and the poetic prolepsis[22] of the lovers' death: there is also a sharp illumination of what men and women in love are like. Othello's sentiments are magnificently commonplace; for he shares with most men the delight of achievement and possession and he feels too the loss of freedom, of the 'unhoused condition', a loss which he has already faced in his large way and put aside. The romantic dangers are there, as with most men, but they do not diagnose his amatory weakness or label him finally. He is not a Tristan or a Lancelot, wholly committed to an intensity in love which is unaware of any freedom outside itself.

Indeed the possibility of development, and the sense of freedom that goes with it, is precisely what the duet most poignantly holds out. Desdemona's love for Othello is also of course wildly romantic – he personifies for her all the romance she has discovered to exist in life – but committing herself to this vision is for her a more matter-of-fact business than it could be for him. Her greeting is as whole-hearted as his, and as characteristic. 'My dear Othello!' – the simple warmth reveals a whole world of feminine actuality behind the male need for hyperbole and symbol. She takes his speech lightly, as the sort of wonderfully gratifying and romantic thing he *would* say – its deeper note doesn't mean much to her except as a stimulus to 'touch wood' and to give her own settled and happy conception of the future. She takes up the word 'comfort' from his speech, the sort of word which in her vision of things presents a concrete and lasting reassurance and satisfaction. The situation has a joyful sense of mutual possibility, the spaciousness which throughout the play is the atmosphere and element of love. Othello's unconsciously romantic sense of an end rather than a beginning is not final: Desdemona's placid confidence touches and lights his own, and he shows the beginnings of a readiness to draw certainty and stability from her, just as she had drawn fire and enthusiasm from him. But this interdependence is not the same as understanding: the singers in the duet are too preoccupied with the vision of their own love really to perceive the nature of their partner's. Desdemona is as much imprisoned in her assumption of love as is Othello in his, and for the same reasons: their kinds of love have produced the relationship in which they find themselves. The helplessness of Desdemona as the tragic climate darkens around her is as much emphasized as is that of Othello in the grip of his jealousy, and it proceeds from the same cause. She cannot break out of her kind of love to tell him what a monster he is being any more than he can break out of his to reflect that after all she is a free agent, and that perhaps a quiet talk would clear the matter up.[23] □

It is interesting to compare Bayley's account with Eliot's and with Leavis's. There is very little that divides the three critics beyond their different evaluations of romantic love. Their way of handling the work is very similar though Bayley seems much more like Bradley on the face of it. What is emerging again is the ease with which, in talking of *Othello*, critics slip into the habits we associate with novel reading. This is because, as Bayley sees so clearly, the play is so like a novel. But he also sees that it is like an opera and that its more obviously unrealistic elements – its verse, for example – have to work even harder to be themselves as a consequence of the work's closeness to the world most easily and effectively handled by the novel. He also points out, by implication, that, as opera can handle the world handled by the novel, then the novel is by no means uncontrived. A 'sub-text' of Bayley's essay is that the novel is a form of the highest art.

This may lead the reader to reflect that the persistent trend in *Othello* criticism that has seen the play in this way may not be a diminution of the work's status as a work of art. It may also help to explain the play's resistance to the eighteenth-century's practical-critical response; the adaptation or the song-and-dance makeover. It makes, finally, interesting sense of the hostility of some twentieth-century critics to the play. Helen Gardner's 'Retrospect' suggests a reason for the antagonism:

■ Wilson Knight's complaint that 'its thought does not readily mesh with our thought' reflects a genuine dilemma for many twentieth-century critics, who find themselves confronted with a work of obviously supreme artistic power and beauty which does not satisfy their characteristic concerns and strongly resists their characteristic methods.[24] □

Bayley's suggested synthesis of opera and social-realist novel is an attempt to bridge this gap perhaps; it is at least an attempt to recognise the paradoxical co-existence of heroic poetry and domesticity and social comedy in the play and to make something of it.

At this point it may be useful to recall the link Gardner makes between adverse reactions to the play in the early twentieth century and the horrors of the First World War:

■ The stigmatizing of Othello as 'unaware' had an obvious relation to the appalling catastrophe of the First World War, and the blow that the image of the professional soldier received from the senseless carnage in Flanders. It became axiomatic in the twenties and thirties that professional soldiers were stupid. Even Wyndham Lewis, who sympathized with the Lion against the Fox, saw Othello as a kind of dazed, unhappy bull with Iago as a clever matador dancing round him.[25] □

It might be possible to put the two together to suggest some convergence between the 'characteristic concerns' and 'characteristic methods' of the critics Gardner is talking about and their hostility to 'the image of the professional soldier'. The world of the novel had produced an image of both the man of action *and* the man of intellect as increasingly isolated and ineffectual figures; a new stage would have to be constructed before either could be seen in a heroic light. Leavis's sneer at 'the cult of T. E. Lawrence' suggests that the man of action may have been temporarily in the lead at the time that his essay was written.

Jan Kott's *Shakespeare: Our Contemporary* (1967) takes a very different view. Under the influence of such developments as the 'Theatre of the Absurd' of Eugene Ionesco and to some extent of Beckett, and the 'Theatre of Cruelty' of Antonin Artaud, Kott looks at Shakespeare as an absurdist *avant la lettre* and as a precursor of the Theatre of Cruelty. These developments in twentieth-century European theatre have much to do with the impact of existentialist philosophies of extreme scepticism. Absurdism owes much to Albert Camus's view that human consciousness is out of place in the universe, as though it were not meant to be but happened by accident; Artaud's Theatre of Cruelty in turn is influenced by existentialist interest in de Sade. De Sade's most influential work is a pair of novels, *Justine* and *Juliette*, in which he shows that virtue is an absurd irrelevancy and vice merely the will following nature. The virtuous Justine is victimised and persecuted and the vicious Juliette prospers. Existentialists saw in this a parable of human existence in a world interested in neither good nor evil.

Existentialism is perhaps a counterpart to and a necessary evolution of the extreme humanism of Dowden: while that fixed the idea of the good in the determined will, the existentialist looked at the world around the determined will and saw no ground for belief or even hope that the will could succeed in its aim, however determined it might be. Kott's essay 'The Two Paradoxes of "Othello"' is a good example of this development. He begins by surveying the development of the operatic and naturalistic versions of *Othello* from Rymer onwards. Neo-classicism leads to an *Othello* trimmed of its horrors; to a Desdemona reposing in a night-cap and the intervention of a dagger in the murder as far less vulgar than the 'stifling' Shakespeare seems to have wanted. Kott seeks to rescue Shakespeare from the creeping Bowdlerisation[26] that these developments have imposed. Many of the critics considered in this Guide have dissented from the dominant form of staging *Othello* in their time, whatever it may be; what is original to Kott is his insistence on the bleakness of the view:

■ There are two other excellent descriptions of Iago [Kott has quoted Coleridge's 'motive-hunting of motiveless malignity']. Carlyle called him 'an inarticulate poet', Hazlitt 'an amateur of tragedy in real life'. Iago is not satisfied with devising the tragedy; he wants to play it through, distribute parts all round, and takes part in it himself.

Iago is a diabolical stage manager, or rather – a machiavellian stage manager. His motives for acting are ambiguous and hidden, his intellectual reasons clear and precise. He formulates them in the early scenes when, for instance, he soliloquizes: 'Our bodies are gardens, to the which our wills are gardeners [I, iii, 321–2].'

The demonic Iago was an invention of the romantics. Iago is no demon. Like Richard III, he is a contemporary careerist, but on a different scale. He, too, wants to set in motion a real mechanism, make use of genuine passions. He does not want to be cheated. 'We cannot all be masters, nor all masters Cannot be truly follow'd [I, i, 42–3].' This is not a demonic statement, but rather one which is obvious to the point of vulgarity. 'Preferment goes by letter and affection [I, i, 35].' This is not a demonic statement either. Iago is an empiricist, he does not believe in ideologies and he has no illusions: 'Reputation is an idle and most false imposition, oft got without merit, and lost without deserving [II, iii, 264–6].'

Of course, Iago is a machiavellian, but machiavellism merely means for him a generalized personal experience. Fools believe in honour and love. In reality there is only egoism and lust. The strong are able to subordinate their passions to ambition. One's own body can also be an instrument. Hence Iago's contempt for everything that benumbs a man, from moral precepts to love.

> I never found a man that knew how to love himself: ere I would say I would drown myself, for the love of a guinea-hen, I would change my humanity with a baboon [I, iii, 314–7].

Iago believes in will-power. One can make everything of oneself, and of other people. Others, too, are only an instrument. They can be moulded like clay. Iago, like Richard III, despises people even more than he hates them.

Says Iago: The world consists of villains and fools; of those who devour and those who are devoured. People are like animals; they copulate and eat each other. The weak do not deserve pity, they are just as abominable, only more stupid than the strong. The world is vile.

Says Othello: The world is beautiful and people are noble. There exist in it love and loyalty.

If we strip *Othello* of romantic varnish, of everything that is opera and melodrama, the tragedy of jealousy and the tragedy of betrayed confidence becomes a dispute between Othello and Iago; a dispute on the nature of the world. Is the world good or bad? What are the limits of suffering, what is the ultimate purpose of the few brief moments that pass between birth and death?

Like Richard III, Iago sets in motion the mechanism of vileness, envy and stupidity, and like him, he will be destroyed. The world, in which Othello can believe in Desdemona's infidelity, in which treachery is possible, in which Othello murders Desdemona, in which there is no friendship, loyalty, or faith, in which Othello – by agreeing to the murder of Cassio – has consented to a secret assassination, such a world is bad. Iago is an accomplished stage manager.

Thou hast set me on the rack [III, iii, 338].

He has proved that world consists of fools and villains. He has destroyed all around him, and himself. He goes to be tortured in a tragedy devised by himself. He has proved that neither the world nor himself deserves any pity. Richard's defeat confirms the working of the Grand Mechanism; just as Iago's failure does. The world is vile. He was right. And the very fact that he was right proved his undoing. This is the first paradox.[27] □

The second paradox concerns Desdemona:

■ Heine felt uneasy about Desdemona having moist hands. He wrote that sometimes he felt sad at the thought that perhaps Iago was partially right. Heine interpreted Shakespeare with far greater pungency than Schlegel, Tieck and all the other sentimental Germans. He compared *Othello* to *Titus Andronicus*. 'In both the passion of a beautiful woman for an ugly Negro is presented with particular relish,' he wrote.[28]

Desdemona is two to four years older than Juliet; she could be Ophelia's age. But she is much more of a woman than either of them. Heine was right. Desdemona is obedient and stubborn at the same time. She is obedient to the point where passion begins. Of all Shakespeare's female characters she is the most sensuous. More silent than Juliet or Ophelia, she seems absorbed in herself, and wakes only to the night.

Nature would not invest herself in such shadowing passion without some instruction [IV, I, 39–41].

She does not even know that she disturbs and promises by her very presence. Othello only later learns about it, but Iago knows this from the outset. Desdemona is faithful, but must have something of the slut in her. Not *in actu* but *in potentia*.[29] Otherwise the drama could not work, because Othello would be ridiculous. Othello must not be ridiculous. Desdemona is sexually obsessed with Othello, but all men – Iago, Cassio, Roderigo – are obsessed with Desdemona. They remain in her erotic climate.

> The wine she drinks is made of grapes; if she had been blest, she would never have lov'd the Moor . . . Didst thou not see her paddle with the palm of his hand? . . . They met so near with their lips, that their breaths embrac'd together [II, i, 249–58].

In Othello's relation to Desdemona a violent change now occurs; a change that cannot be explained fully by Iago's intrigues. It is as if Othello were suddenly horrified by Desdemona. Robert Speaight in his reflections on Othello[30] wonders where their marriage was con-summated. In Venice, or only in Cyprus, the night when Iago made Cassio drunk. Such a question may sound absurd when applied to a Shakespearean tragedy, with its double time of events and synthetic motivation. But, perhaps because Shakespeare leaves no motivation out, this question touches on a dark sphere in Othello's relations with Desdemona. Othello behaves as if he found a different Desdemona from the one he expected. 'She that so young could give out such a seeming . . . [III, iii, 212]' It is as if the outburst of sensuality in a girl who not long ago listened to his tales with her eyes lowered, amazed and horrified him.

> His bed shall seem a school, his board a shrift . . . [III, ii, 24]

From the very first night Desdemona felt herself a lover and a wife. Eroticism was her vocation and joy; eroticism and love, eroticism and Othello are one and the same. Her Eros is a substance of light. But for Othello Eros is a trap. It is as if, after the first night, he got lost in dark-ness, where love and jealousy, lust and disgust were inextricably bound together.

The more violently Desdemona becomes engrossed by love, the more of a slut she seems to Othello; a past, present, or future slut. The more she desires, the better she loves, the more readily Othello believes that she can, or has, betrayed him.

Iago sets all the world's evil in motion and falls victim to it in the end. Desdemona is the victim of her own passion. Her love testifies against her, not for her. Love proves her undoing. This is the second paradox.[31] □

Kott's insight is into the ambiguity of the concept 'nature' as that is handled by the play. He looks at the phrase 'And yet how nature erring from itself' and reflects upon its key components: Brabantio's warning, and the use Iago has just made of it:

■ Respect for father, husband, family, class and estate is consistent with nature. Social order is natural. Everything that destroys it is against nature. Eroticism is nature, too. But nature can be good or evil. Eroticism is nature depraved. The theme of *Othello*, like that of *Macbeth* and *King Lear*, is the Fall. The Renaissance tale of the cunning villain and the jealous husband has been changed into a medieval morality.

OTHELLO	Why, what art thou?
DESDEMONA	Your wife, my lord, your true and loyal wife.
OTHELLO	Come, swear it, damn thyself.
	Lest, being like one of heaven, the devils themselves
	Should fear to seize thee, therefore be double-damn'd,
	Swear thou art honest.
DESDEMONA	Heaven does truly know it.
OTHELLO	Heaven truly knows, that thou art false as hell
	[IV, ii, 34–40].

Angel turns into devil. After animal symbolism, in which eroticism has been enclosed, this is, in frequency, the second semantic sphere of the tragedy. *Othello*'s landscape consisted of the earth without moon and stars, then of the world of reptiles and insects. Now the setting, as in medieval theatre, consists of two gates: of heaven and hell. Even the sober and down-to-earth Emilia turns into a gate-keeper of hell:

> . . . you, mistress,
> That have the office opposite to Saint Peter,
> And keeps the gates in hell . . . [IV, ii, 92–4]

In front of the two gates Othello utters his great closing speeches before he kills himself:

> . . . When we shall meet at count,
> This look of thine will hurl my soul from heaven,
> And fiends will snatch at it [V, ii, 271–3].

But in fact *Othello* is no more a morality, or a mystery, than it is an opera or a melodrama. Nature is depraved and cannot be trusted. Eros is nature and cannot be trusted either. There is no appeal to nature, or her laws. Nature is evil, not only to Othello, but also to Shakespeare. It is just as insane and cruel as history. Nature is depraved but, unlike in a medieval morality, it is not redeemed. There is no redemption.

Angels turn into devils. All of them.

> Turn thy complexion there;
> Patience, thy young and rose-lipp'd cherubin,
> I here look grim as hell! [IV, ii, 63–5]

It is the mad Lear, who continues the argument:

> Behold yond simpering dame,
> Whose face between her forks presages snow,
> That minces virtue, and does shake the head
> To hear of pleasure's name;
> The fitchew nor the soiled horse goes to't
> With a more riotous appetite.
> Down from the waist they are Centaurs,
> Though women all above:
> But to the girdle do the gods inherit,
> Beneath is all the fiends';
> There's hell, there's darkness, there's the sulphurous pit,
> Burning, scalding, stench, consumption [*Lear*, IV, vi, 116–25].

Othello and Lear stay in the same sphere of madness. Nature has been put on trial. Once again Shakespeare's hatred of nature forecasts that of Swift. Nature is depraved, above all in its reproductive function. Love tales, stories of lovers and married couples, are just as ruthless and cruel as the histories of kings, princes and usurpers. In both, dead bodies are carried away from the empty stage.[32] □

His summary is devastating:

■ Othello kills Desdemona in order to save the moral order, to restore love and faith. He kills Desdemona to be able to forgive her, so that the accounts be settled and the world returned to its equilibrium. Othello does not mumble any more. He desperately wants to save the meaning of life, of his life, perhaps even the meaning of the world.

> And say besides, that in Aleppo once,
> Where a malignant and a turban'd Turk
> Beat a Venetian, and traduc'd the state,
> I took by the throat the circumcised dog,
> And smote him thus [V, ii, 350–4].

Othello's death can save nothing. Desdemona is dead, and so is the world of feudal loyalty. The *condottieri* are anachronistic, together with their enchanting poetry, with their rhetoric, their pathos and their gestures. One such gesture is Othello's suicide.

Desdemona is dead, as are the stupid fool Roderigo and the prudent Emilia. Soon Othello will die. All of them die: the noble ones and the villains; the level-headed ones and the madmen; the empiricists and the absolutists. All choices are bad.

DESDEMONA	Would'st thou do such a deed, for all the world?
EMILIA	Why, would not you?
DESDEMONA	No, by this heavenly light!
EMILIA	Nor I neither, by this heavenly light,
	I might do it as well in the dark.
DESDEMONA	Would'st thou do such a thing for all the world?
EMILIA	The world is a huge thing, it is a great price,
	For a small vice [IV, iii, 63–8].

Iago keeps silent. Probably even on the rack he will not utter a word. He has won all the arguments; but only the intellectual ones. In all great Shakespearian dramas, from *Hamlet* and *Troilus and Cressida* onwards, the moral order and the intellectual order are in conflict with one another. They will remain so up to *The Winter's Tale* and *The Tempest*. The world is as Iago sees it. But Iago is a villain. Like our world, Shakespeare's world did not regain its balance after the earthquake. Like our world, it remained incoherent. In Shakespeare's *Othello* everybody loses in the end.[33] □

Kott has only made explicit and affirmed what Rymer recoiled from: 'If this be our end, what boots it to be vertuous?' If Kott is right, that is the challenge of the play.

This chapter ends with a quotation from Helen Gardner's conclusion to her retrospective survey of criticism of the play in the first half of the twentieth century as a piece of concentrated wisdom the like of which is not often discovered. She is reflecting upon J. I. M. Stewart's rather odd attempt to find substance in the so-called 'double time-scheme' (which had been dismissed by earlier critics but whipped up by 'Christopher North' for the Victorians; M. R. Ridley was impressed, Honigmann ignores it):

■ A view which sees in *Othello* the tragic sense that there is something in the very nature of our temporal existence that defeats our highest human needs and aspirations, and that 'To live your life is not as simple as to cross a field', seems more adequate to Shakespeare's play than an attempt to find the root of the disaster in flaws in Othello's nature that made him an easy prey to Iago. It is perilous to garner up one's heart in the heart of another human being, and whoever does so loses control of his own destiny. Passion has its ebbs and flows. The attempt to found the social bond of marriage on passionate love is a great adventure of the human spirit – an attempt to unite contrary values – that brings with it a possibility of agony that those who seek for no such unity in their experience do not risk.[34] □

The next chapter considers essays by critics not always impressed by 'an attempt to unite contrary values'. Such an attempt may seem impracticable or even objectionable in a 'postmodern' world in which any synthesis is open to the objection that it is an ideological construction, at best false, at worst insidious.

CHAPTER SIX

'The Play's the Thing': Some Postmodern Voices

■   *the play's the thing;*
Wherein I'll catch the conscience of the king [*Hamlet*, II, ii, 600–1]. □

MUCH CONTEMPORARY criticism has a preoccupation with the notion that language and signifying practices in general are characterised both by an undermining indeterminacy and by the operations of power. In this chapter recent accounts of *Othello* have been selected that have seen in the play the opportunity to explore these concerns.

The first extracts are from Valerie Traub's discussion of the play in *Desire and Anxiety: Circulations of Sexuality in Shakespearean Drama* (1992). Traub's view is that 'In Shakespearean drama what engenders the female body is her sexuality'. She explains:

■ As the drama positions the female gender within its psychic and narrative frame, 'woman' becomes synonymous with the presence or absence of chastity.[1] □

This is intensely dangerous:

■ To be a woman in Shakespearean drama means to embody a sexuality that often finds its ultimate expression in death.[2] □

It is dangerous because it is powerful:

■ Maid, wife, widow, whore: these are the positions accorded to women in early modern society. They are specifically *erotic* positions, locating women, via an erotic sphere of activity and signification, within the economy of patriarchal heterosexuality. By definition, a maid is virginal, a whore promiscuous; widows and wives can be either lusty or abstinent; all are defined, not merely by their biological sex, but by their sexual activity . . . As a defining characteristic, chastity renders woman's specifically *erotic* power incommensurate with her place in early modern gender and class hierarchies; the social importance accorded to chastity renders woman's erotic power inordinate, even excessive.[3] □

Traub insists that the significance of the plays she is considering in this chapter, *Hamlet, Othello,* and *The Winter's Tale,*

■ is not so much the eventual status of women as reified objects . . . but the *process* by which the drama renders them as such, the *transformation* that occurs as the motive and telos of dramatic action.[4] □

She offers a vision of sexual activity that is plainly relevant to *Othello*:

■ As many critics have argued, masculine identity in the early modern period is constructed in relation to a fantasy of the female body as different, oppositional, other. However, in the act of orgasm, male experience of the female body is not so much that of an object to be penetrated and possessed, but of an enclosure into which the male subject merges, dissolves, and in the early modern pun, dies. Orgasm within the body of a woman calls attention to – makes palpable – the myth of the unity and self-identity of the masculine subject: orgasmic release is precisely too much of a release of the self. Insofar as women act as mirrors for the development of male subjectivity, female erotic mobility threatens the process by which male subjectivity is secured. For men to achieve the fantasy of full subjectivity, women must remain still.[5] □

Desdemona, whether sleeping or dead, is certainly 'still'. In the next extract Traub outlines her theoretical approach:

■ For women in Shakespearean drama, 'chastity' requires being still, cold, and closed; to be 'unchaste' is to be mobile, hot, open. What is striking is the minimal room within which to maneuver; even a minimum of erotic 'warmth' is quickly transmogrified into intemperate heat. Indeed, what the drama enacts is the disappearance of any middle ground, with the rigidity of this bifurcation following a unidirectional narrative: from a projection of too much movement, warmth, openness, to an enclosing fantasy of no movement or heat at all . . . According to Joel Fineman, 'plays are not only a means of representative expression but as such constitute strategies of psychological defense, defending, that is, against the very fantasies they represent'.[6]

My attempt is not to explicate *Hamlet*, *Othello*, or *The Winter's Tale*, but rather to analyze the multiple deployments of a recurring anxiety and the means by which the plays exorcise or assuage it.[7] □

The following extract sees Traub doing just this:

■ In *Othello*, the need to suppress the anxieties that female sexuality engenders is tragically manipulated into the murder of the woman who elicits those anxieties. As critics have noted, Othello is both emotionally vulnerable to Desdemona and ambivalent about women in general, and it is precisely because his anxieties are multivalent and mutually reinforcing that Othello is susceptible to Iago's murderous seduction. Like Brabantio's premonition of Desdemona's elopement – 'This accident is not unlike my dream;/Belief of it oppresses me already [I, i, 140–41]' . . . Othello's belief in woman's power of deception lies just under the surface of his idolization. Othello himself exclaims in reaction to Iago's intimations, 'Think, my lord? By heaven, *he echoes me,*/As if there were some monster in his thought/Too hideous to be shown [III, iii, 109–11] [italics my emphasis]', suggesting that Iago echoes not merely Othello's words, but his thoughts. Indeed, having betrayed her father, Desdemona is suspect to all men except the similarly manipulated Cassio. Brabantio warns: 'Look to her, Moor, if thou hast eyes to see./She has deceiv'd her father, and may thee [I, iii, 293–4].' And Iago voices the same refrain: 'She did deceive her father, marrying you [III, iii, 209].'[8] □

Traub's insight is the suggestion that, for Othello, 'marriage is not only cursed by women's sexual appetites and deception, marriage is itself a curse'. She refers to 'O curse of marriage,/That we can call these delicate creatures ours,/And not their appetites! [III, iii, 272–4]'; resisting the obvious interpretation Traub suggests that 'O curse of marriage' is ambiguous, meaning not only obviously that the autonomy of women's 'appetites' is a curse of marriage – that is, incidental to marriage and a blight upon it – but that marriage is itself a curse because 'we can call these delicate creatures ours,/And not their appetites'. Traub goes on to suggest that it is not only or even primarily the fear of being cuckolded that lies at the heart of the play:

■ As Peter Stallybrass has noted, Iago succeeds in manipulating Othello because 'his is the voice of "common sense", the ceaseless repetition of the always-already "known", the culturally "given".[9] He seduces Othello in multiple ways. By pouring 'this pestilence into his ear,/That she repeals him for her body's lust [II, iii, 351–2]', Iago invokes the cultural suspicion that all women are whores. In this respect, according to Edward Snow, Othello's fear of adultery masks a more basic castration anxiety, a fear of 'thralldom to the demands of an unsatisfiable sexual appetite in woman', brought on by the consummation of his marriage.[10] Othello's murder of Desdemona, then, is a ritualistic effort to repeat and undo his own sexual complicity. Secondly, as Stephen Greenblatt demonstrates, in abusing 'Othello's ears/That he is too familiar with his wife [I, iii, 394–5]', Iago manipulates the Christian doctrine of sexuality that posits even marital sexuality as sinful.[11] Thirdly, Othello's ambivalent relation to Christian society as Moor and alien creates the conditions for internalized racial self-hatred, the logical outcome of the play's representation of the 'Moor's' sexuality as 'lascivious' [I, i, 124], even 'monstrous'.[12]

The racial dynamics of the play are crucial to any understanding of Othello's subjectivity, for, although the primary spokesmen of racist ideologies are Iago, Roderigo, and Brabantio, one of the tragedies of the play is the extent to which Othello internalizes their negative representations of his race. In the first three scenes, the discourses of Iago, Roderigo, and Brabantio set up the following dichotomy: black, dark, evil, animal, hyper-sexual, versus white, fair, virtue, human, chastity.[13] The terms by which Brabantio expresses his refusal to believe in Desdemona's willing love for Othello – 'For nature so preposterously to err [I, iii, 63]' – underscores their culture's appeal to 'nature' as the causal basis of these dualisms. As Martin Orkin argues, much of the play resists these 'natural' categories, not the least of which is Desdemona's love and Othello's spiritual nobility.[14] However, these racist dualisms are reinscribed all the more forcefully by being expressed in Act III, Scene iii by Othello himself. His meditative response to Iago's intimations of Desdemona's infidelity, 'And yet, how nature erring from itself [III, iii, 231]', credits Desdemona's choice of mate as unnatural, a recognition that permeates Othello's final conclusion, 'Her name, that was as fresh/As Dian's visage, is now begrim'd and black/As mine own face [III, iii, 389–91]'. At that moment, Othello marks his acceptance of the racist categories which correlate skin color with the presence or absence of virtue. His inability to maintain trust in Desdemona is directly related to his inability to trust his own racial identity and self-worth . . . In short, Othello's anxiety is culturally and psychosexually over determined by erotic, gender, and racial anxieties, including, I now want to argue, the fear of chaos he associates with sexual activity . . . As a military officer who makes crucial decisions regarding war and peace, life and death, Othello's subjectivity is predicated upon an absolute dichotomy between chaos and stasis . . . Othello associates romantic love with calm and 'content[ment]' and, as the following quote makes clear, the loss of that love with chaos: 'Excellent wretch! Perdition catch my soul/But I do love thee! And when I love thee not,/Chaos is come again [III, iii, 90–2].' Woman has a metaphysical responsibility to represent and maintain peace – a responsibility that correlates with her function as a stable mirror of masculine subjectivity. However, throughout the play, Othello also equates Desdemona's sexuality with chaos and violence. A disjuncture thus exists within Othello's psyche between romantic love (associated with stasis and calm) and sexuality (associated with chaotic violence). Such hostilities, brought to a head by the consummation of his marriage, between the psychic structures necessary to his sense of self and those related to his sexuality must ultimately be reconciled if Othello is not to go mad.[15] □

A useful ambiguity is discovered in the passage that follows:

■ I had been happy if the general camp,
  Pioners and all, had tasted her sweet body,
  So I had nothing known [III, iii, 348–50]. □

Traub points out that Othello could mean that he could have been happy under these circumstances if only he had not known her – that is, 'tasted her sweet body'. However,

■ [H]aving 'tasted her sweet body', Othello is, as Iago suggests, 'eaten up with passion [III, iii, 394]', and as such, Othello becomes more victim than connoisseur of an act that metaphorically connotes the dissolution of boundary distinctions. The love that promised calm and repose actually sparks erotic arousal, and with it the fear of complete chaos: 'Get me some poison, Iago; this night. I'll not expostulate with her, lest her body and beauty unprovide my mind again. This night, Iago [IV, I, 201–203].' The only protection against 'unprovision' is to project onto the loved one the tranquility that she is supposed to (but because of her mobile sexuality, fails to) create . . . The imposition of calm on Desdemona is explicitly offered as a remedy for the 'hot, and moist' palms of her excessively sexual body [III, iv, 39]. Just prior to the murder, Desdemona's moistness and heat are replaced in Othello's imagination by the cool, dry, immobile image of 'monumental alabaster [V, ii, 5]'. Once dead, Desdemona is compared to 'another world/Of one entire and perfect chrysolite' for which Othello would not have sold her, if only she had been true [V, ii, 140–41]. After having realized his error, Othello compares himself to a 'base Indian' who 'threw a pearl away/Richer than all his tribe [V, ii, 345–6]'. Despite the value such idealization appears to ascribe, the comparison of Desdemona to jewels is part of Othello's strategy for containing her distressing erotic mobility. By imaginatively transforming Desdemona into a jewel – hard, cold, static, silent, yet also adored and desired – Othello is able to maintain both his distance from and his idealization of her. By reducing a warm, living body to a static yet idealized object, Othello hopes to master the situation that threatens him . . . Othello's strategy, of course, provides him with only a temporary measure of safety. The unified image of male subjectivity which Desdemona's still body would seem to guarantee is shown to be fractured as soon as the illusion of her guilt is challenged. The terms of self-loathing by which Othello describes and inflicts his own death demonstrate a self-recognition of fragmentation made more devastating because so utterly constituted by racist categories. As the valiant Christian warrior smites the Turkish 'circumcised dog' [V, ii, 353], Othello demonstrates the price for men of woman's failure to comply with her mirroring function: psychic disintegration and death.[16] □

Before leaving the play Traub comments on its relationship to others:

■ The tragic brutality of *Othello* . . . seems to have operated as a kind of exorcism. Although fear of women's sexual power dominates *King Lear* (1605) and *Macbeth* (1606), never again are the strategies employed to combat those fears so vitriolic and vituperative – or so horrifyingly final.[17] □

Though Traub's essay clearly proclaims its contemporary allegiances there are earlier antecedents: Dowden and Bradley are discernible in the interest in Shakespeare's mind and in the interest in Othello's mind, respectively. Wilson Knight's determination to push the interpretation of the poetry as far as it will go is also here and interestingly fruitful. Indeed, it begins to seem that the interest in poetry shown by Knight and the interest in language in history shown by Empson have had, in the long run, the effect rather of reviving the interests of Dowden and Bradley than correcting the approach. Given new critical theories, critics with Traub's interests are exploring as archaeology what to Dowden and Bradley was a common culture.

Unless boundaries to the text are to be drawn, and justified, critical exploration can not be bounded. Leonard Tennenhouse sees in the plays he examines the operations of power, especially that power deriving from hereditary positions in society. His interest in *Othello* has to do with his perception of Jacobean tragedies that they 'offer up their scenes of excessive punishment as if mutilating the female could somehow correct political corruption'. He comments:

■ The women on the Jacobean stage are tortured, hung, smothered, strangled, stabbed, poisoned or dismembered for one of two reasons:

either they are the subject of clandestine desire or else they have become an object of desire which threatens the aristocratic community's self-enclosure. Their innocence notwithstanding, women in *The Revenger's Tragedy* must be poisoned once they become the objects of adulterous desires. The Count Montsurrey in *Bussy D'Ambois* tortures Tamyra for her secret assignations, and Othello murders Desdemona because he assumes she has been guilty of infidelity. True, he is wrong to doubt her innocence. On the other hand, Desdemona has, like the Duchess of Malfi, violated the law of her blood in so marrying. Her marriage to the moor echoes the mismating of the Egyptian and the Roman, the duchess and the steward, the duke and the White Devil as well as those two queens who lust for the bastard Edmund. In other words, it seems that women must be punished excessively when they have blurred within their bodies the distinction between what is properly inside and what must be kept outside the aristocratic community.[18] □

In this extract, Tennenhouse applies this theoretical approach to the play:

■ Resembling nothing so much as an Elizabethan heroine in her capacity for erotic desire as well as in her authority to give herself in marriage, Desdemona contains just the right features for a Jacobean rewriting of the female body. That the Jacobean politics of the body differs significantly from what came before becomes clear as Iago stages his romantic comedy: here the threat implicit in the daughter's initial act of rebellion against the patriarch displays its true nature. It is not only Roderigo whom Iago gulls into seeing the vigor of her Elizabethan eroticism as the poison of adulterous passion. Iago's magic as dramatist is such that he transforms the signs of Desdemona's chaste desire into those of a monstrous betrayal right before Othello's eyes. Self-possessed and capable of speaking the language of the court, Desdemona herself takes on Iago in a court game. 'What wouldst write of me', she asks, 'If thou shouldst praise me? [II, i, 117–18]'. Desdemona continues as if anticipating Iago's words will transform her own words, 'How if she be black and witty? . . . fair and foolish? [II, i, 132–5]' Ironically, too, it is this very power to write herself which Iago turns into a vice and Othello forcibly strips from her character as he strangles her.

When she first appears on the Jacobean stage, Desdemona is nothing if not the embodiment of power. In convincing the senate to side with her against her father, Desdemona seizes hold of two patriarchal prerogatives: the power to speak the language of the law, which in turn gives her the power to give her own body in marriage. The power to marry herself threatens to detach the sexual prerogative from other forms of patriarchal authority, and such a sexual challenge has to be construed as an assault upon patriarchy in Jacobean terms. It is only left to Iago to turn the features of her political rebellion into the signs of unchaste desire. Thus for Desdemona to speak to Lodovico of Cassio's fall from power proves to Othello that she is a 'devil' and 'the whore of Venice'; he translates her exercise of political patronage into an illicit use of her body. However wrong he may seem in regarding her as the embodiment of such monstrous desire, Othello is only reading Desdemona's political features according to the Jacobean politics of the body. But it is ultimately Shakespeare himself who deprives Desdemona of her capacity to speak with the authority of the law, just as he deprives her of any authority to determine the use of her body. His representation of her character differs from that of Iago only in that Shakespeare idealizes where his malevolent counterpart defames. Shakespeare does not differ from Iago in terms of the basis upon which gender distinctions should be made. Either way the female body loses its capacity to exercise patriarchal authority. These political features are returned to the male by way of Othello's vengeance, which operates, then, much as a theater of punishment.

The point I want to stress for purposes of this argument is Shakespeare's collaboration with Iago rather than his condemnation of the malcontent, the collaboration of the two, that is, in purifying political iconography. Thus by the end of the fourth act, Desdemona has completely lost the verbal powers she possessed as the sophisticated lady who challenged Iago in a courtly game of wit during the second act of the play. Grown newly naïve, she must ask Emilia if there really are women in the world capable of cuckolding their husbands. True, Shakespeare uses her loss of verbal power as an idealizing strategy when he makes Desdemona seem all the more innocent as Iago poisons her character. But as she loses the power of speech, she also loses the control over her body she possessed at the opening of the play and, with it, the verbal power to argue for the legitimacy of her sexual behaviour.

Othello may be wrong in taking Iago's interpretation of this comic heroine for the Desdemona whom Shakespeare portrays as the innocent instrument of the malcontent's assault on his ungenerous patron. But there is a way in which Iago's interpretation of her is correct. Even if Desdemona's relationship with Cassio was strictly business, such interest in court dealings as war makes her sexually monstrous according to the Jacobean understanding of power. She may have mingled the two in joining her husband on the iron bed of war, but her body becomes susceptible to misreading because she overturns the natural subordination of female to male when she married Othello in the first place.

When she asks permission to accompany Othello to the frontier, she acknowledges that her own behavior was a violent assault on custom:

That I [did] love the Moor to live with him,
My downright violence, and storm of fortunes,
May trumpet to the world. My heart's subdu'd
Even to the very quality of my lord. . . .
And to his honors and his valiant parts
Did I my soul and fortunes consecrate.
So that, dear lords, if I be left behind,
. . . and he go to the war,
The rites for why I love him are bereft me [I, iii, 249–58].

As Iago reminds the Moor, 'She did deceive her father, marrying you [III, iii, 209]'. If she can overthrow her father's authority, presumably she can overthrow that of Othello as well. For this reason, we may gather, he views her alleged sexual infidelity as the overthrow of his patriarchal authority:

I had been happy, if the general camp,
Pioners and all, had tasted her sweet body,
So I had nothing known. O now, for ever
Farewell the tranquil mind! farewell content!
Farewell the plumed troops and the big wars . . .
Farewell! Othello's occupation's gone [III, iii, 348–60].

An Elizabethan to the end, Othello thinks first of dismemberment – 'I will chop her into messes', and then of poison. Poison would make him a source of her pollution in symbolic terms, rather than the agent of purification. But Iago's Jacobean turn of mind instructs Othello otherwise. It requires a punishment to make the crime legible upon the subject's body. 'Do it not with poison', he thus tells Othello, but 'strangle her in her bed, even the bed she hath contaminated [IV, i, 204–205]'. With this, Shakespeare has Iago distinguish between the act of pollution and that of purification. Mutilation, in other words, becomes the solution to the assault on the authority of the monarch. Now completely given over to the machinations of the Jacobean theater, Othello reenacts the crime upon the female's body – more accurately, upon her mouth – by smothering her. Much as it may seem to diverge from a form of mutilation that displays the permeability of the body, this punishment also points right to the source of the assault upon patriarchy, the woman's political voice. And true to the poetics of punishment, the act which reveals the truth of his crime radically subordinates the material body of the subject in a ritual testimony to the power of blood. By this brief reading of *Othello*, I simply want to suggest that a shift in the strategies of political display can be inferred from Shakespeare's use of the female body. Desdemona poses a specifically Jacobean assault on monarchy when she assumes authority over her body and persuades the senate to assert the priority of a contractual relationship over and against the will of the patriarch.[19] □

The final essay considered in this Guide is by Stanley Cavell. Cavell is a philosopher who has pursued the questions that interest him into literature, especially into Shakespeare's plays. Some may think Cavell is merely using the plays to illustrate, for the non-specialist, recondite matters while others may think that he is revealing the implications of the play. His work certainly moves freely over the boundary between philosophy and literary criticism and it is useful to watch a philosopher approaching the realm of literary criticism as so much literary criticism approaches the realm of philosophy. Cavell's essay 'Othello and the Stake of the Other' is part of his exploration of the meaning of scepticism. For Cavell scepticism is not just a philosophical position abstracted from ordinary life; it must be considered as a form of life and *Othello* gives him an opportunity to discuss an important aspect of it. He begins by considering an argument of Descartes, from the *Meditations*, an argument for the existence of God. Cavell reasons, if Descartes wanted to prove to himself beyond doubt that he was not alone in the world, why did he not seek to prove beyond doubt the existence of another finite being? His answer is that, for Descartes, to prove the existence of another finite being beyond doubt is to prove the existence of Christ, that is the unity of the dual nature of soul and body, in another as in oneself and that could only be proved if one proved the existence of God. The proof of the existence of God is necessary to the proof of one's own existence beyond doubt. Scepticism, for Cavell, is always the attempt to convert the human condition into an intellectual puzzle:

■ Tragedy is the place we are not allowed to escape the consequences, or price, of this cover: that the failure to acknowledge a best case of the other is a denial of that other, presaging the death of the other, say by stoning, or by hanging; and the death of our capacity to acknowledge as such, the turning of our hearts to stone, or their bursting.[20] □

Not to trust, to disbelieve, is in certain circumstances to fall prey to a terrible temptation that Cavell believes is the cause of scepticism: the temptation to deny the problem that the existence of another poses. That problem is, in Cavell's view, the problem of the reality of the metaphysical, a reality scepticism seeks to deny by asserting, to the contrary, that the human problem is an intellectual puzzle.

Though his essay takes the form of an exploration, in fact his questions are tendentious and the piece is best read as the exposition of a view. The view depends upon an unstated but continually implied emphasis upon Othello's demand for proof. This demand in turn implies, for Cavell, the truth he sees underlying the condition of scepticism, that paradox that scepticism is a cover or concealment for the sceptic, preventing the sceptic from acknowledging that the human condition is metaphysical. It is as though an intellectual irritation is better than a metaphysical dismay. This view is contentious of course; it is even 'psycho-analytical'. It depends upon a 'reading into' the condition of scepticism of concealed motives of which even the sceptic himself or herself may be unaware; it uses the work of a French thinker of the later seventeenth century to read the work of an Elizabethan Englishman who lived into the Jacobean age; it is itself, therefore, open to a sceptical view. Yet such scepticism is not founded on a more secure basis than the scepticism Cavell is exploring; in the later twentieth century in literary studies no school of thought can afford merely to dismiss views it may find extravagant.

This extract shows Cavell pursuing his argument through *Othello*:

■ Briefly, to begin with, we have the logic, the emotion, and the scene of skepticism epitomized. The logic: 'My life upon her faith [I, iii, 295]' and '. . . when I love thee not/Chaos is come again [III, iii, 91–2]' set up the stake necessary to best cases; the sense I expressed by the imaginary major premise 'If I know anything, I know this.' One standing issue about the rhythm of *Othello*'s plot is that the progress from the completeness of Othello's love to the perfection of his doubt is too precipitous for the fictional time of the play. But such precipitousness is just the rhythm of skepticism; all that is necessary is the stake. The emotion: Here I mean not Othello's emotion towards Desdemona, call it jealousy; but the structure of his emotion as he is hauled back and forth across the keel of his love. Othello's enactment, or sufferance, of that torture is the most extraordinary representation known to me of the 'astonishment' in skeptical doubt. In Descartes's first Meditation: 'I realize so clearly that there are no conclusive indications by which waking life can be distinguished from sleep that I am quite aston-ished, and my bewilderment is such that it is almost able to convince me that I am sleeping.' (It does not follow that one is *convinced* that one is awake.) When Othello loses consciousness ('Is't possible? – Confess? – Handkerchief? – O devil! [IV, i, 42–3]') it is not from con-viction in a piece of knowledge but in an effort to stave the knowledge off. The scene: Here I have in mind the pervasive air of the language and the action of this play as one in which Othello's mind constantly outstrips reality, dissolves it in trance or dream or in the beauty or ugliness of his incantatory imagination; in which he visualizes possibilities that reason, unaided, cannot rule out. Why is he beyond aid? Why are the ear and the eye in him disjoined? We know that by the time he formulates his condition this way:

> By the world,
> I think my wife be honest, and think she is not,
> I think that thou are just, and think thou are not;
> I'll have some proof [III, iii, 386–9] . . .

he is lost. Two dozen lines earlier he had demanded of Iago 'the ocular proof,' a demand that was no purer a threat than it was a command, as if he does indeed wish for this outcome, as if he has a use for Iago's suspicions, hence a use for Iago that reciprocates Iago's use of him. Nothing I claim about the play here will depend on an understanding of the relation between Iago and Othello, so I will simply assert what is suggested by what I have just said, that such a question as 'Why does Othello believe Iago?' is badly formed. It is not conceivable that Othello believes Iago and *not* Desdemona. Iago, we might say, offers Othello an opportunity to believe something, something to oppose to something else he knows. What does he know? Why does it require opposition? – What do we know?

We have known (say, since G. Wilson Knight's 'The *Othello* Music') that Othello's language, call it his imagination, is at once his, and the play's, glory, and his shame, the source of his power and of his impotence; or we should have known (since Bradley's *Shakespearean Tragedy*) that Othello is the most romantic of Shakespeare's heroes, which may be a way of summarizing the same facts. And we ought to attend to the perception that Othello is the most Christian of the tragic heroes (expressed in Norman Rabkin's *Shakespeare and the Common Understanding*). Nor is there any longer any argument against our knowledge that Othello is black; and there can be no argument with the fact that he has just married, nor with the description, compared with the cases of Shakespeare's other tragedies, that this one is not political but domestic.

We know more specifically, I take it, that Othello's blackness means something. But what specifically does it mean? Mean, I mean, to him – for otherwise it is not Othello's color we are interested in but some generalized blackness, meaning perhaps 'sooty' or 'filthy,' as elsewhere in the play. This difference may show in the way one takes Desdemona's early statement: 'I saw Othello's visage in his mind [I, iii, 253].' I think it is commonly felt that she means she overlooked his blackness in favor of his inner brilliance; and perhaps further felt that this is a piece of deception, at least of herself. But what the line more

naturally says is that she saw his visage as he sees it, that she understands his blackness as he understands it, as the expression (or in his
word, his manifestation) of his mind – which is not overlooking it.
Then how does he understand it?

As the color of a romantic hero. For he, as he was and is, manifested
by his parts, his title, and his 'perfect soul [I, ii, 31]', is the hero of the
tales of romance he tells, some ones of which he wooed and won
Desdemona with, others of which he will die upon. It is accordingly
the color of one of enchanted powers and of magical protection, but
above all it is the color of one of purity, of a perfect soul. Desdemona,
in entering his life, hence in entering his story of his life, enters as a fit
companion for such a hero; his perfection is now opened toward hers.
His absolute stake in his purity, and its confirmation in hers, is shown
in what he feels he has lost in losing Desdemona's confirmation:

> . . . my name, that was as fresh
> As Dian's visage, is now begrim'd, and black
> As mine own face [III, iii, 389–91].

Diana's is a name for the visage Desdemona saw to be in Othello's
mind. He loses its application to his own name, his charmed self,
when he no longer sees his visage in Desdemona's mind but in Iago's,
say in the world's capacity for rumour. To say he loses Desdemona's
power to confirm his image of himself is to say that he loses his old
power of imagination. And this is to say that he loses his grasp of his
own nature; he no longer has the same voice in his history. So then the
question becomes: How has he come to displace Desdemona's imagination by Iago's? However terrible the exchange, it must be less
terrible than some other. Then we need to ask not so much how Iago
gained his power as how Desdemona lost hers.

We know – do we not? – that Desdemona has lost her virginity, the
protection of Diana, by the time she appears to us. And surely Othello
knows this! But this change in her condition, while a big enough fact
to hatch millennia of plots, is not what Othello accuses her of.
(Though would that accusation have been much more unfair than the
unfaithfulness he does accuse her of?) I emphasize that I am assuming
in Othello's mind the theme and condition of virginity to carry their
full weight within a romantic universe. Here is some recent Northrop
Frye on the subject: 'Deep within the stock convention of virgin-
baiting is a vision of human integrity imprisoned in a world it is in
but not of, often forced by weakness into all kinds of ruses and strata-
gems, yet always managing to avoid the one fate which really is worse
than death, the annihilation of one's identity . . . What is symbolized as
a virgin is actually a human conviction, however expressed, that there

is something at the core of one's infinitely fragile being which is not only immortal but has discovered the secret of invulnerability that eludes the tragic hero'. [21]

Now let us consolidate what we know on this sketch so far. We have to think in this play not merely about marriage but about the marriage of a romantic hero and of a Christian man; one whose imagination has to incorporate the idea of two becoming one in marriage and the idea that it is better to marry than to burn. It is a play, though it is thought of as domestic, in which not a marriage but an idea of marriage, or let us say an imagination of marriage, is worked out. 'Why did I marry?' is the first question Othello asks himself to express his first raid of suspicion [III, iii, 245]. The question has never been from his mind. Iago's first question to him is 'Are you fast married?' and Othello's first set speech ends with something less than an answer: 'But that I love the gentle Desdemona,/I would not my unhoused free condition/Put into circumscription and confine/For the sea's worth.' Love is at most a necessary not a sufficient condition for marrying. And for some minds, a certain idea of love may compromise as much as validate the idea of marriage. It may be better, but it is not perfect to marry, as St. Paul implies.

We have, further, to think in this play not merely generally of marriage, but specifically of the wedding night. It is with this that the play opens. The central of the facts we know is that the whole beginning scene takes place while Othello and Desdemona are in their bridal bed. The simultaneity is marked: 'Even now, now, very now, an old black ram/Is tupping your white ewe [I, i, 87–8].' And the scene is one of treachery, alarms, of shouts, of armed men running through a sleeping city. The conjunction of the bridal chamber with a scene of emergency is again insisted on by Othello's reappearance from his bedroom to stop a brawl with his single presence; a reappearance repeated the first night in Cyprus. As though an appearance from his place of sex and dreams is what gives him the power to stop an armed fight with a word and a gesture. – Or is this more than we know? Perhaps the conjunction is to imply that their 'hour of love [I, iii, 299–300]', or their two hours, have each been interrupted. There is reason to believe that the marriage has not been consummated, anyway reason to believe that Othello does not know whether it has. What is Iago's 'Are you fast married?' asking? Whether a public, legal ceremony has taken place or whether a private act; or whether the public and the private have ratified one another? Othello answers by speaking of his nobility and his love. But apart from anything else this seems to assume that Iago's 'you' was singular, not plural. And what does Othello mean in Cyprus by these apparently public words?

> . . . come, my dear love,
> The purchase made, the fruits are to ensue,
> The profit's yet to come 'twixt me and you [II, iii, 8–10].

What is the purchase and what the fruits or profit? Othello has just had proclaimed a general celebration at once of the perdition of the Turkish fleet and of his nuptials [II, ii]. If the fruits and profit are the resumption of their privacy then the purchase was the successful discharge of his public office and his entry into Cyprus. But this success was not his doing; it was provided by a tempest. Is the purchase their (public) marriage? Then the fruits and profit are their conjugal love. Then he is saying that this is yet to come. It seems to me possible that the purchase, or price, was her virginity, and the fruits or profit their pleasure. There could hardly be greater emphasis on their having had just one shortened night together, isolated from this second night by a tempest (always in these matters symbolic, perhaps here of a memory, perhaps of an anticipation). Or is it, quite simply, that this is something he wishes to *say* publicly, whatever the truth between them? (How we imagine Desdemona's reaction to this would then become all-important.)

I do not think that we must, nor that we can, choose among these possibilities in Othello's mind. On the contrary, I think Othello cannot choose among them. My guiding hypothesis about the structure of the play is that the thing *denied our sight* throughout the opening scene – the thing, the scene, that Iago takes Othello back to again and again, retouching it for Othello's enchafed imagination – is what we are shown in the final scene, the scene of murder. This becomes our ocular proof of Othello's understanding of his two nights of married love. (It has been felt from Thomas Rymer to G. B. Shaw that the play obeys the rhythm of farce, not of tragedy. One might say that in beginning with a sexual scene denied our sight, this play opens exactly as a normal comedy closes, as if turning comedy inside out.) I shall follow out this hypothesis here only to the extent of commenting on that final scene.

However one seeks to interpret the meaning of the great entering speech of the scene ('It is the cause, it is the cause, my soul . . . Put out the light, and then put out the light') [V, ii, 1ff.], I cannot take its mysteries, its privacies, its magniloquence, as separate from some massive denial to which these must be in service. Othello must mean that he is acting impersonally, but the words are those of a man in a trance, in a dream state, fighting not to awaken; willing for anything but light. By 'denial' I do not initially mean something requiring psychoanalytical, or any other, theory. I mean merely to ask that we not, conventionally but insufferably, assume that we know this woman better than this man knows her – making Othello some kind of exotic, gorgeous, superstitious lunkhead; which is about what Iago thinks. However much Othello deserves each of these titles, however far he believes Iago's tidings, he cannot just believe them; somewhere he also *knows* them to be false. This is registered in the rapidity with which he is brought to the truth, with no real further evidence, with only a counter-story (about the handkerchief) that bursts over him, or from him, as the truth. Shall we say he recognizes the truth too late? The fact is, he recognizes it when he is ready to, as one alone can; in this case, when its burden is dead. I am not claiming that he is trying not to believe Iago, or wants not to believe what Iago has told him. (This might describe someone who, say, had a good opinion of Desdemona, not someone whose life is staked upon hers.) I am claiming that we must understand Othello, on the contrary, to want to believe Iago, to be trying, against his knowledge, to believe him. Othello's eager insistence on Iago's honesty, his eager slaking of his thirst for knowledge with that poison, is not a sign of his stupidity in the presence of poison but of his devouring need of it. I do not quite say that he could not have accepted slander about Desdemona so quickly, to the quick, unless he already believed it; but rather that it is a thing he would rather believe than something yet more terrible to his mind; that the idea of Desdemona as an adulterous whore is more convenient to him than the idea of her as chaste. But what could be more terrible than Desdemona's faithlessness? Evidently her faithfulness. But how?

Note that in taking Othello's entering speech as part of a ritual of denial, in the context of taking the murder scene as a whole to be a dream enactment of the invisible opening of the play, we have an answer implied to our original question about this play, concerning Othello's turning of Desdemona to stone [Cavell has asked, where does Othello's image of her 'and smooth, as monumental alabaster' at IV, ii, 5 come from?]. His image denies that he scarred her and shed her blood. It is a denial at once that he has taken her virginity and that she has died of him. (But it is at the same time evidence that in suffering the replacement of the problem of God by the problem of the other this man has turned both objects into stone, so that we might at this moment understand his self-interpretation to be that of an idolater, hence religiously as well as socially to be cast out.) The whole scene of murder is built on the concept of sexual intercourse or orgasm as a dying. There is a dangerously explicit quibble to this effect in the exchange

OTHELLO   Thou art on thy death bed.
DESDEMONA   Ay, but not yet to die [V, ii, 51–2].

The possible quibble only heightens the already heartbreaking poignancy of the wish to die in her marriage bed after a long life.

Though Desdemona no more understands Othello's accusation of her than, in his darkness to himself, he does, she obediently shares his sense that this is their final night and that it is to be some dream-like recapitulation of their former two nights. This shows in her premonitions of death (the Willow Song, and the request that one of her wedding sheets be her shroud) and in her mysterious request to Emilia '. . . tonight/Lay on my bed our wedding sheets [IV, ii, 106–7]', as if knowing, and faithful to, Othello's private dream of her, herself preparing the scene of her death as Othello, utilizing Iago's stage directions, imagines it must happen ('Do it not with poison, strangle her in her bed, even the bed she hath contaminated.' 'Good, good, the justice of it pleases, very good.' [IV, i, 204–7]); as if knowing that only with these sheets on their bed can his dream of her be contested. The dream is of contamination. The fact the dream works upon is the act of deflowering. Othello is reasonably literal about this, as reasonable as a man in a trance can be:

> When I have pluck'd the rose,
> I cannot give it vital growth again,
> It must needs wither; I'll smell it on the tree,
> A balmy breath, that doth almost persuade
> Justice herself to break her sword: once more:
> Be thus, when thou art dead, and I will kill thee,
> And love thee after [V, ii, 13–19].

(Necrophilia is an apt fate for a mind whose reason is suffocating in its sumptuous capacity for figuration, and which takes the dying into love literally to entail killing. 'That death's unnatural, that kills for loving [V, ii, 42]'; or that turns its object to live stone. It is apt as well that Desdemona sense death, or the figure of death, as the impending cause of death. And at the very end, facing himself, he will not recover from this. 'I kissed thee ere I killed thee.' And after too. And not just now when you died from me, but on our previous nights as well.)

The exhibition of wedding sheets in this romantic, superstitious, conventional environment can only refer to the practice of proving purity by staining. – I mention in passing that this provides a satisfactory weight for the importance Othello attaches to his charmed (or farcical) handkerchief, the fact that it is spotted, spotted with strawberries.

Well, were the sheets stained or not? Was she a virgin or not? The answers seem as ambiguous as to our earlier question whether they are fast married. Is the final, fatal reenactment of their wedding night a clear denial of what really happened, so that we can just read off, by negation, what really happened? Or is it a straight reenactment, without negation, and the flower was still on the tree, as far as he

171

knew? In that case, who was reluctant to see it plucked, he or she? On such issues, farce and tragedy are separated by the thickness of a membrane.[22] ☐

Cavell's interest in the body, in the fate of the body, derives from his conviction that 'those who are pushed, in attempting to counter a dualistic view of mind and body, to assert the identity of body and mind, are again skipping or converting the problem'[23] just as scepticism, according to Cavell, attempts 'the conversion of metaphysical finitude into intellectual lack'.[24]

■ For suppose my identity with my body is something that exists only in my affirmation of my body. (As friendship may exist only in loyalty to it.) Then the question is: What would the body *become* under affirmation? What would become of *me*? Perhaps I would know myself as, take myself for, a kind of machine; perhaps as a universe.[25] ☐

He sums up the ending of the play like this:

■ So there they are, on their bridal and death sheets. A statue, a stone, is something whose existence is fundamentally open to ocular proof. A human being is not. The two bodies lying together form an emblem of this fact, the truth of skepticism. What this man lacked was not certainty. He knew everything, but he could not yield to what he knew, be commanded by it. He found out too much for his mind, not too little. Their differences from one another – the one everything the other is not – form an emblem of human separation, which can be accepted, and granted, or not. Like the separation from God; everything we are not.[26] ☐

Cavell's discussion offers the reminder that *Othello* supplies opportunities for interpretation every bit as rich as other Shakespeare plays. Perhaps this very fecundity is the best answer to Rymer in the end. By his lights he was right; others have shown that other lights show other truths. Our time is wary of comprehensive explanations and more comfortable with diversity; *Othello* offers a pioneering image of the potential for tragedy in any attempt to embrace diversity. Whatever we conclude, the evidence is that the play has survived criticism so far and shall very probably continue to do so for some time yet.

NOTES

INTRODUCTION

1 Catherine Belsey, *Critical Practice* (London: Methuen, 1980); Bernard Bergonzi, *Exploding English* (Oxford: Clarendon Press, 1990).

2 Brian Vickers, *Appropriating Shakespeare: Contemporary Critical Quarrels* (New Haven: Yale University Press, 1993).

3 Brian Vickers, *Shakespeare: The Critical Heritage*, 6 vols. (London and Boston: Routledge and Kegan Paul, 1979), VI, pp. 41–2.

4 Ibid., II, p. 60.

CHAPTER ONE

1 Martin Coyle, *William Shakespeare: Richard II* (Cambridge: Icon Books, 1998), p. 21ff.

2 T.S. Eliot, 'The Metaphysical Poets', in *Selected Essays* (London: Faber, 1951), p. 288.

3 See, for example, the Introduction to *Poetical Works*, ed. Douglas Bush (Oxford: Oxford University Press, 1966).

4 Brian Vickers, *Shakespeare: The Critical Heritage*, 6 vols. (London and Boston: Routledge and Kegan Paul, 1979), I, p. xi. Hereafter, 'Vickers I', etc.

5 Vickers I, p. xi.

6 Gary Taylor, *Reinventing Shakespeare: A Cultural History from the Restoration to the Present* (London: the Hogarth Press, 1990).

7 The editorial question is very thoroughly discussed in the Arden *Othello* (3rd edition, edited by E.A.J. Honigmann, Walton-on-Thames: Thomas Nelson, 1997). I have used this edition throughout except where I have indicated otherwise. (See also the note in the Introduction, p. 6, which explains some of the inconsistencies within the extracts from the play *Othello*.)

8 Terry Eagleton, *The Function of Criticism from the Spectator to Post-Structuralism* (London: Verso, 1984).

9 E.M.W. Tillyard, *The Elizabethan World Picture* (London: Chatto and Windus, 1943); Robert Weimann, *Shakespeare and the Popular Tradition in the Theater: Studies in the Social Dimension of Dramatic Form and Function*, ed. Robert Schwartz (Baltimore and London: Johns Hopkins University Press, 1978).

10 Vickers I, p. 5.

11 Quoted by Curt A. Zimansky in *The Critical Works of Thomas Rymer* (New Haven: Yale University Press, 1956), p. xlix.

12 Ibid., p. xlix, n. 46.

13 Patricia J. Williams, *The Genealogy of Race: Towards a Theory of Grace* (London: BBC, 1997).

14 Zimansky, p. xxix.

15 Ibid., p. xxvii.

16 These references can be found in Zimansky, pp. xlix-l. Scott and Pope need no introduction; Thomas Babington Macaulay (1800–59) is best known for his *History of England* (5 vols., 1848–61).

17 Zimansky, p. xlix.

18 Zimansky, p. 18.

19 *A Short View of Tragedy*, 1695; Zimansky, p. 171.

20 *The Cambridge History of English Literature*, Third Edition, ed. George Sampson (Cambridge: Cambridge University Press, 1970). p. 237.

21 *Cambridge History of English Literature*, p. 237.

22 Aristotle's *Poetics* became known in England through the Italian translation by Ludovico Castelvetro in 1570. Castelvetro's commentary is notorious for his invention of the three dramatic unities, of action, time and place. Although a simplistic elaboration of Aristotle's view of plot unity, it became the Neo-classical orthodoxy.

23 Zimansky, p. xxiii.

24 Ibid., p. 131.

25 Vickers, I, p. 422.

26 Zimansky, p. 131.

27 George Gascoigne's *Certain Notes of Instruction in English Verse* was published in *The Posies of George Gascoigne* (1575); George Puttenham's *The Art of English Poesy* (1589) is more prescriptive and more exhaustive.

28 Ben Jonson, *The Complete Poems*, ed. George Parfitt (Harmondsworth: Penguin Books, 1988), p. 264.

29 Zimansky, p. 132.

30 Ibid., p. 132.

31 Ibid., p. 132.

32 Vickers II, p. 86.

33 James Boswell, *The Life of Samuel Johnson*, edited and abridged with an introduction and notes by Christopher Hibbert (Harmondsworth: Penguin, 1979), pp. 211–212.

34 Zimansky, p. 133.

35 Ibid., p. 133.

36 Ibid., p. 134.

37 Ibid., p. 134

38 Ibid., pp. 134–5.

39 Ibid., p. 135.

40 Ibid., p. 136.

41 Ibid., p. 136

42 Ibid., pp. 137–8.

43 Ibid., p. 142.

44 Ibid., p. 142.

45 Ibid., p. 143.

46 Ibid., pp. 144–5.

47 *Cambridge History of English Literature*, p. 237.

48 Zimansky, p. 152.

49 Ibid., p. 130.

50 Ibid., pp. 150–1.

51 Ibid., p. 147.

52 Ibid., p. 147.

53 Ibid., pp. 153–4.

54 Ibid., pp. 148–9.

55 Vickers, I, p. 29.

56 Ibid., p. 415.

57 *The Diary of Samuel Pepys*, ed. Robert Latham and William Matthews (London: Bell, 1970), vol. I, 1660, pp. 263–5.

58 Zimansky, p. 155.

59 Ibid., pp. 155–6.

60 Ibid., p. 158.

61 Ibid., p. 160.

62 Ibid., p. 161.

63 Ibid., pp. 162–63.

64 Ibid., p. 164.

65 Ibid., p. 163.

66 Ibid., p. l; Isaac d'Israeli was the father of the novelist Benjamin Disraeli.

67 *Selected Essays*, p. 141 n.

CHAPTER TWO

1 Vickers, II, pp. 72–3.

2 Ibid., pp. 73–4.

3 Ibid., p. 74.

4 Ibid., pp. 74–5.

5 Vickers, II, pp. 259–60.

6 Ibid., pp. 11–12.

7 Ibid., p. 4.

8 Ibid., p. 60.

9 Curt A. Zimansky, ed., *The Critical Works of Thomas Rymer* (New Haven: Yale University Press, 1956), p. xxii.

10 Vickers, II, p. 86.

11 Literally 'god out of the machine', a reference to the resort of the theatres of this age to mechanical devices to display supernatural appearances on stage.

12 Vickers, II, p. 86.

13 Ibid., pp. 217–18.

14 Ibid., p. 301.

15 Ibid., p. 302.

16 Ibid., pp. 523–4.

17 Ibid., pp. 524–5.

18 *Dr. Johnson on Shakespeare*, ed. W. K. Wimsatt (Harmondsworth: Penguin, 1969), p. 141.

19 A vivid description of a scene – a term from Rhetoric.

20 Vickers, II, p. 75.

21 Vickers, III, p. 134.

22 *The Poems and Letters of Andrew Marvell*, ed. H. M. Margoliouth (Oxford: Clarendon Press, 1952), p. 26.

23 Vickers, III, p. 476.

24 *Dr. Johnson on Shakespeare*, p. 142.

25 Ibid. p. 142.

26 Ibid., p. 143.

27 Vickers, V, p. 24.

28 Ibid., p. 23.

29 *Dr. Johnson on Shakespeare*, pp. 109–110.

30 Vickers, V, p. 30.

31 Ibid., pp. 18–20.

32 Zimansky, p. 163.

33 Martin Coyle, *William Shakespeare: Richard II* (Cambridge: Icon Books, 1998), p. 53.

34 *A Defence of Poetry*, ed. J. A. Van Dorsten (Oxford: Oxford University Press, 1966), p. 25.

35 Zimansky, p. 163.

36 Vickers, III, p. 207.

37 Zimansky, p. 163.

38 Vickers, V, p. 29.

39 Vickers, IV, pp. 117–18.

40 Vickers, VI, p. 350.

41 *Dr. Johnson on Shakespeare*, p. 143.

42 Ibid., p. 71.

43 Vickers, VI, p. 240.

44 *Dr. Johnson on Shakespeare*, pp. 71–2.

45 Vickers, VI, p. 230.

46 *Dr. Johnson on Shakespeare*, p. 72.

47 Ibid., p. 143.

48 Ibid., p.73.
49 Ibid., p.73.
50 Ibid., pp.72–3.
51 Zimansky, p.142.
52 Vickers, II, p.189.
53 Vickers, V, pp.5–6.
54 Vickers, IV, p.24.
55 Ibid., p.25.
56 Ibid., p.25.
57 Ibid., p.29.
58 Figures quoted by Vickers, V, p.7.
59 James Boswell, *The Life of Samuel Johnson*, edited and abridged with an introduction and notes by Christopher Hibbert (Harmondsworth: Penguin, 1979), p.212.
60 Zimansky, p.132.

CHAPTER THREE

1 *Dr. Johnson on Shakespeare*, ed. W.K. Wimsatt (Harmondsworth: Penguin, 1969), p.71.
2 Vickers, IV, pp.186–7.
3 Ibid., pp.450–2.
4 'Personification' – a term from Rhetoric.
5 Vickers, IV, pp.266–7.
6 *Macbeth*, ed. K. Muir (London: Methuen, 1951).
7 *Coleridge on Shakespeare*, ed. T. Hawkes (Harmondsworth: Penguin, 1969), p.186.
8 Ibid., pp.186–7.
9 Ibid., p.187.
10 Ibid., p.187.
11 Vickers, II, p.74.
12 *Coleridge on Shakespeare*, p.195.
13 Ibid., p.189.
14 Ibid., p.187.
15 *Ben Jonson: The Complete Poems*, ed. George Parfitt (Harmondsworth: Penguin Books, 1988), p.264.
16 *Coleridge on Shakespeare*, p.187.
17 Ibid., pp.198–90.
18 Curt A. Zimansky, ed., *The Critical Works of Thomas Rymer* (New Haven: Yale University Press, 1956), pp.155–6.
19 Vickers, V, p.441 n.
20 Vickers, IV, p.119.
21 Ibid., pp.360–61.
22 *Coleridge on Shakespeare*, p.190.
23 Vickers, IV, p.451.
24 *Coleridge on Shakespeare*, p.193.
25 Ibid., p.195–6.
26 Ibid., p.195.
27 *Dr. Johnson on Shakespeare*, p.143.
28 Vickers, IV, p.361.
29 *Characters of Shakespear's Plays* (London: R. Hunter and C. and J. Ollier, 1817), pp.43–4.
30 Ibid., pp.45–50.
31 Ibid., pp.42–3.
32 James Boswell, *The Life of Samuel Johnson*, edited and abridged with an introduction and notes by Christopher Hibbert (Harmondsworth: Penguin, 1979), p.212.
33 *Characters of Shakespear's Plays*, pp.42–3.
34 Ibid., p.43.
35 *Coleridge on Shakespeare*, p.196.
36 *Characters of Shakespear's Plays*, pp.54–5.
37 Ibid., pp.54–6.
38 *Shakspere: His Mind and Art*, Tenth Edition (London: Kegan Paul, Trench and Trübner, 1892), p.223.
39 Ibid., p.224.
40 Ibid., pp.224–5.
41 Ibid., p.226.
42 Ibid., p.229–30.
43 *Luria*, published together with *A Soul's Tragedy* as No. VIII of *Bells and Pomegranates* (London: Moxon, 1846).
44 *Shakspere: His Mind and Art*, pp.230–1.
45 Ibid., pp.232–5.
46 Ibid., p.235.
47 Ibid., p.236.
48 Ibid., p.236.
49 Ibid., pp.242–3.
50 Ibid., p.232.
51 Ibid., pp.243–4.
52 A.C. Swinburne, *Study of Shakespeare* (London: Chatto and Windus, 1880).
53 *Shakespearean Tragedy* (Harmondsworth: Penguin, 1991), pp.177–87.
54 Ibid., p.191.
55 Ibid., p.192.
56 Ibid., p.179.
57 Ibid., p.190 n.
58 '[T]o set up the *Grecian* Method amongst us with success it is absolutely necessary to restore not only their Religion and their Polity but to transport us to the same Climate in which *Sophocles* and *Euripides* writ; or else, by reason of those different Circumstances, several things which were graceful and decent with them must seem ridiculous and absurd to us, as several things which would have appear'd highly extravagant

to them must look proper and becoming with us.' Vickers, II, p.60.

59 *Shakespearean Tragedy*, p.71.

60 Ibid., pp.206–7.

61 Ibid., p.204.

62 Ibid., p.204.

63 Ibid., p.215.

64 Ibid., p.215.

65 See *Shakespearean Tragedy*, Lecture I; also Bradley's *Oxford Lectures on Poetry* (London: Macmillan, 1909), 'Hegel's Theory of Tragedy'.

66 *Shakespearean Tragedy*, p.217.

67 Bradley's closing quotation is from Wordsworth's 'sonnet "To Toussaint l'Ouverture"'. François Dominique Toussaint l'Ouverture was governor of St. Domingo, and chief of the African slaves freed by the decree of the French Convention (1794). He resisted Napoleon's edict re-establishing slavery and was arrested and sent to Paris where he died in April 1803. Wordsworth's sonnet was written probably in August 1802. The humanistic assertion of the poem is made to and on behalf of a black revolutionary. Bradley uses this fact to introduce his challenge to racist accounts of the play to which the reader has already been referred.

CHAPTER FOUR

1 *Selected Essays* (London: Faber, 1951), pp.129–31.

2 *The Wheel of Fire* (London: Oxford University Press, 1930), pp.97–100.

3 Ibid., p.102.

4 Ibid., p.103.

5 Ibid., p.104.

6 Ibid., pp.108–9.

7 Ibid., pp.130–31.

8 *The Structure of Complex Words* (London: Chatto and Windus, 1951), p.229.

9 Ibid., p.229.

10 Ibid., p.235.

11 Ibid., p.230.

12 Ibid., p.218.

13 Ibid., p.219.

14 Ibid., pp.219–20.

15 Curt A. Zimansky, ed., *The Critical Works of Thomas Rymer* (New Haven: Yale University Press, 1956), pp.134–5.

16 *The Structure of Complex Words*, p.221.

17 Ibid., p.234.

18 Ibid., p.220.

19 Ibid., p.220.

20 Ibid., pp.221–3.

21 Ibid., pp.226–7.

22 Ibid., p.227.

23 Ibid., pp.228–9.

24 Ibid., pp.228–9.

25 Ibid., pp.230–1.

26 Ibid., p.232.

27 Ibid., p.231.

28 Ibid., pp.232–3.

29 Ibid., p.235.

30 *Scrutiny*, 6:3 (December, 1937), pp.259–83. This essay may also be found in the collection *The Common Pursuit* (London: Hogarth Press, 1984; first published in London by Chatto and Windus in 1952), in which it is entitled 'Diabolic Intellect and the Noble Hero: Or the Sentimentalist's *Othello*'.

31 'Diabolic Intellect and the Noble Hero: A Note on *Othello*', p.259.

32 Ibid., p.259.

33 Ibid., pp.259–60.

34 Ibid., p.260.

35 Ibid., p.261.

36 Ibid., p.262.

37 Ibid., p.264.

38 Ibid., pp.265–7.

39 Ibid., pp.270–71.

40 Ibid., p.281.

41 Ibid., pp.272–6.

42 Ibid., p.276.

43 Ibid., p.278.

44 Helen Gardner, '*Othello*: A Retrospect, 1900-1967', *Shakespeare Survey 21* (1968), pp.1–13.

CHAPTER FIVE

1 Kingsley Amis, *Encounter*, July 1960.

2 Helen Gardner, '*Othello*: A Retrospect, 1900-1967', *Shakespeare Survey 21* (1968), pp.1–13.

3 *Shakespeare Criticism 1935–60*, selected with an introduction by Anne Ridler (London: Oxford University Press, 1963), pp.348–68.

4 Ibid., p.350.

5 Vickers, V, p.29.

6 *Shakespeare Criticism*, p.352.

7 Ibid., pp.353–4.

8 Ibid., p. 355.

9 See 'Easter 1916'; 'Upon a Political Prisoner' and 'In Memory of Con Markiewicz and Eva Gore-Booth'. 'In Memory of Major Robert Gregory' and 'An Irish Airman foresees His Death' give Yeats's general idea of heroism.

10 Aristotle's term for the self-will or pride that leads a man to defy the gods.

11 *Shakespeare Criticism*, pp. 364–5.

12 Ibid., pp. 366–7.

13 Ibid., p. 367.

14 *The Characters of Love* (London: Constable, 1960), pp. 161–2.

15 Ibid., pp. 145–6.

16 Ibid., pp. 146–7.

17 Ibid., p. 147.

18 Ibid., pp. 148–9.

19 Ibid., p. 149.

20 Ibid., pp. 149–50.

21 Ibid., pp. 151–3.

22 'Anticipation' – a term from Rhetoric.

23 *The Characters of Love*, p. 158–61.

24 '*Othello*: A Retrospect, 1900-1967', p. 3.

25 Ibid., p. 5.

26 Thomas Bowdler's *Family Shakespeare* (1818) was a 'cleaned up' version.

27 *Shakespeare: Our Contemporary* (London: Routledge, 1967), pp. 86–7.

28 Heinrich Heine, *Shakespeares Mädchen und Frauen mit Erläuterungen*, Leipzig, 1839).

29 *in actu* means 'actually' and *in potentia*, 'potentially'.

30 *Nature in Shakespearean Tragedy*, London, 1955.

31 *Shakespeare: Our Contemporary*, pp. 94–5.

32 Ibid., pp. 96–7.

33 Ibid., pp. 98–9.

34 '*Othello*: A Retrospect, 1900-1967', pp. 12–13.

CHAPTER SIX

1 *Desire and Anxiety: Circulations of Sexuality in Shakespearean Drama* (London and New York: Routledge, 1992), pp. 25–26.

2 Ibid., pp. 25–6.

3 Ibid. pp. 25–6.

4 Ibid., p. 26.

5 Ibid., pp. 26–7.

6 'Fratricide and Cuckoldry: Shakespeare's Doubles', *Representing Shakespeare: New Psychoanalytic Essays*, ed. Murray M. Schwarz and Coppélia Kahn (Baltimore: Johns Hopkins University Press), 1980, p. 73.

7 *Desire and Anxiety*, p. 28.

8 Ibid., p. 33.

9 Peter Stallybrass, 'Patriarchal Territories: The Body Enclosed' in *Rewriting the Renaissance*, ed. Margaret Ferguson, Maureen Quilligan, Nancy Vickers (Chicago: University of Chicago Press, 1986), p. 139.

10 Edward A. Snow, 'Sexual Anxiety and the Male Order of Things in *Othello*', *English Literary Renaissance* 10 (1980), p. 407.

11 Stephen Greenblatt, 'The Improvisation of Power', *Renaissance Self-Fashioning* (Chicago: University of Chicago Press, 1980), pp. 222–54.

12 Traub refers the reader to Karen Newman, '"And wash the Ethiop white": Feminity and the Monstrous in *Othello*' in *Shakespeare Reproduced: the Text in Ideology and History*, ed. Jean E. Howard and Marion F. O'Connor (New York: Methuen, 1987), pp. 143–62, 'for an analysis of how Othello's "monstrosity" intersects with cultural identifications of femininity as monstrous'.

13 Traub refers the reader to I, i, 87–8, 109–12, 114–15, 124; I, ii, 63, 70–1, 99, 290–1.

14 'Othello and the "plain face of Racism"', *Shakespeare Quarterly* 38:2, Summer 1987, pp. 166–88.

15 *Desire and Anxiety*, pp. 35–7.

16 Ibid., pp. 39–41.

17 Ibid., p. 42.

18 Leonard Tennenhouse, *Power on Display: The Politics of Shakespeare's Genres* (London and New York: Methuen, 1986), p. 116.

19 Ibid., pp. 125–7.

20 Stanley Cavell, *Disowning Knowledge in Six Plays of Shakespeare* (Cambridge: Cambridge University Press, 1987), p. 138.

21 *The Secular Scripture* (Harvard University Press, 1976), p. 86.

22 *Disowning Knowledge*, pp. 128–35.

23 Ibid., p. 139.

24 Ibid., p. 138; This argument is pursued in 'Knowing and Acknowledging' in *Must We Mean What We Say?* (Cambridge: Cambridge University Press, 1976).

25 Ibid., p. 139.

26 Ibid., pp. 141–2.

SELECTED BIBLIOGRAPHY

Bayley, John, *The Characters of Love* (London: Constable, 1960).

Belsey, Catherine, *Critical Practice* (London: Methuen, 1980).

Bergonzi, Bernard, *Exploding English* (Oxford: Clarendon Press, 1990).

Boswell, James, *The Life of Samuel Johnson*, edited and abridged with an introduction and notes by Christopher Hibbert (Harmondsworth: Penguin, 1979).

Bradley, A. C., *Shakespearean Tragedy* (Harmondsworth: Penguin, 1991).

Bradley, A. C., *Oxford Lectures on Poetry* (London: Macmillan, 1909).

Carlyle, Thomas, *Sartor Resartus*, in *A Carlyle Reader: Selections from the Writings of Thomas Carlyle*, ed. G.B. Tennyson (Cambridge: Cambridge University Press, 1984).

Cavell, Stanley, *Disowning Knowledge in Six Plays of Shakespeare* (Cambridge: Cambridge University Press, 1987).

Coleridge, Samuel Taylor, *Biographia Literaria, or, Biographical Sketches of My Literary Life and Opinions*, ed. and introd. George Watson (London: Dent, 1956).

Coyle, Martin, *William Shakespeare: Richard II* (Cambridge: Icon Books, 1998).

Dowden, Edward, *Shakspere; His Mind and Art*, tenth edition (London: Kegan Paul, Trench and Trübner, 1892).

Eagleton, Terry, *The Function of Criticism from the Spectator to Post-Structuralism* (London: Verso, 1984).

Eliot, T.S., 'The Metaphysical Poets', in *Selected Essays* (London: Faber, 1951).

Eliot, T.S., 'Hamlet', in *Selected Essays* (London: Faber, 1951).

Eliot, T.S., 'Shakespeare and the Stoicism of Seneca', in *Selected Essays* (London: Faber, 1951).

Empson, William, *The Structure of Complex Words* (London: Chatto and Windus, 1951).

Gardner, Helen, 'Othello: A Retrospect, 1900–1967', *Shakespeare Survey* 21 (1968), pp. 1–13.

Hawkes, T., (ed.), *Coleridge on Shakespeare* (Harmondsworth: Penguin, 1969).

Hazlitt, William, *Characters of Shakespear's Plays* (London: R. Hunter and C. and J. Ollier, 1817).

Knight, G. Wilson, *The Wheel of Fire* (London: Oxford University Press, 1930).

Kott, Jan, *Shakespeare: Our Contemporary* (London: Routledge, 2nd edn. 1967).

Leavis, F.R., 'Diabolic Intellect and the Noble Hero: A Note on *Othello*', *Scrutiny*, 6:3 (December, 1937), pp.259–83.

Leavis, F.R., 'Diabolic Intellect and the Noble Hero: Or the Sentimentalist's Othello' in *The Common Pursuit* (London: Hogarth Press, 1984; first published in London by Chatto and Windus in 1952).

Pepys, Samuel, *The Diary of Samuel Pepys*, ed. Robert Latham and William Matthews (London: Bell, 1970).

Ridler, Anne, *Shakespeare Criticism 1935–60*, selected with an introduction by Anne Ridler (London: Oxford University Press, 1963).

Sampson, George, (ed.), *The Cambridge History of English Literature*, Third

Edition (Cambridge: Cambridge University Press, 1970).

Taylor, Gary, *Reinventing Shakespeare: A Cultural History from the Restoration to the Present* (London: the Hogarth Press, 1990).

Tennenhouse, Leonard, *Power on Display: The Politics of Shakespeare's Genres* (London and New York: Methuen, 1986).

Tillyard, E. M. W., *The Elizabethan World Picture* (London: Chatto and Windus, 1943).

Traub, Valerie, *Desire and Anxiety: Circulations of Sexuality in Shakespearean Drama* (London and New York: Routledge, 1992).

Vickers, Brian, *Shakespeare: The Critical Heritage*, 6 vols. (London and Boston: Routledge and Kegan Paul, 1979).

Vickers, Brian, *Appropriating Shakespeare: Contemporary Critical Quarrels* (New Haven: Yale University Press, 1993).

Weimann, Robert, *Shakespeare and the Popular Tradition in the Theater: Studies in the Social Dimension of Dramatic Form and Function*, ed. Robert Schwartz (Baltimore and London: Johns Hopkins University Press, 1978).

Williams, Patricia J., *The Genealogy of Race: Towards a Theory of Grace* (London: BBC, 1997).

Wimsatt, W. K., (ed.), *Dr. Johnson on Shakespeare* (Harmondsworth: Penguin, 1969).

Zimansky, Curt A., (ed.), *The Critical Works of Thomas Rymer* (New Haven: Yale University Press, 1956).

SUGGESTED FURTHER READING

Some of the material selected for this Guide is available in the *Casebook* collection of essays on *Othello* edited by John Wain (London: Macmillan, 1971). There is a very full bibliography edited by Margaret Lael Mikesell and Virginia Mason Vaughan: *Othello: An Annotated Bibliography* (New York and London: Garland, 1990).

The following suggestions for further reading are divided into two groups: earlier studies and recent studies. Two journals are to be recommended: *Shakespeare Survey* and *Shakespeare Quarterly*. The former has a very useful summary of 'The Year's Contributions to Shakespeare Studies', which repays browsing. There is a wide field in which to browse.

Earlier Studies

Alexander, Peter, *Shakespeare's Life and Art* (London: James Nisbet, 1939).

Arthos, John, *The Art of Shakespeare* (New York: Barnes and Noble, 1964).

Auden, W. H., *The Dyer's Hand and Other Essays* (London: Faber, 1963).

Bethell, S. L., *Shakespeare and the Popular Dramatic Tradition* (London: P. S. King and Staples Ltd, 1944).

Bethell, S. L., 'Shakespeare's Imagery: the Diabolic Images in Othello', *Shakespeare Survey* 5 (1952), pp. 62–80.

Bodkin, Maud, *Archetypal Patterns in Poetry* (Oxford: Oxford University Press, 1934).

Campbell, Lily B., *Shakespeare's Tragic Heroes: Slaves of Passion* (Cambridge: Cambridge University Press, 1930).

Chambers, E. K., *Shakespeare: A Survey* (London: Sidgwick and Jackson, 1925).

Charlton, H. B., *Shakespearean Tragedy* (London: Cambridge University Press, 1943).

Clemen, W. H., *The Development of Shakespeare's Imagery* (Cambridge, Mass.: Harvard University Press, 1951).

Coghill, Nevill, *Shakespeare's Professional Skills* (Cambridge: Cambridge University Press, 1964).

Craig, Hardin, *Shakespeare: A Historical and Critical Study* (1931).

Draper, John W., *The Humors and Shakespeare's Characters* (Durham: Duke University Press, 1945).

Duthie, George Ian, *Shakespeare* (London: Hutchinson's University Library, 1951).

Evans, Ifor, *The Language of Shakespeare's Plays* (London: Methuen, 1952).

Gordon, George, *Shakespearean Comedy and Other Studies* (London: Oxford University Press, 1944).

Granville-Barker, Harley, *On Dramatic Method, Being the Clark Lectures for 1930* (London: Sidgwick and Jackson, 1931).

Granville-Barker, Harley, *Prefaces to Shakespeare, Series IV, Othello* (London: Sidgwick and Jackson, 1945).

Harrison, G. B., *Shakespeare's Tragedies* (London: Routledge and Kegan Paul, 1951).

Hawkes, Terence, *Shakespeare and the Reason* (London: Routledge and Kegan Paul, 1964).

Heilman, Robert B., 'More Fair than Black: Light and Dark in *Othello*', *Essays in Criticism*, 1 (1951), pp. 315–35.

Heilman, Robert B., *Magic in the Web: Action and Language in 'Othello'* (Lexington, Ky.: University of Kentucky Press, 1956).

Holland, Norman N., *Psychoanalysis and Shakespeare* (New York: McGraw-Hill, 1964).

Holland, Norman N., *The Shakespearean Imagination* (Bloomington: Indiana University Press, 1964).

Holloway, John, *Studies in Shakespeare's Major Tragedies* (London: Routledge and Kegan Paul, 1961).

Joseph, Sister Miriam, *Shakespeare's Use of the Arts of Language* (New York: Columbia University Press, 1947).

Kirschbaum, Leo, 'The Modern Othello', *English Literary History*, 11 (1944), pp. 283–96.

Levin, Harry, *Shakespeare and the Revolution of the Times: Perspectives and Commentaries* (New York: Oxford University Press, 1976).

Lewis, Wyndham, *The Lion and the Fox: the Role of the Hero in the Plays of Shakespeare* (London: Methuen, 1955; 1st pbd. 1927).

Lucas, F. L., *Literature and Psychology* (London: Cassell, 1951).

Mason, Philip, *Prospero's Magic: Some Thoughts on Race and Class* (London: Oxford University Press, 1962).

Matthews, G. M., ed. Arnold Kettle, *Shakespeare in a Changing World* (New York: International Publishers, 1964).

Muir, Kenneth, 'The Jealousy of Iago', *English Miscellany*, ed. Mario Praz, 2 (1951), pp. 65–83.

Murry, John Middleton, *Shakespeare* (London: Cape, 1936).

Nicoll, Allardyce, *Shakespeare* (London: Oxford University Press, 1952).

Ribner, Irving, *Patterns in Shakespearian Tragedy* (London: Methuen, 1960).

Ridley, M. R., *Shakespeare's Plays: A Commentary* (1937).

Ridley, M. R., 'On Reading Shakespeare: Annual Shakespeare Lecture of the British Academy, 1940', *Proceedings of the British Academy*, 26 (Oxford: Oxford University Press, 1940).

Rosenberg, Marvin, 'In Defense of Iago', *Shakespeare Quarterly*, 6 (1955), pp. 145–58.

Rossiter, A. P., ed. Graham Storey, *Angels With Horns* (London: Longman's, Green, 1961).

Sewell, Arthur, *Character and Society in Shakespeare* (Oxford: Clarendon Press, 1951).

Shapiro, Stephen, 'Othello's Desdemona', *Literature and Psychology*, 14 (1964), pp. 56–61.

Siegel, Paul N., 'The Damnation of Othello', *Publications of the Modern Language Association*, 68 (1953), pp. 1068–78.

Siegel, Paul N., *Shakespearean Tragedy and the Elizabethan Compromise* (New York: New York University Press, 1957).

Speaight, Robert, *Nature in Shakespearian Tragedy* (London: Hollis and Carter, 1955).

Spencer, Theodore, 'The Isolation of the Shakespearean Hero', *Sewanee Review*, 52 (1944), pp. 313–31.

Spivack, Bernard, *Shakespeare and the Allegory of Evil: The History of a Metaphor in Relation to His Major Villains* (New York: Columbia University Press, 1958).

Spurgeon, Caroline F. E., *Shakespeare's Imagery and What It Tells Us* (1934).

Stewart, J. I. M., *Character and Motive in Shakespeare: Some Recent Appraisals Examined* (London: Longman's, Green, 1949).

Stoll, Elmer Edgar, *Othello: An Historical and Comparative Study* (Minneapolis, 1915).

Stoll, Elmer Edgar, *Art and Artifice in Shakespeare: A Study in Dramatic Contrast and Illusion* (1933).

Traversi, Derek, *An Approach to Shakespeare* (1936).

Ure, Peter, *Shakespeare and the Inward Self of the Tragic Hero* (Durham: Durham University Press, 1961).

West, Robert H., 'The Christianness of *Othello*', *Shakespeare Quarterly*, 15 (1964), pp. 333–43.

Recent Studies

Adamson, Jane, *'Othello' as Tragedy: Some Problems of Judgment and Feeling* (Cambridge and New York: Cambridge University Press, 1980).

Adler, Doris, 'The Rhetoric of Black and White in *Othello*', *Shakespeare Quarterly*, 25 (1974), pp. 248–57.

Alexander, Nigel, 'Thomas Rymer and *Othello*', *Shakespeare Survey*, 21 (1968), pp. 62–77.

Altieri, Charles, 'Criticism as the Situating of Performances: Or What Wallace Stevens Has to Tell Us About *Othello*'; *American Criticism at Work*, ed. Victor A. Kramer (Troy, New York: Whitston Publishing, 1984), pp. 265–95.

Altman, Joel B., '"Prophetic Fury": *Othello* and the Economy of Shakespearian Reception', *Studies in the Literary Imagination*, 26 (1993).

Bamber, Linda, *Comic Women, Tragic Men: A Study of Gender and Genre in Shakespeare* (Stanford: Stanford University Press, 1982).

Bates, Catherine, 'Weaving and Writing in *Othello*', *Shakespeare Survey*, 46 (1993), pp. 51–61.

Bayley, John, *Shakespeare and Tragedy* (London: Routledge and Kegan Paul, 1981).

Berry, Ralph, 'Patterns in *Othello*', *Shakespeare Quarterly*, 23 (1972), pp. 3–19.

Bradshaw, Graham, *Shakespeare and the Materialists* (Ithaca and London: Cornell University Press, 1993).

Bristol, Michael D., 'Charivari and the Comedy of Abjection in *Othello*', in *True Rites and Maimed Rites: Ritual and Anti-Ritual in Shakespeare and His Age* (Urbana and Chicago: University of Illinois Press, 1991).

Buchman, Lorne M., 'Orson Welles's *Othello*: A Study of Time in Shakespeare's Tragedy', *Shakespeare Survey*, 39 (1986), pp. 53–67.

Callaghan, Dympna, *Woman and Gender in Renaissance Tragedy: A Study of 'King Lear', 'Othello', 'The Duchess of Malfi' and 'The White Devil'* (New York and London: Harvester Wheatsheaf, 1989).

Cohwig, Ruth, 'Blacks in English Renaissance Drama and the Role of Shakespeare's Othello', in *The Black Presence in English Literature*, ed. David Dabydeen (Manchester: Manchester University Press, 1985), pp. 1–25.

Colie, Rosalie, *Shakespeare's Living Art* (Princeton: Princeton University Press, 1974).

Dauber, Antoinette B., 'Allegory and Irony in *Othello*', *Shakespeare Survey*, 40 (1987), pp. 123–35.

Doran, Madeleine, 'Good Name in *Othello*', *Studies in English Literature*, 7 (1967), pp. 195–217.

Everett, Barbara, '"Spanish" Othello: The Making of Shakespeare's Moor', *Shakespeare Survey*, 35 (1982), pp. 101–112.

Felperin, Howard, *Shakespearean Representation: Mimesis and Modernity in Elizabethan Tragedy* (Princeton: Princeton University Press, 1977).

Gohlke, Madelon, '"All That is Spoke is Marred": Language and Consciousness in *Othello*', *Women's Studies*, 9 (1982), pp. 157–76.

Grady, Hugh, 'Iago and the Dialectic of Enlightenment: Reason, Will and Desire in *Othello*', *Criticism*, 37 (1995), pp. 251–50.

Greenblatt, Stephen, *Renaissance Self-Fashioning from More to Shakespeare* (Chicago: University of Chicago Press, 1980).

Hankey, Julie, *Othello – William Shakespeare* (Bristol: Bristol Classical Press: Plays in Performance, 1987).

Hawkes, Terence, *Shakespeare's Talking Animals* (London: Edward Arnold, 1973).

Holderness, Graham, John Turner and Nick Potter, *Shakespeare: The Play of History* (London: Macmillan, 1988).

Homan, Sidney R., 'Iago's Aesthetics: *Othello* and Shakespeare's Portrait of an Artist', *Shakespeare Studies*, 5 (1970), pp. 141–8.

Homan, Sidney R., *When the Theater Turns to Itself* (Lewisburg: Bucknell University Press, 1981).

Honigmann, E. A. J., *Shakespeare: Seven Tragedies; The Dramatist's Manipulation of Response* (1976).

Hunter, G. K., '*Othello* and Colour Prejudice', *Proceedings of the British Academy*, 53 (1967), pp. 139–63.

King, Rosalie, '"Then murder's out of tune": The Music and Structure of *Othello*', *Shakespeare Survey*, 39 (1986), pp. 149–59.

Jardine, Lisa, *Still Harping on Daughters: Women and Drama in the Age of Shakespeare* (London: Harvester Wheatsheaf, 1989).

Jones, Emrys, *Scenic Form in Shakespeare* (Oxford: Clarendon Press, 1971).

Josipovici, Gabriel, *Writing and the Body: The Northcliffe Lectures, 1981* (Sussex: Harvester Press, 1982).

Kahn, Coppélia, *Man's Estate: Masculine Identity in Shakespeare* (Berkeley: University of California Press, 1981).

Kirsch, Arthur, *Shakespeare and the Experience of Love* (Cambridge and New York: Cambridge University Press, 1981).

Kirsch, Arthur, *The Passions of Shakespeare's Tragic Heroes* (Charlottesville and London: University Press of Virginia, 1990).

Long, Michael, *The Unnatural Scene: A Study in Shakespearean Tragedy* (London: Methuen, 1976).

McAlindon, T., *Shakespeare's Tragic Cosmos* (Cambridge: Cambridge University Press, 1991).

Mason, Harold A., *Shakespeare's Tragedies of Love* (London: Chatto and Windus, 1970).

Matheson, Mark, 'Venetian Culture and the Politics of *Othello*', *Shakespeare Survey*, 48 (1995), 123–33.

Muir, Kenneth, *Shakespeare's Tragic Sequence* (London: Hutchinson, 1972).

Neely, Carol Thomas, 'Women and Men in *Othello*: "What should such a fool/Do with so good a woman?"' in *The Woman's Part: Feminist Criticism of Shakespeare*, ed. Carol Ruth Swift Lenz, Gayle Greene and Carol Thomas Neely (Urbana: University of Illinois Press, 1980).

Neely, Carol Thomas, *Broken Nuptials in Shakespeare's Plays* (New Haven: Yale University Press, 1985).

Neill, Michael, 'Changing Places in *Othello*', *Shakespeare Survey*, 37 (1984), pp. 115–31.

Neill, Michael, 'Unproper Beds: Race, Adultery and the Hideous in *Othello*', *Shakespeare Quarterly*, 40 (1989), pp. 383–412.

Nevo, Ruth, *Tragic Form in Shakespeare* (Princeton: Princeton University Press, 1972).

Newman, Karen, *Fashioning Femininity and English Renaissance Drama* (Chicago and London: University of Chicago Press, 1991).

Novy, Marianne, *Love's Argument: Gender Relations in Shakespeare* (Chapel Hill: University of North Carolina Press, 1984).

Orkin, Martin, 'Othello and the "plain face of Racism"', *Shakespeare Quarterly*, 38:2 (Summer 1987), pp. 166–88.

Rabkin, Norman, *Shakespeare and the Common Understanding* (London: Collier Macmillan, 1967).

Reid, Stephen, 'Othello's Occupation: Beyond the Pleasure Principle', *Psychoanalytic Review*, 63 (1976), pp. 555–70.

Rogers, Stephen, '*Othello*: Comedy in Reverse', *Shakespeare Quarterly*, 24 (1973), pp. 210–20.

Ross, Lawrence J., 'Shakespeare's "Dull Clown" and Symbolic Music', *Shakespeare Quarterly*, 17 (1966), pp. 107–28.

Snow, Edward A., 'Sexual Anxiety and the Male Order of Things in *Othello*', *English Literary Renaissance*, 10 (1980), pp. 384–412.

Snyder, Susan, '*Othello* and the Conventions of Romantic Comedy', *Renaissance Drama*, 5 (1972), pp. 123–41.

Snyder, Susan, *The Comic Matrix of Shakespeare's Tragedies: 'Romeo and Juliet', 'Hamlet', 'Othello', and 'King Lear'* (Princeton: Princeton University Press, 1979).

Stockholder, Katharine S., 'Egregiously an Ass: Chance and Accident in *Othello*', *Studies in English Literature*, 13 (1973), pp. 256–72.

Styan, John L., *Shakespeare's Stagecraft* (Cambridge: Cambridge University Press, 1967).

Styan, John L., *Drama, Stage and Audience* (Cambridge: Cambridge University Press, 1975).

Vaughan, Virgina Mason, *Othello: A Contextual History* (Cambridge: Cambridge University Press, 1994).

West, Robert, *Shakespeare and the Outer Mystery* (Lexington: University of Kentucky Press, 1968).

Wine, Martin L., *Othello: Text and Performance* (London: Macmillan, 1984).

ACKNOWLEDGEMENTS

The editor and publisher wish to thank the following for their permission to reprint copyright material: Constable (for material from *The Characters of Love*); Penguin (for material from *Shakespearean Tragedy; Coleridge on Shakespeare*; and *Dr. Johnson on Shakespeare*); Cambridge University Press (for material from *Disowning Knowledge in Six Plays of Shakespeare*); Faber (for material from 'Shakespeare and the Stoicism of Seneca', in *Selected Essays of T.S. Eliot*); *Shakespeare Survey* (for material from '*Othello*: A Retrospect, 1900–1950'); Chatto and Windus (for material from *The Structure of Complex Words*); Routledge (for material from *Shakespeare: Our Contemporary; Desire and Anxiety: Circulations of Sexuality in Shakespearean Drama*; and *Shakespeare: The Critical Heritage*); Hogarth Press (for material from 'Diabolic Intellect and the Noble Hero: Or the Sentimentalist's *Othello*', in *The Common Pursuit*); Oxford University Press (for material from *Shakespeare Criticism 1935–60*); Methuen (for material from *Power on Display: The Politics of Shakespeare's Genres*); Yale University Press (for material from *The Critical Works of Thomas Rymer*).

There are instances where we have been unable to trace or contact copyright holders before our printing deadline. If notified, the publisher will be pleased to acknowledge the use of copyright material.

Nicholas Potter teaches at Swansea Institute of Higher Education. He has published on Shakespeare with two colleagues, Graham Holderness and John Turner, in *Shakespeare: The Play of History* (1998) and *Shakespeare: Out of Court* (1990) and elsewhere. He has interests in the Modern period, has published on Edmund Blunden, T.S. Eliot and E.M. Forster, and has recently contributed to a forthcoming *Encyclopaedia of Modernism*.

INDEX

Columbia Critical Guides Series